CHINA'S LONELY REVOLUTION

SUNY series in Chinese Philosophy and Culture
———————
Roger T. Ames, editor

CHINA'S LONELY REVOLUTION

The Local Communist Movement of
Hainan Island, 1926–1956

JEREMY A. MURRAY

Front cover image: An example of Li weavings, published in *The Li Tribes of Hainan Island* (Die Li-stämme der insel Hainan) by Hans Stübel. Berlin: Klinkhardt and Beirmann, 1937. Reprinted with permission from publisher Klinkhardt and Biermann.

Published by State University of New York Press, Albany

© 2017 State University of New York

All rights reserved

Printed in the United States of America

No part of this book may be used or reproduced in any manner whatsoever without written permission. No part of this book may be stored in a retrieval system or transmitted in any form or by any means including electronic, electrostatic, magnetic tape, mechanical, photocopying, recording, or otherwise without the prior permission in writing of the publisher.

For information, contact State University of New York Press, Albany, NY
www.sunypress.edu

Production, Jenn Bennett
Marketing, Michael Campochiaro

Library of Congress Cataloging-in-Publication Data

Name: Murray, Jeremy A., author– 1978
Title: China's lonely revolution: the local Communist movement of Hainan Island, 1926–1956 / Jeremy A. Murray
Description: Albany : State University of New York Press, [2017] | Series: SUNY series in Chinese philosophy and culture| Includes bibliographical references and index.
Identifiers: ISBN 9781438465319 (hardcover : alk. paper) | ISBN 9781438465302 (pbk. : alk. paper) | ISBN 9781438465326 (ebook)
Further information is available at the Library of Congress.

10 9 8 7 6 5 4 3 2 1

Voor onze ouders
For our parents

Els and Stuart Murray
Patricia and George Jakovich

CONTENTS

ACKNOWLEDGMENTS ix

INTRODUCTION 1

CHAPTER 1
Cultivating and Exploiting a "Primitive" Island: From Hainan's
Early History into the Twentieth Century 11

CHAPTER 2
Political Prospects in the Early Republic: Revolution, Warlords,
and Diaspora, 1912–1926 33

CHAPTER 3
From Globetrotters to Guerrillas: Hainan's Early Communists 57

CHAPTER 4
An Outrage of Little Consequence: The Japanese Invasion and
Occupation of Hainan 75

gallery of photographs follows page 94

CHAPTER 5
New Allies: The Baisha Uprising and the Li-Communist
Alliance, 1943 95

CHAPTER 6
Holding Aloft Hainan's Red Flag: Disobedience and Survival
in the Civil War, 1946 119

CHAPTER 7
Sharing Victory: The Communist Conquest of Hainan Island 143

CHAPTER 8
Bringing Hainan to the Nation's Heel: Anti-localism in the Early PRC 163

EPILOGUE 185

NOTES 189

BIBLIOGRAPHY 219

INDEX 235

ACKNOWLEDGMENTS

My advisors, Joseph Esherick and Paul Pickowicz, instructed me at the University of California, San Diego (UCSD) with wisdom, care, and inexhaustible patience. They provided structure, direction, and meaning to seven formative years, and it will take me many more years to bring to full fruition all of the seeds they planted with their guidance and examples. For now, I present this earnest effort with profound gratitude to Paul and Joe.

I have benefited from the inspired and inspiring teaching of many dedicated scholars. At UCSD, Roberto Alvarez, Suzanne Cahill, Takashi Fujitani, Lu Weijing, Richard Madsen, Jeremy Prestholdt, David Ringrose, Sarah Schneewind, Stefan Tanaka, and others enriched my learning. Ye Wa assisted me in making sense of the Peng Chengwan survey. Eugenia Lean and Madeleine Zelin at Columbia University encouraged me to continue my studies in Chinese history. At the State University of New York, Albany, Jim Hargett, Anthony DeBlasi, Susannah Fessler, and Charles Hartman launched me into the study of history and of China, which now brings me full circle to State University of New York Press! Thanks to series editor, Roger Ames, and also Jessica Kirschner for helping to guide this work to publication. I am also very grateful to Christopher Ahn and Jennifer Bennett for taking the manuscript through the production phase. I am grateful that Nancy Ellegate saw value in the work, and welcomed me on board. Thanks also to three anonymous readers who provided incisive comments. Xiaorong Han took great care in providing instruction and direction, and Gregor Benton encouraged me to continue the project as it wavered between dissertation and book. I have benefited from the expansive expertise of the above scholars, and I thank them for their instruction and guidance.

Funding for the project has come from the University of California Pacific Rim Research Program, the U.S. Department of Education's Jacob K. Javits Fellowship Program, the California State University San Bernardino (CSUSB) Office of Academic Research, the CSUSB Center for International

Studies and Programs, and my CSUSB History Department. Joyce Hanson, Tim Pytell, Ward McAfee, Michal Kohout, and all of my CSUSB colleagues have made my time here constantly pleasant and rewarding.

The staff members of the Hainan Provincial Archives in Haikou were always eager and diligent in their support of my research through many visits. I have also benefited from the expert guidance and assistance of the staffs of the University of Oregon Special Collections and University Archives, the Hoover Institution, the Columbia Center for Oral History and C.V. Starr East Asian Library, the Missions Etrangères de Paris, the National Archives of Australia in Canberra, the UCSD library, and the CSUSB Pfau Library.

The graduates of the Modern Chinese History PhD program at UCSD comprise a wonderful group and I am very proud to count myself among them. For their help in countless ways, I thank Emily Baum, Jeremy Brown, Jenny Huangfu Day, Miriam Gross, Brent Haas, Christian Hess, Dahpon Ho, Ellen Huang, Matthew Johnson, Justin Jacobs, Judd Kinzley, Jomo Smith, Elya Zhang, Zheng Xiaowei, and many others.

I dedicate this work to my mother, Els Murray, and to my father, Stuart Murray. Their lives and work are my first and best inspiration. My siblings, Aaron Murray, Timothy Murray, and Rachel Turetsky, and their families, sustain me with their love. My great friend William Langran and his family welcomed me and mine in Hong Kong. The Monson family and the Tanner family have made life out west a little more like home with their warmth and generosity. My wife, Katherine, is my love, comfort, and constant joy, and along with Alexander, I can see her love and care woven throughout this book.

INTRODUCTION

The best place to begin an examination of the Communist movement on Hainan island is with the proud and unique declaration made by its leaders in 1950: "For twenty-three years, the Red flag did not fall (*Ershisan nian hongqi bu dao*)." In no other major Chinese territory can this claim of continuity in the Communist revolution be made. From the Chinese Communist Party's (CCP) origins in Shanghai, to Jinggangshan and other base areas, to the hallowed ground of Yan'an, all major territories of the CCP were overcome by the Nationalists, the Japanese, regional governors, or a combination of these, before they were later retaken and incorporated into the People's Republic of China (PRC). Hainan's geographical insularity, and the contingency and perennial historical trends connected to this "islandness," played a crucial part in shaping the distinctive history in the period examined here.

In Hainan, the Communist presence grew and shrank throughout the more than twenty-three years from its founding in 1926 until its incorporation in the PRC in early 1950. But even during times when there were only twenty-six known members of the Hainan movement, seeking refuge in the ancestral village of their leader, Feng Baiju (1903–1973), and even when they lost all communications with the mainland Communist leadership, they endured as a continuous force on the island. The persistence of Hainan's revolution sometimes came at the price of ideological purity. Pragmatism, improvisation, and isolation became its defining features. The solitude and remoteness of Hainan shaped the movement, as Feng and others sank deep roots on the island, drawing on the movement's local pride, as well as its unflagging and tenacious impetus to survival. In this work I aim to incorporate motivations such as regionalism and ethnicity into a study of the revolution as it was experienced there. Hainan Communist leaders and their mainland counterparts held widely divergent perspectives of the movement's direction and its path forward. Some perceptions, or misperceptions, on both sides of the narrow Qiongzhou Strait that divided Hainan from the mainland, were grounded in perennial notions about one another's culture. Some of these misperceptions and prejudices persist today, and continue to shape the way that Hainan's history is remembered and written.

For more than two millennia, the nearly 13,000 square-mile teardrop-shaped island has been China's Hainan. Since the Han Empire established a garrison there in the late second century BCE, Hainan has been a part of the Chinese cultural and political realm. While its indigenous inhabitants, known in Chinese as the Li people, have frequently clashed with Han Chinese on the island, Hainan has never produced a noteworthy political or military movement that sought independence from China. There has never been a question as to Hainan's allegiance and belonging.[1] This sets Hainan apart from other troublesome border regions of China, including Tibet, Xinjiang, Manchuria, Mongolia, and Taiwan.

And yet the relationship has rarely been a comfortable or mutually beneficial one. Both islander and mainlander have viewed each other with suspicion, the former fearing exploitation and the latter secession or instability. Between 1926 and 1950, the Chinese Communist Party established a political and military presence on Hainan, and even after its success, these enduring frustrations and anxieties continued to define its relationship with the mainland regime. Ultimately, these long-standing trends between Hainan and the mainland have continued to hamper the island's development and progress, in terms of culture, politics, and economics. This is the history of Hainan's Communist movement in the context of the first half of the twentieth century. Trends that shaped this movement continue to play out in the island's politics, its economic potential, and its cultural identities.

Hainan lies just about ten miles off the southern Chinese mainland, with Guangdong's Leizhou peninsula stretching to nearly touch the island. Leizhou dips into the South China Sea, and continues as an underwater ridge all the way to the northern coast of Hainan. This has made the Hainan or Qiongzhou Strait a dangerous passage for centuries of sailors and fishermen. In May of 1950, Hainan was incorporated into the new Beijing regime of the PRC with the defeat of the Nationalist forces on the island. On the island, an insurgent Communist force had fought the Japanese occupation (1939–1945) as well as the Nationalist forces on the island (1927–1950). In the spring of 1950, they joined with a massive landing operation of the People's Liberation Army (PLA) from the mainland to achieve victory. The history and collective memory of the war-weary Hainan Communists was based on the ideal of perseverance and continuity over twenty-three years of struggle, sometimes with no support or communication from the mainland

Communists. Fiercely patriotic and eager to be given a provincial seat at the national table (a seat that would not be granted until 1988), the Hainan Communists, like their 1911 revolutionary predecessors, were proud of their local identity, forged in a local struggle with local characteristics.

From the perspective of the mainland Communist landing forces of the spring 1950 campaign, Hainan's revolutionary success was seen to be not nearly as hard-fought or long-awaited as other conflicts in their recent memory. The mainland Communist Fourth Field Army had reached the southern provinces far more quickly than even the most optimistic plans of the Communist leadership. With some valuable experience gained in previous failed amphibious attacks, they had crossed the narrow Qiongzhou Strait and liberated Hainan in a mere two weeks. Two weeks of fighting, from the mainland forces' and the PRC leadership's perspective, brought Hainan under Communist control. In this coup, half of Nationalist territory was won and lost, and Chiang Kai-shek (1887–1975) and his forces hunkered down on the other half—Taiwan—which some believed would be the next battlefield of the Chinese civil war. Instead, Taiwan was soon to be a Cold War bulwark following the outbreak of the Korean War a month later and the resulting aid of Chiang's somewhat reluctant but supportive American allies.

The Hainan Communists were dedicated to the national revolution, even though questions of loyalty, commitment, and belief in the revolution would later become an issue. The mainland Communists had been able to supply little or no support through much of that struggle, and the Hainan Column had turned to the island's local Han and indigenous Li population in an alliance that allowed them to survive in the mountainous southern interior. So deep were the roots of the Hainan Communist movement that it led them to disobey central directives to move their forces off the island following the Japanese defeat in 1945. When the mainland Communist leadership ordered the Hainan Column to abandon the island in 1946, and withdraw their forces north to Shandong, or east to Vietnam, the Hainan command responded this was impossible, and that they respectfully refused to obey the orders. This 1946 disobedience and the anti-localism campaigns of the early PRC represent the culmination of more than two decades in Hainan's revolutionary movement, and I aim to make sense of this longer history.

The successful military campaign that came in 1950 was due to the cooperation between a massive "people's navy" composed largely of commandeered or volunteered fishing craft launched from the mainland, with support from the local Hainan Column. Shortly after the victory, as in other newly acquired territories especially in the south, the regional and national administration implemented accelerated and jolting land reform to catch them up with other longer-held regions. The Hainan Communists had held insufficient territory to allow the completion of land reform on the entire island prior to May of 1950. Further, mainland Communist leaders judged that the land reform and redistribution that had been carried out in the limited Communist territories of Hainan was incomplete and too moderate to satisfy national standards.

By 1951, a flood of "southbound cadres" (*nanxia ganbu*) arrived on Hainan to replace local Hainan cadres and revolutionary veterans. The local cadres' connections allegedly made them too soft on the island's landlords and big capitalists. Mutual resentment grew between the old revolutionaries of the Hainan Column and the newly arrived southbound cadres. Many of the new cadres were young urban intellectuals or even students, some from the distant northern reaches of China, now sent into Hainan's towns and villages to overturn the local order. With the Korean War underway and the implementation of a series of national campaigns, regional and national administrators were suspicious of any local leadership that might obstruct the project of building a unified nation-state. The urgency of rapid industrialization and centralized command overruled the popularity, moderation, and revolutionary credentials of local leaders, like Feng Baiju on Hainan, the man who most embodied the spirit of the Hainan Column.

Through the early 1950s, local leaders around China were systematically removed from positions of power in the "anti-localism" (*fan difang zhuyi*) campaigns. The culmination of the centralization of political and economic control in Beijing came with the Anti-Rightist Movement (the larger umbrella campaign that encompassed the "Anti-Localism Campaigns") and then the Great Leap Forward. These two catastrophic events removed from power the moderate and critical voices within the political structure and then implemented one of the most devastating economic campaigns in human history, leading to the starvation of tens of millions by 1961. A generation of local leaders were silenced and sidelined after having helped bring about the military and political victory of the CCP.[2] Decades later, vindication would come with the loosening of state economic controls and the granting of provincial status and increased autonomy on Hainan.

Finding the place where Hainan's Communist movement fits into the greater revolutions and wars of resistance of the first half of the twentieth century requires focusing on the military history of the Hainan Column. Military history is no longer confined to the biographies of eminent generals and their tactical successes and blunders. The works of Gregor Benton, Hans Van de Ven, Edward McCord, Stephen Averill, and others have expanded the discipline to include the political, social, economic, and cultural dimensions of modern Chinese military history.³ It is the inspiration and example of these works that drive my own research on this topic. While the biography of Feng Baiju and other leaders of the Communist Hainan Independent Column are important, my examination of the Hainan Communist movement is not limited to a telling of their lives alone. And while the specific operations and fortifications of the Hainan guerrilla forces are relevant to the narrative of the movement, I do not restrict the aim of this study to a military atlas of maneuvers throughout the Communist fight against the Japanese and the Nationalists.

In the early period of academic study of the Chinese revolution by non-Chinese scholars, in the 1950s, 1960s, and 1970s, a lack of archival access to the Chinese mainland led to an excessive focus on ideology in the form of political and intellectual history. Western political and social scientists were locked out of the PRC, and Chinese Communist historians were likewise politically constrained in the telling of their own recent history. The jingoistic narratives of the Cold War dominated the histories about the first half of the twentieth century throughout the world in this period. In many cases, and due in part to Chinese nationalism and American anxieties about China's rise in the twenty-first century, simplistic mutual depictions continue in popular culture, though today this type of polemic continues to be produced more out of a desire to rile up a like-minded reader; but it is no longer attributable to a lack of access to sources.

Since the late 1970s, many of the nearly forgotten histories of the Chinese civil war, and the War of Resistance against Japan were collected and compiled through projects like the *Wenshi ziliao* (roughly translated as "literary and historical materials"), which exploded with other projects in the 1980s, into millions of pages of individual recollections of the wars. Today, oral historians continue their work in China, and they now have access to localities like Hainan: as one example, Sato Shojin of Japan's Osaka Sangyo University has spent years working on Hainan, seeking an accurate and complete account of the atrocities of the Japanese occupation of Hainan (1939–1945).

Based on personal accounts and increased access to official archival sources, both Chinese and foreign historians have begun to construct a richer historical account of the years that had once been nothing more than a source for Cold War propaganda. Naturally, these and other new histories continue to be driven by the ideology and political concerns of the present, and of the historian. But the recently increased freedom in recounting the history of China during the first half of the twentieth century has allowed for new voices to be added to what was once only the orthodox Western or Chinese account of the rise of Mao Zedong (1893–1976) and the CCP.

The new voices have brought new actors onto the stage of the civil war and the War of Resistance. They have served to effectively decenter the narratives of the revolution. While still in the middle of the Cold War, Chalmers Johnson showed the Chinese nationalist origins of resistance and revolutionary energy to be the source of the Communist success.[4] In doing this, he broke down the myth of a monolithic, international Communist entity, connected through a tiered system with Moscow at the top, and the tiniest Chinese village at the bottom. (In some powerful currents of political thought, a monolithic Communist history still prevails, owing to myopic scholarship and the institutional inertia of academic and governmental institutions.[5]) Today, the deconstruction of international monolithic Communist history is being pushed further, past Johnson's national level and to the subnational nature of revolutionary movements. Abandoning the nation-state as a unit of analysis here does not mean that we should move immediately to the global or international, as some theorists and historians have done. Stephen Averill and others have begun to move us toward an understanding of the local origins of the Chinese Communist movement.[6]

Regional characters and motivations drove the revolution in its early days, and continued to be a defining force through the civil war and War of Resistance. It was not simply national resistance to the Japanese threat that allowed the Communists to harness this energy and drive them to victory. Our increased access to official and nonofficial sources from wartime China allows the historian to no longer essentialize the experience of the Chinese revolution across the profoundly diverse regions and people within the PRC. Local histories are becoming more and more richly textured with increasing scholarly access to provincial and national archives, as well as to sources like the *wenshi ziliao*, and in Hainan another similar series called *Qiongdao Xinghuo* (Hainan Spark). As with any other locality, understanding Hainan requires us to focus on the local actors who have been celebrated and criticized in the national history. In this way, we discover another history, another identity, and even another patriotism. In traveling to China and interacting with regional and peripheral sources of revolutionary history, I discovered a remarkable and inexhaustible wealth of voices and perspectives that have fueled my work. It has been both energizing and daunting to encounter the printed and living history of Hainan.

Some of the major themes and questions that came to the surface and drove my research on Hainan include the center-periphery relationship in China's Communist revolution; the questions of ideological correctness versus opportunism of regional or national leaders; the shifting itinerary of the revolution's ideology and adherence to a new or old itinerary; the importance of biography and charismatic leadership within the Chinese revolution versus the social and economic impetus toward revolutionary activity; the interaction of the Chinese revolution with indigenous peoples, and their overlapping or conflicting aims; and others. Central to Hainan's Communist revolution was the tension between ideological purity and pragmatic survival. The latter was often the path that Feng Baiju and the Hainanese leadership chose, and they took this path in the name of holding aloft the Red flag for more than twenty-three years from their founding days until their final victory.

In chapter 1, I introduce Hainan's perennial relationship with the mainland, characterized by unrealized hopes for development. Centuries of history saw the formation of a distinct Hainanese culture, which connected its population not only to the Chinese mainland, but also to Southeast Asia and to the distinctive and deep roots of Hainan's own identity. This chapter aims to sketch out a landscape on which the remainder of the narrative will unfold, and is therefore not a chronological telling of Hainan's early history. In chapter 2, the more chronological element of the study begins, with a study of the cosmopolitan revolutionaries who helped overthrow the last dynasty of China in 1911 as they gradually shift their political plans from international ambitions, to national service, and finally, to local survival. In chapter 3, the early Communist movement on Hainan is founded in 1926, but becomes increasingly isolated from its mainland CCP leadership. Guangdong warlord, Chen Jitang, loosely affiliated with the Nationalist rulers, nearly annihilates the Hainan Communists. In chapter 4, the Japanese invasion of China in July of 1937 leads to the occupation of Hainan in 1939, and an uneasy alliance between the Hainan Communists and Nationalists. In this alliance, the relative autonomy of both parties from their respective mainland authorities in their negotiations is striking. As on the mainland, this united front soon breaks down, and the conflict between the Nationalists and Communists on Hainan resumes even during the Japanese occupation, as on the mainland. In chapter 5, an alliance with the indigenous Li people of the island's interior allows for the Communists and the Li to survive in the mountainous southern central region of Hainan. In chapter 6, with the end of the Japanese occupation, the mainland leadership reestablishes contact with the Hainanese Communists after years with no radio or messenger communication. In 1946, in an effort to consolidate its national forces, and in negotiations with Chiang Kai-shek and the Nationalists, the mainland Communist leadership, then based in Yan'an, orders the Hainan Communists to abandon the island to either northern China or Vietnam

(Indochina). By this time, the Hainan Communist movement is so deeply rooted in the island that its leadership refuses to attempt this movement, and communicates their inability and unwillingness to carry out the orders to leave Hainan. In chapter 7, the successful military conquest of Hainan is completed through a combined effort of the local Communists and mainland landing forces. The views of the campaign diverged radically between Hainan and the mainland, and veterans of the campaign hold irreconcilable views of the same events, and perhaps differing views of the revolutionary path forward. In chapter 8, the mainland consolidation of power leads to the further souring of relations between the Hainanese and mainland Communists leaderships. Anti-Localism Campaigns uproot or demobilize the Hainanese political and military leadership, based on accusations of nepotism, "localism," and overly moderate policies. While limited development of Hainan's tropical agriculture moved forward in the years that followed, the trauma of this rupture between the two Communist leaderships lasted for more than three decades. To some extent, these bitter roots of the Communist revolution on Hainan continue to shape the island's remembered past and lived present at the time of writing.

In Haikou Park, Feng Baiju's memorial pavilion and mausoleum are meticulously groomed with blooming gardens all year round. Feng stands above all other sons and daughters of the island as the symbol of Hainan's struggles in the twentieth century. I was conducting research for this project when the traditional Qingming Festival or tomb-sweeping holiday was officially reinstated in April 2008, and I strolled to the park to see how the holiday would be observed at Feng's tomb. Government and military personnel stood in solemn lines and presented Feng with huge wreaths as offerings. Brief speeches recounted Feng's life, and his contribution to the Hainanese people and the Communist Party. Then, throughout the day, fewer official delegations of young parents and toddlers placed fruit and flowers along the pedestal of Feng's monument and the nearby pillar commemorating all of Hainan's revolutionary martyrs.

By the early afternoon, the pavilion was quiet and nearly deserted. I struck up a conversation with two young police officers, since their duty prevented them from retiring with the rest of the crowd for the usual afternoon nap to escape the heat. I had brought "ghost money," and I told them that I hoped to burn it in front of Feng's resting place. The senior of the two told me sharply that it was strictly not allowed in the park; the other officer looked less certain. Apparently, there was some room for debate on the point. The younger officer switched from Mandarin to Hainanese as they discussed the matter among themselves.

"Ah, you're Hainanese," I said, with some relief, because their People's Armed Police uniforms meant that they might not be locals. They turned back to me. I realized my interjection might have been interpreted as a challenge to their Hainanese loyalty: How could they not allow this little ritual? The officer who had initially forbidden the offering turned and walked briskly to his police booth. He returned with his canteen and said with some officiousness, "Fine, you can burn it. Here." The spot he seemed to choose casually was centered exactly in front of Feng's tomb in the back of the pavilion. I had brought no matches, and so I imposed further on them to break the law against having an open flame in the park by using the officer's cigarette lighter. Then, as an impromptu ceremonial group, we took a quarter hour to burn two bundles of money, mostly in silence. As the fire dwindled, the senior officer looked to me and the other officer: "Done?" We both nodded, and his overbearing demeanor disappeared as he knelt and reverently scooped one, two, three handfuls of water from his canteen onto the tiny pile of ashes.

This is my effort to tell a chapter in the history of Hainan, where local identities and loyalties persist, and where a regional patriotism still prevails. As in any large country, regional and provincial loyalties develop and can be a source of both pride and conflict with the national culture and the central government. In framing the narrative of the Hainanese revolutionary movement, the Chinese nation and the mainland Chinese Communist movement must play an important part. The perspectives of the Hainanese and mainland leadership are both important, and examining them reveals that not only the power relations, but also the perceptions were, and are, asymmetrical. Actions are misinterpreted from both sides, and actors sometimes move easily from one side to the other. Much of this work examines a local movement that aimed to act in a way that embodied patriotism and the greatest loyalty to China and to the central Party authorities. And yet the movement's work was observed with a wary eye from the Party center, with concern that the local group was promoting a local agenda that was essentially separatist.

Taiwan is an obvious comparison in any study of Hainan. Taiwan's history and its present political status are, of course, hotly disputed, and its relationship with the mainland is still a major source of tension and volatility. From the perspective of mainland Chinese regimes, Taiwan, Xinjiang, and Tibet are examples of why regionalism and local identities must always be closely monitored, and maintained as subservient to the larger national cultural and political agendas. Hainan, as a southern island far from the political center of China, has also sometimes been suspected by central authorities of working toward a separatist or "localist" goal.

Hainanese regional identity is strong, but it is not separatist, nor has it ever been. The problem of excessive local autonomy is still seen from the mainland within the context of separatist realities elsewhere, and so although there is no independence movement on Hainan, movements toward increased autonomy are closely monitored in Beijing, especially based on the island's history and the honored heroes of its Communist revolution. Perception and misperception of cultural and revolutionary identities are therefore at the center of this work.

CHAPTER 1

CULTIVATING AND EXPLOITING A "PRIMITIVE" ISLAND

From Hainan's Early History into the Twentieth Century

This chapter provides some of the cultural, political, economic, and social landscape of early Hainan, including the islanders' complex relationship with mainlanders and other external observers in the early twentieth century. Rather than a strict chronological telling of Hainan's history, I lay out some characteristics of the island and its place in the region and the world. In addition, using mostly contemporary accounts, I develop some of the most prominent and recurrent themes in the island's history through the early twentieth century. In chapter 2, I begin a more chronological exploration of Hainan's history.

An Outsider's Story

It is often in violence toward unwelcome visitors that we first hear anything at all from the Hainanese in the early historical record. Until the twentieth century, like many regions at the margins of empire, Hainan island's native inhabitants could not tell their own stories beyond their home region. The indigenous Li people and the settled Han Chinese of the island had their history written for them by guests, some welcome and some not. These voices are heard only indirectly in descriptions of battles or magistrates' records of the interrogations of captives.[1] Only in the 1920s did Hainanese actors begin to make their own voices heard in sustainable political terms, advocating their position as loyal, but increasingly autonomous, members of the Chinese polity.

Before the 1920s, for written sources on Hainan, we must look to the stories told by the island's guests—the outsiders' stories. In the early decades of the twentieth century, a growing interest developed around Hainan for political, military, economic, and religious reasons. Through the writings of mainland Chinese and foreign observers of Hainan, the island's social and political ecology begins to come into focus in this time period. These sources provide an outsider's understanding of Hainan, and the island world out of which clearer Hainanese voices emerged.

Beginning in the spring of 1919, Peng Chengwan (1880–1978) led a six-month survey tour of Hainan, commissioned by the National Assembly in Beijing and with cooperation from prominent southern political leaders. Throughout the tour, Peng assessed the conditions of the island with a focus on Hainan's potential for development. At the time of his survey, Hainan's island neighbor, Taiwan, had already been under Japanese rule for a quarter century. Flourishing in many ways as a Japanese colony, Taiwan's success reinforced Hainan's still unrealized potential as another "treasure island" (*baodao*). Next to Taiwan, the lack of development on primitive Hainan was a reminder of the political and economic weakness of the new Chinese republic founded in 1912. Less than a decade before Peng's survey, he and some of his colleagues had served the now defunct Qing empire (1644–1911), and in 1919 they were working to establish the ambitious boundaries of the Chinese nation-state. The establishment of the republic's borders was not a foregone conclusion, however, and there were challenges from within and without the former Qing borders.[2]

In his thorough report published the following year, Peng Chengwan began with a note on this topic of Hainan's neglected potential:

> With its riches in lumber, mining, salt, rubber, coconuts, and coffee . . . if Hainan's natural resources are developed, the island's wealth could very well surpass that of Singapore or Taiwan. . . . It could soon become a tropical breadbasket of China, and it is a pity that it remains an undeveloped stone field. . . . It could become a land of plenty. In my humble opinion, in order to develop the natural wealth and benefit of Hainan, we must improve transportation and communications there, and make of Hainan a regional hub; further, we must guide the indigenous Li people, and teach them to be the pioneers and trailblazers of Hainan.[3]

Developing infrastructure and gaining cooperation from the Hainanese people, especially the indigenous Li, were the two stubborn challenges that Peng Chengwan perceived in plans for development that would benefit the island and the mainland. Neither obstacle had an easy solution, and they occupied most of his attention in the survey.

While comparisons between Hainan and its more developed neighbors were both unavoidable and painful, they also imbued Peng's mission with a sense of urgency. Peng and several other contributors to the report noted that development on Hainan could not be delayed due to several key factors. Cen Chunxuan (1861–1933), a leading figure in southern politics, wrote in his preface to the report that effective development of Hainan's resources could be the saving grace of the weak Chinese economy. Timely action was essential, since Hainan's prime location in the South China Sea, along with its great economic potential, made it a tantalizing site for foreign imperial development.[4] While foreign powers had not yet developed Hainan, Cen's concerns reflected an awareness in China that Hainan could be carved away in another "scramble for concessions" as had occurred twenty years earlier. This rush by foreign governments to carve out "spheres of influence," urban concession areas, and outright colonies had followed the Japanese naval defeat of the Qing in 1895 and coincided with the catastrophic Boxer Uprising from 1898 to 1901. In the opening chronicle ("Chronique") of an 1898 issue of the sinology journal, *T'oung Pao*, the editor commented on a Li uprising on Hainan:

> We know that Hainan Island is located in the waters of the French possessions of Tong-king, and therefore in the French sphere of influence. The French flag flies there already. If the Chinese regular army fails to restore order, we will be required to intervene energetically. Indeed, it is becoming increasingly urgent to see French influence affirmed in southern China where disorder is a permanent condition, and definitely and firmly plant the French flag on the entire island of Hainan.[5]

Hainan remained the object of covetous imperial designs through the early republic, indeed until the eve of the Japanese occupation that began in 1939.[6] Cen's call to strengthen China's hold on Hainan in 1920 was echoed by a second contributor to Peng Chengwan's survey, who noted the urgency of establishing clear Chinese claims to sovereignty on Hainan through economic development and modernization guided by the mainland regime.[7] A third contributor to the survey, Li Genyuan (1879–1965), pointed out that modern colonial powers in the region, like Japan on Taiwan, the British in Malaya and Hong Kong, the French in Indochina, and the Americans in the Philippines, were all developing their respective regions. To prove itself worthy of being considered a modern nation among equals, China must take immediate action to develop Hainan.[8] Li Genyuan was another prominent figure in the shifting southern revolutionary movement. At the time of the survey, he was stationed on Hainan with a popular fighting force that had recently defeated Long Jiguang (1860–1921), a former ally of the notorious "father of the warlords," Yuan Shikai (1859–1916).[9] Long and other militarists had tried to use Hainan as a temporary refuge from the battles raging on the mainland.

Other outsiders came to the island from Europe or the United States, sometimes as diplomats or merchants, but most of them were Christian missionaries. As early as the 1630s, Jesuits came to Hainan in hopes of educating and converting the locals. More than two centuries later, B.C. Henry, a Protestant American missionary observed a graveyard that marked the plots of hundreds of Chinese Catholic converts, as well as German and Portuguese Jesuits who died and were buried on the island in the 1680s.[10]

Like Peng Chengwan, the American Presbyterian missionary and schoolteacher, Mary Margaret Moninger (1891–1950) first came to Hainan as an outsider. Unlike Peng, the Iowa native made Hainan her home for much of her life, studying the local Hainanese dialect, directing mission work, and educating the young women of the island. She lived there from 1915 until 1942.[11] After a few years of living on Hainan, she was already a seasoned resident and she wrote a book about the island to inform an Anglophone audience, and also to invite other Presbyterian missionaries who might consider mission work there. In 1919, four years after arriving on the island, Moninger wrote:

> For the new missionary coming to the island there are the usual pitfalls—the despair at the beginning of language study, the dirty streets of the Chinese town, the strange climate and the longing for home and home friends. But the language is a fascinating study with all its interests and ramifications, the dirty streets are full of human interests, one attack of malarial fever dispels our fear of it, letters and papers link us to the homeland, and the new friends, both among the members of the mission and among the Chinese, prove beyond a shadow of a doubt the promise in Matthew 19:29: "And everyone that hath left houses, or brethren, or sisters, or father, or mother, or children, or lands, for My name's sake, shall receive an hundredfold." So we bid you a hearty welcome, you who we hope will hear the call and come

to labor in this far corner of the Master's vineyard, and promise you a hearty greeting as you too enter into our goodly heritage.[12]

Peng Chengwan and Margaret Moninger published their impressions of Hainan within a year of each other. Their backgrounds and interests in Hainan diverged greatly, but they observed many of the same places and activities. They shared the view that Hainan was a remote and largely neglected place especially in its relationship with the Chinese republican government. Peng's account is a sober analysis of the obstacles to modern development, as well as an appraisal of the island's strengths. Both obstacles and potential strengths are found in the people of the island, and especially in the indigenous Li people living in the island's interior. Moninger's text portrays a quiet island, peopled by farmers and fishers who led slow, rural lives when they were free from the violence between natives and newcomers, bandit raids, or the activities of mainland armies temporarily garrisoned there.

Moninger's account of Hainan in the early twentieth century actually dovetails surprisingly well with the official Chinese Communist history of prerevolutionary Hainanese society written decades later—one of bucolic self-sufficiency that was preyed upon by exploitative militarist and imperialist forces.[13] While Peng also notes the predatory mercantile forces on Hainan, his account is chiefly concerned with the benefit Hainan could have for all China. Moninger's observations provide a more intimate portrait of Hainan from the perspective of an outsider to China who was increasingly at home on the island. And so, amid the paradoxes of Hainan in this period, it was possible in 1919 for an Iowan schoolteacher to take the role of host on the island, and a Beijing official to be the outsider. Using these and other sources, a picture of the unique island begins to emerge.

Geography and Social Ecology

Hainan's neglect is evident in the inaccurate mapping of its territory as late as the nineteenth and twentieth century. Its harbors were never properly measured so that only in the past seventy-five years have the best natural ports in the south been developed into modern naval docks, beginning with the Japanese occupation (1939–1945). Until that time, visitors to the island approaching from the Chinese mainland immediately to the north risked running aground on the hazardous shoals of Haikou and Qiongzhou harbors along Hainan's northern coast.[14] At the shortest crossing, these ports are just more than ten miles across the Qiongzhou Strait from Guangdong's Leizhou Peninsula.

Despite this proximity, travel to and from Hainan was inconvenient at best through the Strait, and the poorly charted shoals and inlets made the short trip impossible for all but the most expert pilots and sailors even into the nineteenth and twentieth century. In 1882, the American missionary, B.C. Henry, visited Hainan, and in his 1886 account, Hainan was "here laid open for the first time to the reading world [being] of much special interest from a political, a commercial, a geographical, and an ethnographical point of view."[15] As with Peng and Moninger, he felt that he was opening Hainan to the outside world. Henry wrote of his trip to Hainan:

> Our journey from Hong-kong to Hoi-how [Haikou] was made in a wretched little steamer. . . . All arrangements of the ship were admirably fitted to produce discomfort and disgust, which were intensified by the slowness of speed, two days and the intervening night being consumed in traversing the two hundred and ninety miles between the two ports. . . . [T]he rocks and the currents are so treacherous and the channel so intricate, that no ship will go through in the night.[16]

Henry goes on to describe the extreme inconvenience of the shallow, muddy harbor around Haikou, where every passenger and every piece of cargo must make a three-mile trip to shore on a smaller boat designed for this purpose, taking five hours in Henry's case. In his survey, Peng Chengwan also acknowledged the limits of Haikou as a harbor more than thirty years later, and recommended instead the further development of Hainan's southern fishing towns, Yulin and Sanya, the former as a naval base. The republican government was unable or unwilling to act on Peng's prescient survey, however, and only under Japanese occupation and today under the People's Republic of China (PRC, 1949–present) did these natural deepwater southern ports enjoy the attention that connected Hainan to more convenient maritime travel, commerce, defense, and most recently, tourism.[17]

Haikou would require significant investment in order to serve as a safe and commercially viable harbor. Peng noted that even if one negotiated the difficult shoals and tides, policing piracy was another perennial challenge, and resources for government protection of the sea lanes to the mainland were extremely limited. A military presence in the south of Hainan, therefore, would establish a clearer authority in the region not only for dealing with piracy but also for asserting maritime sovereignty. These maritime claims, so crucial to the twenty-first-century discourse on the South China Sea, were not enforceable by Beijing at the remote southern end of the island.[18] At the time of his survey, official mail to and from the island only made the trip twice a month, and depending on the season, conditions, and destination, could take anywhere between one day and three weeks to reach the mainland.[19]

Peng's survey includes maps of six ports, some with depth markings and dotted lines that indicate ambitious plans for prospective jetties and other harbor development. Studies of Hainan's geography in the first half of the twentieth century, however, reflect a relative dearth of knowledge both in mainland China and among foreign observers. Even on the most fundamental geographic attributes of the island, it seems that the lack of political and economic interest was reflected in the lack of cartographic accuracy. From extant survey statistics between 1927 and 1987, measurements of the island's area have fluctuated by tens of thousands of kilometers, with the largest and most inaccurate measurements coming as late as a Chinese survey in 1927.[20] In earlier Chinese maps, Hainan's cartographic neglect is reflected in one Qing-era map of 1817 that depicts Guangdong coastal settlements with striking accuracy, while Hainan itself is both misshapen and not to scale.[21]

Hainan island's area is between 13,100 and 13,200 square miles, or between about 33,920 and 34,180 square kilometers. (It should be noted that these are the figures for Hainan *island*, and the current Hainan *provincial* area is significantly larger including most of the South China Sea and various smaller islands.)[22] In 1928, a French observer with access to Chinese records noted Hainan island's area to be as high as 14,700 square miles (more than 38,000 square kilometers).[23] Ten years later, *National Geographic* also overestimated the island's size at about 14,000 square miles (more than 36,200 square kilometers), almost a thousand square miles off the mark.[24] It is significant that these estimates of Hainan's size incorrectly suggested that it was larger than its neighbor, Taiwan. They also naturally reflected the significant lack of knowledge of Hainan's most basic geographical characteristics. By the middle of the twentieth century, no thorough survey of the island had been conducted in such a way as to provide an accurate figure of the island's geography. Only in 1956 did survey figures finally begin to stabilize and home in on a number closer to the island's geographical reality noted above.[25]

The inaccessibility of the island's interior and the hostility of the Li people who lived there had once been the reason for this ignorance. But trade routes gradually increased the contact between the southern highlands and the coastal settlements so that Peng could declare in 1919 that Hainan's interior was not, in fact, as remote as the prejudices of his fellow mainlanders might suppose. While the inconvenience of traveling between Hainan and mainland China was an obstruction to commerce and development, Peng noted that the natural waterways of the island were conducive to passenger and commercial traffic aboard a range of vessels. These included everything from steamboats, to junks, to rafts, and finally, to large hollow gourds serving as flotation devices to safely cross a mountain stream.[26]

Six rivers flow from the island's highest mountain, Wuzhishan, or "Five-Finger Mountain," named for its five prominent and narrow peaks. The rivers run through the lush forests that cover the southern mountains, and the main branches run to the western coast, flowing into the Gulf of Tonkin. Wuzhishan is in the south-central mountainous region of the island. The northern portion of the island is relatively flat with extremely fertile soil, watered by streams that flow from the southern highlands to the eastern central region. Water also comes from the heavy seasonal rains that sweep over the island through the late summer, autumn, and early winter. Besides bringing occasionally dangerous seasonal typhoons, these rains blow in from the northeast and make the northeast of Hainan rich farmland, and historically it has been the wealthiest part of the island. In 1920, the island's farmers mainly grew rice, but also exported lumber, sugar, rubber, coconuts, live pigs, bananas, and coffee.[27]

The southern mountain forests produced the lumber, but a lack of modern or efficient transportation prevented this industry from developing into a major part of the Hainanese economy. In the final years of the Qing, overseas Hainanese living in Singapore pushed investment in Hainan's agriculture for export to Southeast Asia, especially in bananas and coffee. Beginning in 1906, improved cultivation methods spurred an increase in tropical agriculture that carried into the PRC era, but still did not serve as a basis for significant modern development.[28] Peng hoped that the mining potential of the island could be realized, but again infrastructure limitations prevented that until the Japanese occupation of 1939 brought a light-rail connecting the Shilu iron mines of western Hainan with the natural southern ports.[29] Here again, Peng's survey is prescient in proposing mining development for the island that would only be realized by later regimes.

As of a 2006 study, agriculture in Hainan continued to make up nearly 50 percent of the island's economy, a larger proportion than any other province. In the early republic, agriculture encompassed an even larger portion of the economy.[30] Margaret Moninger noted in 1919, "Agriculture is preeminently the industry of this tropical island. Nearly all other industries are side issues, to be worked in the leisure periods." She wrote of the various other sideline industries of the island: "The factory whistle is not heard in Hainan. . . . The industries of the people are the simplest kind, requiring no complex machinery, and no power other than that supplied by man and beast. . . ." Moninger goes on to playfully list the vocations of the Hainanese that she has observed using every letter of the alphabet (including Q for "Quacking" to describe the work of shady medical practitioners, and V for "vermicelli" to describe Hainan noodle shops).[31] The production of dyes, incense, fans, glue, rope, and salt were other significant occupations in Hainan in 1919, but all of them were handicrafts and cottage industries even while factories had begun to appear in mainland cities. Still in 1931, according to another member of the Presbyterian mission community, "Manufacturing is practically nil. Some weaving is done on home looms, some firecracker shops make their own products. . . . The recent influx of kerosene and gasoline tins has given the tinsmiths a new field of endeavor . . ." but clearly the island had been passed by in the early years of Chinese industrialization.[32]

Han-Li Relations on Hainan

Peng Chengwan hoped to accelerate modern development on Hainan, and change the persistent mainland biases about the island's backward ways. He believed that steady investment and development of Hainan would win the favor of the islanders. Though various claims to the island overlapped through the first half of the twentieth century, Peng believed that responsible government and adequate investment would win Hainan for Beijing. Peng praised Hainan's potential as a breadbasket (*tianfu*), a term usually reserved for the fertile western province of Sichuan. His blunt assessment of the Li problems and the island's undeveloped infrastructure led to his recommendation for tax relief and central government investment in Hainan. Neither was forthcoming, however, and perceptions of the island continued to waver between another potential Taiwan, and a remote and primitive island ruled by a weak mainland government.

In Edward Schafer's study of Hainan's early history, *Shore of Pearls*, he gave full range to the contradictory perceptions of the island from a mainland perspective. It could be Heaven or Hell, and in the mainlander imagination, tropical islands can often be both, simultaneously representing paradise and the inferno.[33] Shafer's focus was on Hainan from its earliest history until 1100, which was the year one of China's most beloved scholar-officials, Su Dongpo, perished on a return journey from his exile on Hainan. In imperial China, Hainan was the most remote destination of banished officials, and Schafer conveyed the shame and mortal fear associated with banishment to the island. But Su Dongpo's wit and genius made his ordeal seem less miserable than another official's experience on Hainan might have been, as is apparent from this preface and poem written during his exile in 1098.

> Having drunk some wine, I went out alone for a walk and visited the house of four Li families, Tzu-yün, Wei, Hui, and Hsien-chüeh.
>
> > Half-sober, half-drunk, I call on the Lis;
> > Bamboo spikes, rattan creepers tangle every step.
> > Following the cow turds I find my way back—
> > Home beyond the cattle pen, west and west again.[34]

Su Dongpo and many other imperial officials were sent to Hainan in exile, and while there, they were charged with governing the wild Li people as well as the Han Chinese settlers of the island. In the preface to this poem, Su wrote that he was stumbling home after a night of drinking with four different households of the indigenous minority Li people. Su is remembered on Hainan as a great official and an adopted son of the island. His playful poems reflect his good spirits during his exile and his good rapport with the local people, but for the Hainanese, he also worked tirelessly to establish academies and teach countless skills from efficient farming methods to geomancy and water management.

These issues of Li conflict and transportation were also central to the Ming official, Hai Rui (1513–1587), who suppressed several Li uprisings, and aimed to open better roads and more military outposts on the island.[35] But unlike Su or Hai Rui, most tenderfoot officials were not equipped for a life in the frontier wilds of Hainan. A special term was used for such environments—*zhangqi*, best translated as "miasma" but conveying also a sense of natural dangers more terrible than the malaria that it usually denoted. Hainan was described in this way even through the twentieth century.[36]

It was Chinese official convention to think of Hainan in such savage terms, but the island's current label as a luxuriant and heavenly "Hawaii of Asia" is also not without precedent. Even in the early days of the Japanese full-scale invasion of China, and two years before the occupation of Hainan, the island was being heralded as the "Paradise of China."[37] Still, even under such a title, in 1937 Han Chinese mainlanders generally found the aboriginal Li population to be bizarre, barbaric, and sometimes terrifying.

They have the piercing eyes of the eagle, the cunning of the fox, and also at certain times a feline bestiality. They feel they are disliked by the Chinese, and consider themselves as hunted beasts, which, if they come out of their dens, run the risk of being ill-treated. Born free, high in the hills, they have got into the habit of running over mountains and valleys. They know every single path or secluded spot of the forest where they wander about with a gun, ready to shoot a bird, as much as to rob a traveler. Poor, they have nothing to lose on their expeditions but often on the contrary, everything to gain.[38]

The Li people, lacking an accurate census of their population, were estimated to constitute about 15 percent of the island's population, which meant they numbered around half a million in the early twentieth century. Hainan's population in 1950, at the time of the Communist takeover was approximately 2.3 million, and at the time of writing is about 8.2 million. The rest of the island's non-Li population was a mixture of mostly Fujian and Guangdong Han Chinese, with less than 1 percent of the population made up of Miao (Hmong) and Hui people.[39]

In assessing Han-Li relations on Hainan, Peng Chengwan shamed previous and current mainland administrations of the island. He outlined the history of Han-Li relations, and his narration of historical trends and the state of affairs in 1919 was pessimistic. "Past officials would bend all their mental efforts to the task of achieving internal peace [on Hainan] but all of their work was not sufficient to solve the problem." Officials complained of the difficulty of pacifying Hainan's interior. Simply put, Li uprisings or disturbances on Hainan constituted *the* perennial issue for the island's officials. "Since the Han Dynasty [more than two millennia earlier, when Han settlement of coastal Hainan began] there has not been a single dynasty that has not had trouble in their dealings with the Li."[40]

The Li were and are not simply a single tribe of ethnically distinct people inhabiting Hainan's interior from prehistoric times. They were granted official status as an ethnic minority (*shaoshu minzu*) of the People's Republic of China when these groups were established in the ethnic identification project during the early years of the PRC.[41] The Li, led by Wang Guoxing, played an important role in preserving and aiding the Communist revolution on Hainan, and as a result, they were one of the earliest groups granted this status as an official national minority group, which allowed them certain privileges, and in their case, an "autonomous" territory in southern-central

Hainan. But the PRC's broad categorization of the Li is not adequate to understand the complexity of these people of Hainan who are thought of as the indigenous Hainanese.

Indeed the origins of the Li on Hainan predate any written history, and the lack of a written Li language prevents accurate speculation on the earliest dates of their settlement on the island. Similarities in costumes, crafts, rituals, and a simple subsistence lifestyle characterize the people I will continue to refer to here as the Li.[42] Early Han settlers on the island encountered the Li people, who were already living in the island's "belly," the southern mountainous jungle region of Hainan. The Han newcomers found the flatter and more fertile plains of northern Hainan more suitable to the lifestyle they had known on the mainland. Interaction between the Han and Li peoples was sporadic and often violent for most of the two thousand years between the earliest Han settlement, and Peng's survey.

For the Han, the rugged mountains and jungles of the south were not suited to their agrarian tradition or their walled villages; and in turn, the Li people needed little from these settlers. But with the newly arrived Han came the availability of some things that would make the lives of the Li easier, and the Han wished to trade for some luxury items that the Li could bring them from the jungles. Plentiful rice, salt, and fish would relieve some of the burden on Li hunters, and ease the environmental strain of their slash-and-burn growing techniques. A special local incense was the main commodity available to the Li that was sought by Han merchants. The divine smell of Hainan's "sinking wood" (*chenxiang*) incense filled the ceremonial halls of Beijing and all those throughout China who could afford it.[43] The incense itself was actually at a stage in the rotting of an aloeswood or agarswood tree, and its nickname of "sinking wood" was apt, as its density was greater than water. The early interactions between Li and Han were based mainly in this trade, but besides this limited exchange of goods, from the perspective of Qing officialdom, the wild Li of the island's interior were better off left alone.[44]

Han migration to Hainan also was a factor in contributing to the complexity of the Li people. Coming mainly from Guangdong to the north, and Fujian to the northeast, most Han settlers remained on the coasts and the northern plains of Hainan, but for various reasons, some of the newcomers ventured farther inland, and sometimes settled in Li villages. From earliest times, Li villages and Li families welcomed some Han guests as participants in their community. And reciprocally, some Li changed their dress—and under Qing rule, their hairstyle—and joined the coastal community. These were known in imperial Chinese vocabulary as "cooked" (*shu*) Li, while those Li who maintained their own culture separate from the coastal settlements were known as the "raw" (*sheng*) Li. This was a common cultural and political distinction in Confucian Chinese encounters with frontier peoples and different ethnic groups. It reflected the universalizing aspect of Han Chinese civilization, which placed all peoples on a spectrum of civilization and barbarity, with the possibility to move along that spectrum based on increasingly "civilized" dress, customs, and often, obedience to imperial rule. But Li uprisings were common, especially in the troubled last century of Qing rule. Most of these uprisings were related to unaddressed Li complaints pertaining to exploitative, violent, and rapacious behavior on the part of Han merchants in their territory.[45]

In his survey, Peng lists some of these newcomers who had joined the Li, based on his interviews with Li villagers throughout the island. Chinese from what is today Yunnan, as well as natives of Southeast Asia traveled to Hainan and sometimes settled in Li villages. Some criminals evaded punishment by fleeing to Hainan, and they sometimes began their lives anew as part of a Li village and family. Soldiers garrisoned on Hainan sometimes deserted to the villages and tribes that they had been sent to pacify.[46] Japanese sailors and merchants also occasionally joined the Li community, as did some Chinese traders whose conduct the Li chiefs considered sufficiently upright and respectful. A small number of descendants of exiled officials, and even some Ming loyalists who fled to Hainan to escape the Manchu rule of the Qing dynasty, also joined the Li people in Hainan's interior.

Despite this complex makeup of Hainan's Li people, most imperial efforts to pacify Hainan put the Li into a single group, just as the PRC authorities have done. And it was the suppression of this homogenized group that most frustrated peaceful Chinese rule of the island. Peng researched the long and troubled history of Li-Han conflict on Hainan, and he drew many conclusions that placed the blame clearly with the Han newcomers to the island, of which he himself was naturally another. His observations are based on extensive interviews across the island, from top officials to the supplications of the poorest villagers, including inhabitants of most regions of the island and most cultural groups. He also used the compiled resources of centuries of official records to compose his survey. His resulting observations provide a broad impression of the general trends in political, social, and economic conditions on the island. His survey is meant for advisement and policy recommendations, and not for historical richness or anecdotal entertainment. So his tendency is to sketch trends rather than provide statistical and anecdotal substantiation of his case.

The poor quality of the civil officials posted to Hainan was a crucial problem, in Peng's view. This view was shared by the Minister of Transportation, Zhao Fan, who also wrote a preface to Peng's survey. Zhao noted that improving the quality of the local and mainland officials serving on

Hainan was central to further developments there. Peng and Zhao blamed the middle officials, the magistrates who were sent to Hainan to govern the Li and Han there. It was their clumsiness, according to Zhao, that accounted for the Li uprisings, though he makes no mention of another likely problem—the perennial and systematic exploitation of the Li people, and the encroaching settlements, by newly arrived Han mainlanders.[47]

The problem of poor quality officials had not been solved, according to Peng, and the recent officials posted to Hainan were no improvement on the long line of inadequate administrators sent to govern Hainan. Their laziness and corruption prevented the deft handling of the ethnic conflict on the island. In keeping with the commonly invoked Confucian attack on mid-level bureaucrats, these officials, sweating in the tropical heat, were always slow to address the minor appeals of the Li, and they brushed off the concerns of the tribal subjects. As a result, minor conflicts gained momentum. Villages were linked through counsels among Li leaders. Arrow heads were passed through the villages as a signal for a counsel, and the chiefs of villages and tribes convened to share their complaints. This led in turn to significant uprisings, that might have been settled by some earlier action taken by the official, who had likely hoped to kick the problem along to his successor, after his three-year term.[48] While Peng is most likely indicating an important failing in the character of many officials posted to Hainan, it bears noting that this is a stock Confucian critique, leveled at both mid-level bureaucrats and their moral shortcomings. Classical Confucianism favors the ethical cultivation of a supreme group of officials to rule through benevolent example, and in this model, failures of government can be pinned on the personal failings of an individual magistrate, rather than a systematic failure of governance or a subject's unanswered and legitimate grievance.

The grievances of the Li people were long-standing issues mainly stemming from neglect of their political concerns and exploitation at the hands of avaricious merchants. At the top of Peng's list were the greedy merchants who exploited the innocence and naïveté of the Li people. Again we may fault Peng for engaging in a classic Confucian anticommercial argument, though the record does indeed bear out the regularity of duplicity on the part of Chinese merchants in their interactions with the Li. An American missionary, B.C. Henry, noted near the end of the nineteenth century that the Li "are victimised in many ways, as to the weight and quantity of the goods they bring on the one hand, and in the payment they receive, either in money or goods, on the other."[49] Other outside sources confirm that the Li-Han troubles were often related to the merchants who traveled into Li territory to sell and trade, well into the twentieth century. These merchants, however, did not constitute a uniform group, and were often made up of criminals escaping the law on the mainland, agents of the Chinese military or civilian government, or members of the Li community who had been integrated into the coastal or northern Hainan Han villages. Some of the merchants, then, were trusted by the Li communities, whereas some divided the communities and exploited them.[50]

During the Qing and earlier dynasties, in response to duplicity, exploitation, or violence from the coastal Han community, the Li launched raids. In 1919, though, Margaret Moninger wrote, "Of late years, no great [Li] raids have taken place, but in earlier times whole ruined villages were witness to their enmity with the Chinese."[51] The 1910s and 1920s saw a shift in Li-Han relations, as Moninger observed. During the temporary garrisoning of Long Jiguang's soldiers on Hainan, the Li took part in uprisings led by Hainanese Han fighters against the mainlanders. In these sporadic and poorly documented uprisings, a precedent was established for cooperation between the Li and Han of Hainan in a common cause.[52]

While these occasional political alliances between the Li and Han developed, economic practices were slow to change. Among other products, the merchants brought alcohol, cigarettes, and opium into Li villages in the late Qing and through the early republican period. The drugs were sold to the Li people on credit at first. The prices were inflated, but the unfamiliar and appealing idea of credit, according to Peng, made the Li eager to accept the novel drugs for what seemed like a minimal price. These debts accumulated, and once a year, the merchants would settle the accounts, and collect on the debts. For those Li who could not pay the debts, according to Peng's study, the merchants took several courses of action. They sometimes demanded the precious few animals that the Li possessed as payment of their liquor and cigarette debts. The same merchants who made these claims had often brought the same livestock into the jungles in the first place and traded them to the Li.[53]

Further, according to Peng's survey, cattle were not the only precious collateral claimed by exploitative merchants in exchange for the debts that the merchants had encouraged the Li to pile up throughout the year. If the Li debtor in question had a daughter, the merchant might take her in exchange for the debt. If the debtor had no daughter, his son might be taken; and if he was childless, he could be taken into bondage or servitude himself.

In summary, Peng wrote that there was a huge and perhaps unbridgeable gap (*honggou*) between the Han and the Li populations. In the language of the recent revolution and the social upheaval that was taking place throughout Chinese cities even as Peng conducted the survey, he wrote that the most recent Li movement (*yundong*) could be described as the Li people's anti-Han revolution (*geming*).[54] And here, Peng finally broke with the paternal language of his Qing predecessors. Like Han or Manchu observers of the Li who came before him, and the Communists who would come later in the 1950s and 1960s, Peng criticized the administration of the island by the local officials who could not resist the temptations of graft and corruption, being so far from the punishing hand of Beijing. In describing the Li movement as something more than violent and unruly bandits who were reacting to oppressive and extractive individual officials, Peng was taking a longer and less conventional view. The Li were a force to be reckoned with as the original hosts of Hainan, and in the next three decades, the Japanese and the Nationalists would learn this firsthand. The Li were the cultural, political, economic, and geographical heart of the island.

Peng Chengwan was not the only outside observer who took a keen interest in the Li people as an essential element to the development of Hainan. Ten years after Peng's survey, the German anthropologist, Hans Stübel made two trips to Hainan to observe the Li people, out of which came his encyclopedic volume, *Die Li-stämme der insel Hainan* (The Li tribe of Hainan Island). Stübel traveled to Hainan in 1931 and 1932, and published his lavishly illustrated tome on Li ethnography in 1937. Ten years later, when Hainan was under Japanese occupation, Tokyo University's Kunio Odaka published *Economic Organization of the Li Tribes*. Using maps made by the Japanese Nitrogen and Electric Company, and enjoying the hospitality of the Ledong Japanese Marine base, Odaka published his study on a smaller group of Li villages with an emphasis on their usefulness to the Japanese governance and economic development of the island.[55]

These three surveys—Peng's in 1920, Stübel's in 1937, and Odaka's in 1942—all point to the Li as a crucial factor in the development of Hainan. Clearly separable from the Han majority of the island, the three observers saw the Li as a great potential resource. Of course, the three men did not plan to completely circumvent any interaction with the mainly coastal-dwelling 85 percent of Hainan's Han inhabitants and relate only to the Li people. But the latest of the three observers, Odaka, hoped to separate the Li from the Han, and to think of the Li as a buffer between the Japanese and those Chinese of the island who were hostile to Japanese rule and economic development.

While Peng's view of the Li people was perhaps more accurate than his predecessors, his plans for dealing with them was similarly shortsighted. He pointed them out as an obstacle to development and he noted the strength and potential of exploiting the Li in making Hainan a new breadbasket for China. And for Peng, the "training" or "breaking" (*xun*) of the wild Li people was an essential ingredient to this formula of development. Stübel's aim in his survey of the Li people was less explicit in its plans for the development of the island. This is to be expected considering that the German interest in the region was minimal at this time, especially compared with the Beijing officials of the 1920s and the Japanese occupiers of the early 1940s. Stübel's sought to establish the lineage of the Li people as traced through their material culture.

Odaka, on the other hand, is perfectly explicit in the preface to his study when he outlines his goals for this study of the Li.

> This survey of the condition of the social and economic organizations of the Li of Hainan has been undertaken in the hope that the information obtained will be useful to the [Japanese] administration in governing them. . . . As part of the policy to maintain order, it is necessary to use the Li section of the island as a buffer region against the Chinese, especially against the guerillas, in order to provide a stable background for our military bases. As to the problem of developing the island, it is not necessary to utilize its natural resources, but the Li themselves must be utilized as a source of labor.[56]

Odaka believed that the Li people were potential allies for the Japanese against the coastal Han Chinese of Hainan.[57] In the 1910s and 1920s, the Li situation was only one of a two-part problem preventing the successful development of Hainan. The other was the poor infrastructure, which was in a sense, the other side of the same coin. "Civilizing" the Li, or changing their ways of agriculture, education, and political organization, would be impossible without adequate communication and transportation networks on the island.

Transportation, Communication, Isolation

Peng Chengwan's assessment of the transportation infrastructure on Hainan was mixed. Some aspects of the transportation system were predictably primitive compared to the mainland, like the complete lack of railroads and paved roads. But in other areas, like water transport and access to the island's interior, Peng sought to dislodge stubborn mainlander opinions about Hainan as hopelessly backward and in need of endless investment. He did not suggest Hainan was not in need of great attention and funding, but he urged a more pragmatic and informed approach to the specificities of Hainan's strengths and weaknesses in its transportation infrastructure.

In 1919, Peng Changwan found three automobiles on Hainan island. They had been recently brought to Hainan by a businessman who purchased them in Hong Kong. In December of 1918, the cars arrived in Haikou to local excitement, according to Peng. They sat six passengers each, and were in constant need of repair. This was still the dawn of motoring throughout the world, but even so, the three vehicles already appear pathetic in Peng's description. They jostled their passengers relentlessly along the ten-kilometer road between Haikou and neighboring Fucheng in the north.

At the time of their purchase, the company, headed by one Li Jinlong, had boasted that they would be able to run the cars from Haikou to Ding'an, dozens of kilometers away, and then on to the relatively cosmopolitan town of Wenchang on the northeastern coast of the island. Wenchang was the ancestral home of the famous Song family and many prominent generals, as well as being the traditional home of the political and cultural elites of Hainan, supplying the island's government with most of its low-level officials and educated workers.

But the plan to connect Wenchang and Haikou by automobile was abandoned when it became apparent that the cars simply could not sustain the pounding that the bumpy roads would inflict on them; nor could they escape the muddy ruts and washouts that resulted from any significant rainfall. So the planners adjusted their goals. The ten-kilometer trip from Haikou to Fucheng was much more modest, but it still was not easy. The huge puddles were too deep for the cars to cross in wet weather. The automobiles were already out of date and they would have needed constant repair even without the hazards of tropical weather and poor quality roads.

Peng wrote of the cars with somewhat amusing language, but he also expressed a cautious optimism about the enterprise. Of course, he noted, these cars were merely a novelty to wealthy Haikou dwellers who could pay 40 *jiao* for a ride to Fucheng and another 40 for the ride back. Li Jinlong's initial investment in buying the cars was 20,000 *yuan*, according to Peng, and the investment seemed at first to be symbolic considering that one fully loaded car brought only 4.8 *yuan* for a round-trip from Haikou to Fucheng. But Peng praised Li's initiative with this little business, noting that the three cars could make sixty round-trips each day, bringing in a maximum potential net income of 864 *yuan* for the small company. Of course, this was considering all conditions were perfect, the cars did not break down en route, and every car was fully loaded with passengers.

In reality, Li Jinlong's business actually did manage to turn a tidy profit in several months between the arrival of the automobiles in December of 1918, and the time of Peng's survey visit in the spring of 1919. On average, Li's company turned 100 *yuan* in profits every day, significantly less than Peng's ambitious and fanciful calculations for the venture, but still, a brisk business. Peng was impressed with the industriousness of this businessman, and the cleverness of the Hainan people more generally. He concluded that it was not merely a symbolic venture, but held promise for future enterprises in transportation innovation.[58]

What Peng Chengwan could not have known in 1919, or when the survey was published a year later, was that this little enterprise was in fact a harbinger of a later trend of Hainanese professionalization in work related to the automobile. Especially in the Southeast Asia Hainanese communities, auto mechanics and chauffeurs became vocations in which the Hainan community was most prolific.[59] The number of cars on Hainan island was not significant through the early and mid-twentieth century, but in 1920, Peng Chengwan saw potential in the development of Hainan's infrastructure through efforts like Li Jinlong's.

While praising the industrious Li Jinlong, Peng Chengwan still did not avoid the blunt conclusion that Hainan's roads would need extensive investment and labor in order to sustain anything more than this modest motoring route between two northern towns. Horse and ox carts were more suited to the transportation realities of Hainan, and these—especially ox carts—were not in short supply. Horses were not as common. At the end of Qing Dynasty in 1911, a unit of the Hunan Army's cavalry that was stationed in Hainan was abruptly demobilized. The demobilization left the cavalrymen with no vocational opportunities or assets, except for the thirty or forty steeds of their unit. Again, Peng takes this chance to make an example of the industriousness and enterprising savvy that combined into good business potential on Hainan. Several of the cavalrymen joined together and formed a company that provided the use of their horses and carts for the transportation of people and goods. Peng notes wryly that the steeds were generally more reliable than Li Jinlong's automobiles, and they usually got their passengers to their nearby destinations in about the same amount of time.[60]

Peng's optimism for change on Hainan was not misplaced. Less than a decade later, M. Savina, a French observer who visited Hainan in 1928, referred to the northern Hainanese towns of Haikou and Qiongzhou as the island's "pride," noting that they offered access by automobile and even airplane. Savina wrote that on his visit, wireless telegraph, telephones, and electricity were common in Haikou, and that the city featured large boulevards, lined with modern buildings and stores. The city walls that one observer noted in 1919, had been destroyed by 1928, and the city was moving toward a more modern design that allowed migrant workers to move in and out of the city more freely. For Savina, this prevented an accurate estimate of the northern city's population of about sixty thousand, but it also was a sign of a move away from the strict and stultifying distinction between rural and urban workers.[61]

Three years later, in 1931, a Presbyterian mission newsletter noted the increasing profile of automobiles and related occupations: "the advent of the Ford and its competitors has given rise to new professions, the chauffeurs especially being persons of considerable economic importance . . . The motor car is the factor most responsible for material change in Hainan during these past fifty years and is perhaps the forerunner of many modern improvements yet to come."[62] Li Jinlong's little motoring business had indeed inspired a trend on Hainan.

Besides the anecdotal examples of the Hunan cavalry horses and Li Jinlong's three-car automobile company, Peng Chengwan was eager to note that Hainan's transportation infrastructure had significant potential, and in fact was already quite developed in several ways. According to Peng's findings in 1920, tales of the dangers and inaccessibility of the island's interior were greatly exaggerated among mainland and foreign prejudices. Peng disabused the reader of notions about Hainan's completely inaccessible interior.

He wrote of an amusing example during the late Qing, when several conflicts erupted between imperial troops and the local Li people of the interior. Feng Zicai (1818–1903), a general in the imperial army and hero of the Sino-French War in 1885, led Qing forces in suppressing a Li uprising in 1887. At the conflict's resolution, Feng memorialized the emperor, reporting the successful campaign and adding that he would take this opportunity to improve access to the island's remote interior regions by building new roads.[63]

The new roads, according to Feng Zicai, would connect the southern ports to the Li villages, where luxury goods like incense, teak, and sandalwood could be bought from the Li. Feng claimed that these interior villages had never been connected to the coastal villages and cities, and that his work would bring these Li people and their products into the imperial fold for the first time in the history of the Chinese empire. These claims of inaccessibility correspond to similar ones made by the Americans, B.C. Henry and Leonard Clark, in 1886 and 1938, respectively. All three men claimed to be the ones to first bring the island's interior into contact with the outside world. But all three of these outsiders seem to exaggerate the remoteness of the island's interior villages. Feng Zicai was certainly familiar with the work of the Ming official and Hainan native, Hai Rui, who had advocated the construction of two military highways bisecting the island's central Li territory from north to south and east to west. In his memorial application for the highest civil service degree, Hai Rui connected the two aims on Hainan of improved transportation and Li pacification.[64] While these proposed highways had not been constructed by the time of Feng Zicai's campaigns against the Li, the dual concerns remained, as they did for Peng Chengwan in 1919.

Peng read Feng's reports and visited these Li villages along some of the routes that Feng claimed to have opened only a few decades earlier. He visited with the Li people in these villages, and talked with them about their conflicts with the imperial armies, and their contacts with traders. Peng discovered that Feng's claims to have been the one to open these routes for the first time had been hugely exaggerated. Some old Li tribesmen laughed when Peng asked them about having been newly connected to the coastal Han by Feng's 1887 efforts. Indeed, they had heard of Feng Zicai making such claims, like a frontiersman who was bringing the civilization of the empire to the Li villages.

Feng Zicai had ordered teams of Li villagers dragooned to "build" the roads. In reality, according to Peng's findings in the survey, young men of the Li villages did indeed accompany Feng with their tools. But they were walking along the roads that had existed for centuries, and paths that connected one village to the next, and eventually connected to coastal towns. Still, in a grand and ceremonious way, Feng ordered that these roads were to be "opened." The confused Li men trimmed a few branches that hung in the road, pulled some errant weeds and plants that had sprouted in the paths, and Feng claimed victory in his endeavor. Today, at the top of Wuzhishan, a mighty rock inscription still testifies to Feng Zicai's efforts: "Single-handedly holding up the heavens."[65] In his survey, Peng refers to Feng's "so-called 'opening of the roads'" (*suowei kailu*), noting that even the most remote Li villages had been connected to the coast and the Han people for centuries.

Though the story was not always one of hostility, as the earlier description of Li-Han conflict may suggest, the lives of the interior Li villages were led in voluntary seclusion. Peng could not avoid this conclusion in his survey. He had to acknowledge that the lack of "civilization" among the Li was not due to a lack of trying, or a lack of contact.[66]

When the Hainanese Communist movement took root as a militia and guerrilla military struggle, the poor infrastructure of the island served as a boon to their efforts, for it prevented an organized counterinsurgency by either the Nationalists or the Japanese. And making common cause with much of the Li population in fighting the Japanese and the Nationalists, the Hainan Communists were allowed to operate in the island's mountainous interior, which had once been terra incognita for international and mainland Chinese geographers and surveyors.

While this chapter has served as an introduction to some of the trends in Hainan's relationship with mainland China and the region, the following will examine Hainan's specific political and cultural world and some of its prominent actors in the early twentieth century, and the landscape out of which the Communist movement there emerged. The cultural and ethnic dimensions of the island and its relationship with the mainland was the main factor in the shape that the Hainan Communist revolution would take in the decades to come.

CHAPTER 2

POLITICAL PROSPECTS IN THE EARLY REPUBLIC

Revolution, Warlords, and Diaspora, 1912–1926

Isolation in a Disintegrating National Polity

From the fall of the Qing in 1911 until the founding of the People's Republic of China in 1949, Hainan island became increasingly isolated from politics on the national stage. The island's government had only occasional significant contact with the central authorities from 1911 to 1930, when the leadership of Guangdong Province (which then included Hainan) effectively declared its regional independence. Peng Chengwan's 1920 survey was an exception to this trend, and thus it is a rare insight to Hainan in this period beyond the writings of foreign missionaries and other travelers. In the early republic, Hainan's turn away from the central government reflected the broader political atmosphere throughout China in which provincial leaders gained strength in relation to a weak national authority in Beijing.

By the late 1910s, Chinese advocates of a more federalized national polity put forth their ideas in newspapers and political debates, and gained support among some members of the National Assembly as well as prominent citizens in their home provinces. The impetus for increasing regional power, however, came from extremely divergent perspectives, including a diverse spectrum of voices from the most progressive intellectuals to the most conservative warlords. The lack of common ground prevented the federalist issue from becoming a clear and strong political platform, and weakened it in the face of the eventual rise of the centralized authority of the Nationalist Party in the mid-1920s.[1]

Though federalism ultimately failed as a ruling philosophy in the early republic, provincial militarism gave several provinces de facto autonomy in the 1910s and 1920s, if not a stake in a harmonious federated government. Some called these regional military governors "warlords," but whatever their label, they forced a rough-hewn federalism on the weak central government, in the absence of any centralizing ruler or ruling platform. The various revolutionary credos that had brought about the end of imperial China in 1911 actually shared few specific aims other than opposition to Qing rule by the minority Manchus. The project to construct a national consciousness from these diverging factions, therefore, produced a brand of patriotism that was initially weaker than residual local and provincial identities. According to historian John Fitzgerald, in his assessment of the *longue durée* of Chinese provinces in history, "Attempts to balance the age-old demands of center and province in the twentieth century were compounded by an additional problem common to revolutionary states: the need to build new state structures on unorthodox ideological, social and economic foundations."[2]

Many regional leaders opposed the new project of cohesive, modern nation-building, and instead chose to strengthen their regional bases rather than throwing in their lot with the feeble national government. Hainan had its own regional leaders, and in keeping with the traditional Chinese adage, *Tian gao huangdi yuan* (Heaven is high and the emperor is far away), in China's deep south, the great distance from central authority made their brand of regionalism especially potent. While China does not have exactly the same historically fraught divide between north and south as the United States, cultural and political divisions between northern and southern China have been strong in most periods of its history, with hostility and resentment near the surface even in times of peace. In their recent examinations of the Taiping Rebellion (1850–1864), which largely split the country into a rebellious south and a north that hoped to preserve the empire, Stephen R. Platt and Tobie Meyer-Fong cast the conflict as the seminal event of the nineteenth century; both authors draw numerous comparisons with its contemporary American Civil War.[3] The legacy of Qing success in suppressing this conflict, according to both authors, was not simply the reinforcement of the dynasty's rule, but more significantly, it provided traction for the growing resentment in an alienated south that continued to hum with revolutionary energy until the dynasty's demise in 1911 and beyond.

In another of John Fitzgerald's works, this one on Guangdong separatism, he notes that the Guangdong ruler, Chen Jitang (1890–1954), effectively declared the independence of his province (which included Hainan) when he withdrew his support for the Nationalists' Nanjing government in the early 1930s. From 1911 through the end of the 1920s, Guangdong's regional rulers had changed often and violently. Guangzhou (Canton) was an early center of the revolutionary movement that overthrew the Qing government in 1911, and then continued to resist the rule of the republican government under Yuan Shikai (1859–1916), which lasted from 1912 until Yuan's death in 1916, and continued under his several militarist protégés. Guangdong political leaders remained at odds with most in the parade of short-lived northern regimes that followed, but also saw the occasional violent appearance within their region of a militarist ally of Beijing who made some temporary political and territorial gains.

By the time of Chen Jitang's effective declaration of independence, it was actually not the northern warlords, but the new revolutionary regime in Nanjing that he was cutting ties with. Chiang Kai-shek (Jiang Jieshi, 1887–1975) and the Nationalists had successfully ousted the Beijing government in 1927 and moved the capital south to Nanjing. The persistence of regional power was proven in Chen's actions, even opposing the new southern regime that shared its Guangdong political origins. Southern independence took on a new ferocity in this era. It is noteworthy that in the 1930s, Guangdong, as the southern birthplace of China's republican revolution, became one of the most autonomous territories in China, maintaining strained relations with the Nanjing government that it helped to create.[4]

Chen Jitang's effective independence was the culmination of two decades of southern separatism and revolution. This regionalism frustrated calls to patriotism and unity in these formative and troubled decades. We mark certain events as watersheds in the nationalist and patriotic history of China, such as the May Fourth Movement of 1919, the May Thirtieth Movement of 1925, and, of course, the long anti-Japanese resistance struggle beginning in the early 1930s. But in such a vast country as China, these events did not easily or immediately galvanize a population and transform the disintegrated nation into a modern national polity. Doubtless events as traumatic as the Japanese invasion served to create a strong negatively defined sense of national identity—a culture of resistance that is as coherent as any foundation for modern nationalism. And yet even the Japanese invasion (let alone the urban-based and intellectual-driven May Fourth and May Thirtieth movements) certainly had varied impacts throughout the country that cannot be painted in one retroactive hue of countrywide experienced nationalism. In Hainan, the period from 1911 through the Japanese invasion of the island in 1939 saw the development of a revolutionary movement that was distinct in the quality of being shaped by local and regional events.

It was in this context of disunity, as a district under the administration of Guangdong, that the Communist movement on Hainan began to take shape in the mid-1920s. Hainan's leaders did not hope to construct an independent satrapy on the island, but rather a provincial administration that was increasingly tied to the national government. Local conflicts and persistent militarism frustrated their efforts to incorporate the island into the national polity. The causes of the inward turn on Hainan were many, including factors such as the island's obvious geographical isolation; strained and tenuous relations between Hainan islanders and the once-supportive "bourgeois" overseas Hainanese community; a perennial perception, on the part of some Hainanese, of mainland political envoys (including Communists) as officious and exploitative; a stubbornly provincial and perhaps simplistic Hainanese perception of anti-imperialism and class struggle.

From the mainland and abroad, Hainan's inward turn and isolation was reciprocated in the low estimation of the island's importance even to the point of Sun Yat-sen's (1866–1925) alleged willingness to sell off Hainan's economic sovereignty to the Japanese in exchange for guns and cash, which was not uncharacteristic of Sun's efforts to essentially mortgage portions of the country that were not always within his control. Hainan's revolutionaries played their part in the national Chinese revolution, whether it was the 1911 revolution, the Nationalist conquest, or the Communist revolution. The prominence of some of them would bring the island of Hainan into a position of newfound importance in national politics, or at least this was the expressed hope of many political activists whose roots and priorities were in Hainan in the twentieth century.[5] After the fall of the Qing in 1911, Hainanese progressives and revolutionaries in the early republic were tied especially close to the mainland southern revolution and Sun Yat-sen. One similarity in the republican movement of the early twentieth century on Hainan was the international orientation of these early revolutionaries, though there was also a streak of antiforeign animosity on Hainan that sometimes came to the surface in violence.

Haikou housed several consulates and had been forcibly opened as a treaty port hosting foreign trade since the Treaty of Tianjin in 1860 ended the second Opium War.[6] The implications of this foreign presence on Hainan were widely known—extraterritoriality, missionary activity, and foreign tariff control. Anti-imperial sentiment was sometimes expressed in an organized way through student groups and fundraising in Southeast Asia, Japan, and around the world, but it could also erupt in seemingly random acts of violence, labeled outrages of "Boxerism" by the foreign press, recalling the antiforeign and anti-Christian movement of the turn of the century.

In the early twentieth century, minor disturbances that brought to mind this recent harrowing experience for foreigners in China often led to an increased gunboat presence around Haikou or requests for this, as well as executions and heavy indemnities. One such incident was the murder of Reverend George D. Byers, of the American Presbyterian Mission Society in June of 1924 in Jiaji (then called Kachek by foreigners). The ensuing legal battle reflected the Byzantine complexity of American and Chinese diplomacy and governance, as well as the Presbyterian Church authorities. The challenges to the resolution of the diplomatic crisis that resulted from the Byers killing involved the sensitivities of a strong new nationalism developing throughout China, and even at the ends of the earth in Hainan.[7] But banditry such as the Byers incident is obviously not the kind of patriotic anti-imperialism expressed in student protest or worker strikes. Anti-imperialism, xenophobia, and nativism seem to overlap in a complex and sometimes messy way on Hainan. One American observer who had been a guest of Byers only weeks before his murder suggested that indeed the line between Hainan's soldiers and bandits was a blurry one. He wrote in 1925, "A few of these immature rowdies in ragged semi-uniform commonly miscalled soldiers of China were loafing and gambling about Kachek [Jiaji], but I saw none at all in Hainan compared with Canton [Guangzhou] and many another place on the mainland. It seems there were plenty [of soldiers], but most of them were up country fighting the bandits, for robbery and brigandage were rampant in many parts of the island."[8]

The unclear distinction between banditry and soldiery was a common problem in China in this era, and indeed one observer's brigand was another's patriotic militiaman. But suspicion of foreigners had a very long history in Hainan, going back even to the Ming dynasty. In 1583, a vessel carrying Franciscan friars and laymen through the South China Sea was forced by a tropical storm to seek shelter on Hainan. Their hosts on Hainan presumed that they were all foreign spies and sent them to Guangzhou (Canton), where local Portuguese authorities purchased their freedom.[9]

The French Catholic history on Hainan was also a long one, but by the early twentieth century, their interest in Hainan had expanded significantly since their neighboring mainland holdings in Indochina put the island within its "sphere of influence." Besides proselytizing and tariff control, the French on Hainan were also the most dominant foreigners in the coolie trade, supplying workers to projects around the globe. These workers often lived in a legal gray area between outright slavery and volunteer servitude. In the center of Haikou, French traders had set up a prominent barracoon, or holding pen for their human wares. In 1913, local activists frustrated the operation of this French business. In the few records of this event, an unnamed member of the Revolutionary Party (Gemingdang) initiated an act of sabotage to the French going concern. In what was later called the "Pigsty Smashing Incident," the barracoon was destroyed and one of its minders killed. Although there are few sources on the incident, Chinese sources remember it as a blow struck for anti-imperialism on Hainan, because thirty of the chained coolies were freed instead of being shipped off by their French masters.[10] The Pigsty Smashing Incident and the murder of Reverend Byers represent localized incidents that are only vaguely connected to the anti-imperialism and Chinese nationalism that intellectuals and political leaders on the Chinese mainland and in the global Chinese community were expressing so eloquently at the same time. In some ways, they represent both ends of the spectrum of political activism and revolutionary violence on Hainan, with brigands on one end and liberators on the other. The reality was, of course, rarely this clear.

But the Hainanese revolutionary movement was also connected to this level of revolutionary rhetoric beyond its shores. In the late Qing and early republic, some Hainanese merchants and activists took part in the cosmopolitan revolutionary movement. Hainanese identity was perhaps paradoxically a mixture of both virulent nativism and wealthy cosmopolitanism. The revolutionary impetus of the 1910s was both the republican consciousness of Hainan's diaspora and the hot-blooded Hainanese nativist resistance to extractive foreign presences on the island, sometimes referred to in Chinese as *paiwai*, which can mean a kind of antiforeignism that essentially resists all outside forces. This thread within the fabric of Hainanese identity would be woven closely into the Communist movement on the island, and give rise to concerns among the mainland Communist leadership that Hainan would be difficult to bring into a subordinate relationship with central rule.

In the late 1920s, the Communist movement on Hainan became a violent and localized conflict that effectively shed the national, let alone international, ideology, and spirit. The line from Hainan's globe-trotting merchants and newspapermen like Lin Wenying (1873–1914) to Communist guerrilla leaders like Feng Baiju (1903–1973) is a clear one, and both ends of the trajectory represent an important side of the island's cultural and revolutionary character. But the path from one to the other was not a smooth or consistent one.

Lin Wenying and Hainan's Diaspora from the Qing to the Early Republic

In the early years of the republic, Hainan's prominent leaders did not think of the island as being isolated in every sense. Thousands of Hainanese people left their island to find work throughout the world, and often maintained connections to their island home through remittances and Hainanese associations in their new homes. While some of the Hainanese diaspora anticipated a short stay, many made permanent homes abroad, in the Americas, Australia, Europe, and especially in neighboring Southeast Asia. At the time of writing, the Hainanese provincial government claims that three million Hainanese live abroad, more than a third of the total 8.5 million people living on the island itself (as of a 2007 census).[11]

Song Yaoru (Charlie Soong, 1863–1918), a native of Wenchang, Hainan, was perhaps the most famous of Hainan's wandering sons. Song was the patriarch of the most powerful family in twentieth-century China, with three daughters who married Sun Yat-sen, H.H. Kung (Kong Xiangxi, 1881–1967), and Chiang Kai-shek; and a son, T.V. Soong (Song Ziwen, 1891–1971) who would rise nearly to the pinnacle of political and economic power in China. In spite of (or perhaps because of) the huge popularity of Sterling Seagrave's account of the Song family, academic historians generally overlook Song's importance in modern Chinese history.[12] Song was certainly an important financier of Sun Yat-sen's revolutionary efforts, and as a Hainanese was comfortable traveling the world.[13] Born to a family of little means, he built his fortune on personal and professional affiliations and on bible sales, to ultimately live a life of cosmopolitan comfort.

Hainan's merchants and politicians like Song were aware of, and deeply involved in, the anti-Qing revolutionary movements throughout the region and throughout the world in the final years of the Qing. The island's central location in eastern Asia was reflected in the cosmopolitan outlook of its merchants, intercontinental migrant workers, and its progressive leaders in the late Qing and the early republic. In the first decade of the twentieth century, as the Qing monarchy attempted to reform itself, revolutionary activists traveled throughout the world raising money to fund their plots to overthrow the ruling Manchus, and Hainanese were prominent among those late Qing and early republican revolutionaries. While nationalism grew among this global network of revolutionary organizers and financiers, provincial loyalties also served to rally revolutionary and republican enthusiasm. Newspapers, for example, were printed and read in communities of Chinese abroad with a provincial or regional target audience in mind.[14]

In a study of Guangzhou (Canton) in the first two decades of Communist rule, Ezra Vogel examined the regional foundations on which the People's Republic of China (PRC) was built. He noted that certain "Cantonese traits" were pervasive not only in that city, but throughout Guangdong Province, the expansive southern region, and even among the overseas communities that traced their ancestry to that area.[15] In his study of Guangdong during the revolution that ended the Qing, Edward Rhoads found that a globally connected merchant class had begun to challenge the traditional gentry in the southern region. The prominent role of merchants in the revolutionary movement reflected the outward and worldly orientation of the coastal Guangdong population, and also that of Hainan, where regional domestic and international trade flourished. In the final years of the Qing, the merchant class had begun to expand its local power and influence, especially following the 1905 abolition of the Confucian examination system that had once been the only channel to political power. New chambers of commerce and educational institutions formalized and reinforced the power of prominent local merchants, and strengthened this distinct attribute of the southern coastal elites.[16]

But southern Chinese bonds were even stronger and more complex than these new political and economic developments. In the early and mid-seventeenth century, Ming loyalists had retreated to the south for their last stand during the conquest that brought it low and in the early years of its successor, the Manchu Qing. For the Ming loyalists and any Chinese simply fleeing the Manchu conquerors, Hainan became a temporary refuge at the end of the earth. Today, one of the great tourist attractions of all China is a rock formation on the southern coast of Hainan called *Tianya haijiao*, which roughly translates as "the edge of the earth." Hainan was a hotbed of Ming loyalism, and as the Manchu Qing dynasty became more and more a fact of life, those loyalists melted into the population of Hainan, as in other parts of China. But for many, their resentment remained, either in specifically anti-Manchu racial hatred, or in more generally rebellious societies that could become bandits, criminal gangs, or more organized resistors of imperial rule. The southern coast caused anxiety for those shipping through the South China Sea, for seasonal piracy was a constant lure for young men who could not sustain themselves on terra firma, whether due to drought or warfare, flood or famine. The most organized and violent of these movements produced by the southern provinces was of course the Taiping Rebellion (1850–1864). Its millenarian and anti-Manchu reason for being dovetailed with the rebellious secret societies of the south, some of which still professed allegiance to the Ming loyalists of centuries earlier.

Sun Yat-sen had been an especially inspiring figure among overseas Chinese, many of whom were connected to Hainan through birth or through kinship and native-place associations that were a primary structure within the societies of overseas Chinese. During the tumultuous nineteenth century, emigration from southern China increased dramatically to meet the labor needs of imperial and domestic infrastructure projects of the Western powers throughout their realms. From South Africa, to Cuba, to Peru, to Southeast Asia, and the American West, Chinese laborers were important in building and working the cities of the world.[17]

In the 1910s, 1920s, and 1930s, there was a surge of Hainanese migration and movement between the island and mainland southeast Asia, as well as to the Philippines, Hong Kong, and Singapore. Junks full of Hainanese immigrants sailed on the strong but dangerous late summer and autumn monsoon winds. Those junks that successfully navigated the rough seas would land on the shores of Malaya. The men would sometimes find their way to their Hainan contacts waiting in Malaya, but, according to Victor Purcell, the Malay Immigration Department functioned "very satisfactorily." Many of these Hainan immigrants were apprehended by the Malay authorities, and promptly shipped back to Hainan.[18]

Hainanese coherence abroad remained strong in native place associations and the usual Chinese provincial clustering occurred of Hainanese within certain occupations, in this case, as domestic servants and mechanics. In 1919, the American missionary, Margaret Moninger, noticed the significance of the ties of Hainan to Southeast Asia. "Many of the men develop the wanderlust and go by junk to Siam, the Straits Settlements, or Burma, where they become house servants or ships' boys, work on rubber plantations or in mines, or possibly go into business in shops." Moninger noted that it was common to meet Hainanese who spoke perfect English, acquired during long stays in British Malaya or Hong Kong. She also remarked on the death rituals that connected Hainan island to the communities of Hainanese who traveled abroad: ". . . many of the men die in the south, and down country here one will sometimes see a row of eight or ten graves, in such regular order as to excite curiosity. On inquiry, these are found to be the graves to which the souls of the deceased have been called, and in which a frog or some other small animal has been buried with all the usual ceremonies." Moninger also wrote that some of these men who traveled to British colonies returned to visit Hainan after having converted to Christianity. Some of them, having gone abroad for their work without their wives, and being about to set out alone again, implored Moninger and other missionaries to accept their wives into their mission schools.[19]

While many of these overseas Chinese (*Huaqiao*) became part of a permanent community in their new respective homes, many also continued to travel back and forth between their adopted homes and their native China. But even those who did not return to China maintained their strong cultural identity, often resisting the hyphenated designation of Chinese-Americans, Chinese-Africans, and so on.[20] This group of overseas Chinese had a distinct character and place in Chinese society when and if they did return. In some instances, the Chinese government deemed parts of the Chinese population as overseas Chinese even though they had moved permanently back to their native province. Under the Communist regime beginning in 1949, for example, 20 percent of Guangdong's population living within that province (then including Hainan) was considered to be *Huaqiao*, or overseas Chinese, simply because of their connections or their personal experience in foreign countries.[21]

In the waning years of the Qing, worldly revolutionaries like Lin Wenying organized anti-Manchu propaganda everywhere they could.[22] Lin, like Song Yaoru, traced his ancestral roots to Wenchang, the northeastern city that produced many of Hainan's most prominent scholars and wealthiest merchants. He was actually born in Bangkok, Siam (Thailand) to a wealthy family, the son of a Wenchang merchant and a Thai mother. According to Philip Kuhn's study of Chinese emigration in this period, the marriage of Chinese merchants, craftsmen, and political refugees to Thai women was common. "Siam afforded flexibility to the [Chinese] immigrant," and "Siamese tolerance" prevailed until the early twentieth century.[23] Throughout most of the Qing dynasty there seems to have been an easy flow of Chinese into and out of Siam, without a local effort to assimilate or expel the Chinese immigrants. The twentieth century saw the increasing importance of rigid racial definitions, a discourse probably accelerated by the increasing dominance of Western powers in the region. Emerging ideas of racial and national belonging became stronger than cultural and imperial sources of identity and belonging. Thai, Vietnamese, Chinese, and other labels became racial denotations as the foundation of building new nation-states, and they also became powerful tools in division, exclusion, and persecution.

In the early years of the twentieth century, the Chinese in Siam became a scapegoat for the young King Rama VI (1881–1925), who translated the "fashionable European anti-Semitic clichés" into anti-Chinese denouncements in his native country.[24] It is not clear whether Lin Wenying or his family were personally affected by Rama VI's anti-Sinitism, or how prevalent that that attitude was in Thailand. Lin spent much of his adult life traveling between Japan, China, and back to Siam, studying and organizing revolutionary forces. By the time of Rama VI's reign and the promotion of Siamese/Thai nationalism beginning in 1910, Lin had begun to focus his efforts away from Siam and toward China and his ancestral home in Hainan.

In 1903, at the age of thirty, Lin Wenying had traveled to Tokyo to study politics at Tokyo University of Law and Government. Two years later, in August of 1905, he had joined the Tongmenghui (Revolutionary Alliance)—the party often credited as the political center of the anti-Qing revolution—after hearing a speech by Sun Yat-sen, who would later become the first president and civilian leader of the Chinese republican government. After graduating in 1907, Lin returned to Siam, where he became a professional revolutionary, occasionally working closely with Sun when the latter was in Siam. According to one biography of Lin, the closeness of their purpose and their fraternal bond was reflected in the fact that the two "brothers" even shared a bed during their work together when it was necessary for Sun to keep a low profile while in Siam. This account also notes that the bed that they shared is currently housed in a Bangkok museum. Sun's time spent raising funds and revolutionary fervor is especially remembered in Bangkok's Chinatown, where the Thai government immortalized him by renaming a street "Soi Sun Yat-sen."[25]

Lin Wenying represents the earliest generation of Hainan revolutionaries, and Chinese Communist historians claim him as such in the Communist pantheon although his death predates the founding of the Chinese Communist Party by seven years.[26] Lin traveled throughout the region, often with Sun Yat-sen, giving speeches and raising funds for the revolutionaries who fought for the overthrow of Manchu rule and the establishment of a new Chinese republic. Although his revolutionary credo, like Sun's, did not have a more elaborate platform than this, a Chinese republic that was free of the Manchu yoke was enough of a rallying cry in the Qing dynasty's final years. In the final decades of the Qing and into the early republic Hainan also produced rebels and secret societies that challenged both the dynasty and the new militarist rulers, but rather than claiming the mantle of these leaders, Hainan's Communist movement traces its origins beyond the island's shores, and to civilian men like Lin Wenying. Lin would not meet a peaceful end, but he was not a man of violence. He was most importantly a revolutionary propagandist and fundraiser, and a newspaperman, like some of the other early Hainanese revolutionary leaders.

Following the successful overthrow of the Qing government, Lin and others like him returned from their self-imposed exiles and their international fundraising tours, and rediscovered their homes in China proper. Though Lin had been born in Siam, his Wenchang father had raised him to call China his home country, and it was to Hainan that he returned. But the continuity of leadership that straddled the 1911 divide was not as revolutionary a change as men like Lin had hoped and worked for. Still, some of those allied with the more radical elements of the revolution did return to Hainan, and tried to continue their work of realizing an open and democratic government and society. Like Sun Yat-sen at the national level, the new government gave Lin a post as a leader of the provisional Hainan revolutionary regime; but also like Sun, the civilian Lin was installed and removed by a more powerful military man who was a holdover from the collapsed Qing government. On the national level, it was Yuan Shikai (1859–1916) who quickly pushed Sun aside; on Hainan, it was the Qing military official, Liu Yongdian (1878–1933) who took power from Lin.[27]

Confronted with this challenge, Lin proved less adept in local politics than he had been in the broad-strokes rhetoric of anti-Manchu revolutionary fundraising. The details of the handover of power between Liu Yongdian and Lin had not been clearly established before Lin returned to Hainan. When Lin arrived in Haikou to take up his position in the new government, Liu did not allow him and the new revolutionary government to move into the seat of power in Hainan. Lin quickly grew frustrated with this lack of cooperation, and instead of returning to Wenchang to wait for Liu's cooperation, he decided to set up what seems to have been a theatrical temporary headquarters in the market center of Haikou, the district's capital. This temporary office seems to have been a flamboyant and conspicuous claim to Lin's right to rule.

Then, in a clumsy attempt to assert his new authority on Hainan, Lin ordered the eviction of fruit and vegetable peddlers from the marketplace that was now his political headquarters. In swift response to Lin's clearing of the market, the fruit and vegetable sellers rallied together and raided Lin's "headquarters," finding Lin himself, and beating him until he sustained serious injuries. Lin's rival, Liu Yongdian, came to Lin's aid with an armed guard, but not before Lin's suspicions had grown about Liu's involvement in the peddlers' rioting. The wounded Lin left Hainan, and as he left, he flung accusations at Liu for having riled up the rioters in the market.[28] Lin then went on to serve for a short time in the National Assembly in 1912, but with the March 1913 assassination of Song Jiaoren, Yuan Shikai had pushed aside the newly chosen government. The "second revolution" by some of the southern provinces tried and failed to counter Yuan in the summer of 1913, and Lin's open criticism of Yuan Shikai and his allies put him in danger.[29]

In 1913, when Sun Yat-sen and many of his supporters had fled to Japan and out of Yuan Shikai's reach, Lin brashly returned to Hainan. He turned away from direct participation in political life, and established Hainan's first locally published revolutionary newspaper, the *Hainan Daily* (*Qiongdao ribao*), published out of a secret office. In its pages, he continued to spread revolutionary and republican thought, and he openly expressed his ties to, and support for, Sun Yat-sen. It was through Sun's introduction that Lin connected with a progressive businessman, the powerful Hainanese merchant, Chen Jiafu, who agreed to fund Lin's new paper.[30] It is worth noting that Lin Wenying, who is considered to be Hainan's first revolutionary, needed the introduction of Sun, a Cantonese, to fund a newspaper on his ancestral home island. In 1913–1914, Sun Yat-sen and other opponents of Yuan Shikai found refuge out of Yuan's reach, but the political environment of Hainan was more dangerously confined and its leaders even more provincial in their mind-set than those of the mainland. There was no refuge on Hainan, no safe house as in British Hong Kong, Japan, or the foreign concession areas of Shanghai. Lin had personally realized this in the recent market square incident, when he had been punished by the peddlers for misunderstanding local conditions, and drubbed out of the city and off of the island.

But with his newspaper, Lin targeted a more supportive readership with his message of democracy and progressive reform. With *Hainan Daily*, Lin built up an avid core readership among Hainan's students and city dwellers. At its height, the paper had a circulation of two thousand, and in its pages, readers could learn of the developments in the world socialist movements as well as the latest in national politics. Even more provocatively, Lin began the deadly work of criticizing Hainan's local leaders.[31]

By late 1913, Long Jiguang (1867–1925) and Chen Shihua, had replaced Liu Yongdian in the Hainan and Guangdong leadership. Their poorly concealed involvement in the opium trade was one way that they filled their coffers throughout the region. In late 1913, following an opium purchase in Lin Wenying's home county of Wenchang, he published an account of the drug traffic through Hainan in his own paper. The article in the *Hainan Daily* was specific in pointing out the culpability of high Hainan officials in the drug trade. Opium consumption was frequently noted by foreign visitors to the island as one of the most detrimental aspects of Hainan society. Most of these observers were Christian missionaries, and missionaries made opium one of their chief enemies in their Chinese work. Perhaps for this reason, the debilitating effects of opium on Hainan are emphasized in the writings of B.C. Henry and Margaret Monginger, but the drug's impact on social and financial stability was certainly a scourge, as well as clearly becoming a part of routine corruption in regional politics. Near the end of the Qing, Henry wrote, "The principal important trade is done in opium, which comes in legitimately through the European houses, illegitimately through Chinese under foreign names, and by the usual methods of smuggling. The country is flooded with it, and its baneful effects are seen far and wide. All the officials use the drug, and in some places almost the whole male population is addicted to the opium pipe."[32]

Opium had been responsible for so much of the Qing's weakness, and in his 1913 article, two years after that dynasty's fall, Lin pointed out that the new leadership was continuing to take part in the trade some believed to have brought the once-great dynasty to its collapse. This would be the final political blow that Lin could strike. Someone tipped off the authorities to the location of his paper's headquarters. By early spring of 1914, on direct orders from Beijing and Yuan Shikai, Lin Wenying was imprisoned. Lin's methods in the early republic had been similar to the organizing and writing that he had done abroad in his early revolutionary days. But in the close quarters of Hainan and under a regime that was perhaps even more oppressive than its imperial predecessor, he was not allowed to continue his work. Lin was secretly murdered in prison on the night of April 2, 1914.[33] Perhaps the perpetrators feared a public outcry at the trial and execution of Lin, as an increasingly popular figure on the island.

But others followed Lin in writing about the excesses and harsh rule of the Hainan regime, as well as their provincial and national masters in Guangzhou and Beijing, and even writing of socialist developments in Europe and throughout the world. On the mainland, the New Culture Movement of the late 1910s fostered a generation of thinkers and politicians who were driven by nationalism and anti-imperialism, and who worked to eradicate the remnants of traditional China, whether it was the paternalism of Confucius or the absolute power of an emperor. Following Yuan Shikai's death in 1916, national power was greatly weakened, and regions like Guangdong were largely out of the central government's power. Sun Yat-sen returned from Japan and he cultivated a support base in the south, with the goal of national unification pushed into the future. For his friend, Lin Wenying, Sun arranged for a mausoleum to be built in Wenchang, and he personally inscribed the characters on the placard: "Tomb of Lin Wenying, Revolutionary Martyr."[34] Lin's death was a loss to the movement for the free voices of Hainan, and it marked a transition in Hainan's revolution. In the decades that followed, many of the revolutionary leaders on Hainan were local figures with more of an investment in the welfare of the Hainanese people and less of Lin's early emphasis on international political trends. This did not mean that they were unaware of, or unconcerned with, national and international developments, but rather that local conditions, and the priority of endurance and survival demanded that for many of Hainan's revolutionaries, the political and military focus shifted to the island's local struggle.

Hainan's Anti-Imperialism and Inward Turn

Prior to Lin Wenying's death, he and others had advocated for Hainan to be granted provincial status, free of the provincial rule of Guangdong province. Lin and others implored the central government to grant the island increasing autonomy through a national decree that would acknowledge Hainan deserved to take more responsibility for its own fate. Citing previous wise rulers who had granted Hainan such autonomy, Lin and his allies pushed for this cause, referring to the works of Zhang Zhidong and Li Hongzhang in the late Qing, and even referring back to the golden age of the Tang (618–907).[35] One significant similarity in all of these late Qing and early republican appeals was that they were directed at the national government and were based not on current conditions, but on historical precedent and potential future developments. By the early 1920s, Hainanese political actors turned their focus away from the national and international stage, and directed their attentions to developments closer to home. The new government seemed to be even more of a disappointment than the previous one. Lin Wenying began this shift with his final newspaper work, but his organizational roots were with Sun Yat-sen and abroad, and the successful implementation of this local work would have to emerge from local Hainanese political actors.

For their part, many merchants protested local leadership when they refused to pay taxes to Hainan's local warlord, Deng Benyin (1879–?), who had been a military force in the region since early 1921, connected to the southern political and military leader, Chen Jiongming. Deng had been ensconced on Hainan since early 1923. His relations with both Beijing and Guangzhou fluctuated between open hostility and cooperation, amidst the chaotic shifting of the southern warlords and revolutionaries.[36] His connections with Chen Jiongming kept him in power until Chen was defeated by Nationalist revolutionary forces in 1925.[37] Deng's politics do not seem to have been as nuanced as Chen Jiongming, whose relationship with the Nationalist and Communist Parties shifted between accommodation and hostility. Deng's rule frustrated most attempts at local political organization, and while growth for the Communist Party began on the mainland in the early 1920s, on Hainan the CCP was only able to gain a foothold after Deng's removal in 1925.[38]

Under the rule of warlords through the 1910s and early 1920s, revolutionary political organization on Hainan that was connected with mainland or national groups was effectively oppressed. Rather than aiming for provincial status, and incorporating Hainan into the national and international world, revolutionaries and reformers on Hainan shifted their focus increasingly to the local political scene. Carrying on Lin Wenying's legacy of targeting misrule on Hainan through journalism, Xu Chengzhang (1892–1928) attacked the Hainanese and outsiders who governed on behalf of the early republic.

Unlike Lin, Xu was born in Hainan, in northern Qiongshan County. Both of the men were members of the Tongmenghui and both worked to bring about the end of the Qing dynasty. Both Lin and Xu also opposed the national government of Yuan Shikai and those who ruled on his behalf on Hainan. In 1917, Xu enrolled in the Yunnan Military Academy in Kunming, in south-central China. Whereas Lin raised funds in Siam, the home country of his mother and his birthplace, Xu brought Hainanese concerns to Yunnan, Hong Kong, and Guangzhou in his early organizational work. As part of Guangdong Province, Hainan's provincial affairs were based in Guangzhou, and after his military training, Xu first organized newspaper offices there.[39]

The New Culture and May Fourth Movements of the late 1910s swept Xu and thousands of others into patriotic activity that opposed foreign imperialism, domestic disunity, and Confucian cultural conservatism. While the May Fourth Movement was defined in large part by its patriotic impetus, notably, the spread of May Fourth ideology on Hainan reflected Hainan's local character. One Guo Qinguang (1895–1919), a student at Beijing University, was killed following the famous patriotic May Fourth demonstrations in Beijing, dying of his wounds after having been beaten by police. According to the official Communist Party history of Hainan, it was Guo's death, and not news of the massive protests, that was the most important factor in leading more than one thousand Hainanese students to take to the streets in protest.[40] A Hainanese brother had been killed while studying in Beijing, and this roused the Hainanese students to protest, seemingly with more zeal than the original cause of the May Fourth protests, namely the ignominious cession of the German Shandong territories to Japan at the Treaty of Versailles.

Meanwhile, Hainan was also not immune to the high politics of imperialism and diplomacy. Japanese strength was growing, as was apparent from the Shandong cession, and British and French interests, among others, included concerns about Japanese designs on the strategically central island of Hainan, as is apparent from British intelligence reports of the early republican period. Though the British did not control the island directly in any period, they were the main power behind the Imperial Customs, which administered trade in key Chinese ports, including Haikou. By June of 1922, a British naval intelligence officer filed a confidential report to the British Foreign Office, and referred to Hainan, noting that, "it is undesirable that Japan should annex a group of islands on the route between Hong Kong and Singapore and extend her influence to the southwards under the guise of commerce."[41]

British interest in Hainan was mainly based on concerns over Japanese development of the island, rather than on Chinese activity on the island. This reflected concerns over Japanese increasing strength, which was also evident in the Washington Conference of 1921–1922, in which the Western Powers tried to hamstring Japanese development, especially in terms of naval strength. This was an ongoing regional focus for both British and French interests in the region, and both powers continued to voice concern over apparent Japanese designs on Hainan until the Japanese occupation actually began in February 1939.[42]

In the May Fourth era and after, while most of China's intellectuals were engaging foreign forces either to study Western culture or to challenge Western and Japanese imperialism, on Hainan it was a period of increased isolation even as the foundation of the Chinese Communist Party on the island was laid. Xu Chengzhang's was to continue the final work of Lin Wenying, and he focused on criticizing the corrupt local leadership. After his military training in Yunnan and newspaper work in Guangzhou, Xu returned to Hainan in 1920, and began plans for a newspaper that would publish progressive and revolutionary articles. The content of the articles included the latest in communist and socialist theories, news of revolutionary movements throughout the world, and also, critiques that were specific to Hainan's political scene. In this way, the three tiers of international, national, and local politics continued to occupy the revolutionaries of Hainan.

By 1923, Xu had joined the Chinese Communist Party, formed two years earlier in Shanghai, and he began to recruit adherents and to propagate its philosophy of class struggle in his writings. The internationalism of Xu's generation had changed though. From Lin Wenying's incorporation of overseas Chinese through the direct funds and cooperation of Southeast Asian Chinese, Xu Chengzhang focused on the ideas of international revolution, but when it came to action, this would be constrained by the island's shores. His propaganda work in spreading the ideas of Marxism among Hainanese students and intellectuals, and his membership in the Chinese Communist Party make his work the beginning of the official Chinese Communist history on Hainan.[43]

The inward turn that continued with Xu's leadership was a pragmatic one, resulting from both local unrest and official attempts to limit contact between radical elements on Hainan and communities abroad; but the revolutionaries also had their own reasons for limiting contact with communities of Hainanese in Southeast Asia and focusing their efforts on their home island. Xu and others had reason to be suspicious of the participation in their movement of their Hainanese comrades in Southeast Asia, many of whom were wealthy merchants and prominent, legitimate members of society in their adopted home countries, and not the natural allies of a Communist revolution.

In 1922, Xu Chengzhang reflected on a year of publishing his paper *Hainan Xunbao* (*Qiongya Xunbao*), and he remembered the early struggles of the newspaper's organizers. (*Xunbao*, which has no English equivalent, is a term for a paper published every ten days.) In the summer of 1920, there was an attempt to transition the staff of one newspaper (also called *Hainan Daily* but not the same publication as Lin Wenying's paper) into the staff of the planned *Hainan Xunbao*. Some of the staff and contributors were abroad at the time. The funds that they had raised to make this transition and establish the new paper were stolen, possibly by an overseas investor who suddenly withdrew his support and also absconded with the rest of the staff's funds.[44] The theft of these funds represented the weakening of the once strong ties between the Southeast Asian Hainanese and the struggle of the Hainan islanders.

The rhetoric of race noted above might also have soured relations between Siamese (now Thai) hosts of Chinese communities there, but it was economic and class concerns that seem to have caused the erosion of support for Chinese revolutionaries abroad among their fellow overseas Chinese. Many of the prominent Chinese living throughout Southeast Asia were businessmen and merchants, and they might have perceived radical revolutionary politics of organizers like Lin Wenying and Xu Chengzhang as a threat to the stability of the trade networks that supported their businesses. Fundraising for newspapers, guns, and other tools of revolution continued even after the success of the 1911 revolution, as in the case of Xu's *Hainan Xunbao*. Eventually, after more than two decades of giving funds to the cause of revolution in China, it is understandable that Chinese merchants in Southeast Asia would grow skeptical and withdraw their support for revolutionaries "whose behavior barely distinguished them from the Qing officials from whom so many emigrant merchants had been glad to escape."[45] The theft of the funds for Xu's paper was a setback, but only a temporary one, and it moved Xu and others in the Hainan political scene still farther toward the localization of the Hainanese movement. Now this localization was also connected to an economic radicalization that led the Hainanese revolutionaries away from their prosperous cousins in Southeast Asia.

In his April 1922 article, Xu does not write that this theft of his newspaper's funds led directly to the decision to establish *Hainan Xunbao* in Haikou, as opposed to in Hong Kong, Guangzhou, or somewhere in

Southeast Asia. But the decision to establish the paper's office in Haikou, he wrote, reflected the shift in making Hainan island more than a symbolic homeland and revolutionary rallying cry.[46] Over the next decade, Hainan would become a revolutionary base in its own right, first for the revolutionary forces of the united Nationalist and Communist Parties, and then of the Hainan Communist movement.

Xu acknowledged that most Hainanese were pessimistic about their ability to control their own fate and win the fight for a fair and representative government—one that listened to and responded to the needs of the people who lived on the island. He noted that he had seen the darkest of times, with his newspapers forced to shut; the death of his predecessor, Lin Wenying, murdered in prison without trial; the Hainanese student, Guo Qinguang, killed during the May Fourth protests in Beijing.[47] But in 1922, Xu gave his readers cause for optimism. Many of Hainan's most promising revolutionary leaders were returning to the island and helping to organize the workers in Haikou and the farmers across the island. Like Xu they were publishing their beliefs and distributing them, and a radical movement was gaining momentum.

Xu thus cautiously celebrated the victory of having continuously published *Hainan Xunbao* for a year. He wrote that the ruler of Hainan, Chen Shihua along with Long Jiguang, had attempted to keep the 4 million Hainanese cut off from the outside world (here, in his population figure, it seems Xu is including both Hainanese abroad and those living on the island, because the island's population at the time was below 3 million). In this effort to close down free presses, Chen Shihua had bloodied his hands by ordering the murder of Lin Wenying. In shutting down Lin's *Hainan Daily*, Chen had deprived the people of Hainan of a "representative organ of public opinion."[48] Xu acknowledged that this was a dark time in the isolation of Hainan at the national and international level, but he urged optimism and local action, for there were those who would not accept this leadership and would continue to fight.

Only a few months after the April 1922 publication of Xu's article, however, another incident, though it remained largely secret at the time, seems to reflect an even greater degree of Hainan's isolation, even from Sun Yat-sen's growing southern revolutionary regime. Sun and his allies were using Hainan as a bargaining chip to secure monetary and military aid for their southern government, according to Japanese newspapers cited in a study of China's maritime frontiers in the early republic by Ulises Granados.[49] If Hainanese political organizers had known that mortgaging the island was in the offing by their Cantonese allies, it surely would have been a disappointing shock. The revolutionaries on Hainan in the 1910s and

1920s continued to be closely connected to Sun Yat-sen and the southern revolutionaries through the early shared work of Sun and Lin Wenying. Xu Chengzhang and others carried on this work. As the southern regime gained strength and support in the early 1920s, these revolutionaries continued to work as Hainanese representatives of Sun's Nationalist Party, and later as early members of the Chinese Communist Party and allies of the Nationalists. They were dedicated to the anticipated national revolution that would be launched from the south to reunite all of China and drive out the unscrupulous militarists who often seemed to be leashed to foreign interests.

Hainan for Sale

It seems, however, that this Hainanese dedication to Sun's revolution was not reciprocal, according to the findings of Granados as well as contemporary official British intelligence observers. In June of 1922, while Sun and Chen Jiongming battled for supremacy in the south, Sun fled his offices in Guangzhou (Canton), leaving documents later collected by British foreign service officers. Among these documents was an agreement between Sun's southern government and the Japan-China Forestry, Mining, and Industrial Society. In a communication from the British consul in Guangzhou to the British embassy in Beijing, the document is fully reproduced. Among the details:

> . . . The President of the Southern Government, Dr. Sun Yat-sen signed this agreement with the representatives of the Japan-China Forestry, Mining and Industrial Society, to help the Southern Government to extend: –
>
> 1. The said company agreed to supply the Southern Government with 20,000 latest model rifles, 5,000,000 rounds of ammunition, 72 field guns, 15,000 shells, 120 machine guns and ammunition.
>
> 2. The said company agreed to assist the Southern Government with 5,000,000 gold yen.
>
> 3. The said company are [sic] prepared to enter into another contract as regards further requirements of funds and arms with the Southern Government.
>
> 4. The Southern Government agreed to hand over the development of Hainan Island, all islands on the [Guangdong] coasts

to the said company, and also the fishing rights from south of Amoy to Hainan.

5. The Southern Government agreed to give the first call for forestry and mining rights of the province of [Guangxi] to the said company.

6. The said company have the right to develop Hainan and all islands of [Guangdong], but no military or naval constructions may be constructed. The Southern Government have the right to stop any such works and pull them down. . . .[50]

There are thirteen more related conditions listed in the document. The British consul who was responsible for sending this information on to his superior does not qualify his report with the possibility that it is false propaganda of Chen Jiongming's supporters intended to discredit Sun Yat-sen's patriotism. Indeed this seems unlikely because it was not broadly publicized, though a French Catholic priest named Savina noted during his 1929 visit to Hainan that he had heard of Sun's willingness to essentially sell off the island several years earlier. "In short, China has always regarded Hainan as a dumping ground, a discharge outlet [exutoire], a *refugium peccatorum* [lit., refuge of sinners], and a negligible quantity. A few years ago, the father of the Chinese revolution, Sun Yat-sen, wanted to cede (read sell) Hainan to a foreign power that I could name, for the modest sum of 14 million dollars. It is perhaps because of this that we now see his portrait revered in all the houses of the island!"[51]

If Savina's allegation and the document exchanged between Sun's government and the Japanese company were indeed genuine, they represent Sun's willingness to completely amputate Hainan's economic sovereignty in exchange for the weapons and cash that might win some more territory on the mainland. Although this document seems to have remained relatively secret, or at least in the realm of rumor and allegation, it seems that the revolutionary efforts on Hainan were more isolated than ever in the early 1920s, and that their dedication to the southern revolutionaries—indeed evident in Sun's portrait hung in many of the island's homes—was not a reciprocal relationship.

Rebel Origins of Hainan's Feng Baiju

Feng Baiju (1903–1973) was born in the northern Hainan village of Changtai, in Qiongshan County. According to biographies of Feng, his father Feng

Yunxi, was a prominent local member of one of the most common among the anti-Qing rebellious groups, known as the Triads or the "Three Dots Society" (*Sandianhui*), which was one name of a wide array of secret societies in the final decades of the dynasty.[52] The meaning of the "three dots" of their name, according to some interpretations, reveal how the many antigovernmental and antinorthern movements flowed together among bandits, triads, pirates, and revolutionaries—the dots were a reference to the three strokes written to the left of the Chinese character for the family name of the Taiping rebel leader, Hong Xiuquan (洪秀全 1814–1864).[53]

During the final years of the Qing's effective governance, in the late eighteenth century, many of the older secret society organizations had been smashed and scattered, some finding refuge in surrounding areas including Southeast Asia, where they maintained connections to provincial Chinese societies.[54] As the Qing state became less efficient in dealing with domestic and foreign challenges, the secret societies were allowed to gain strength, and in the view of one scholar of the organizations, they began to take over those duties of governance that the Qing was no longer able to fulfill. As they gained strength, the secret societies also took on some of the duties once the domain of native-place societies and mutual aid societies, such as organizing overseas communities and coordinating and facilitating migration and settlement by providing housing and what became essentially legitimate organizations.[55]

This combination of antigovernmental, antinorthern, and anti-Manchu sentiment strengthened the potential foundation of support for the revolutionaries of the south. The slick cosmopolitan merchants and newspapermen who were the brains behind the early revolutionary movement in the last decade of Qing rule were a far cry from the pirates and peasants who supported the Taipings. But the shared opposition to the Manchus was notable, and antinorthern enmity ran deep even among many of the most progressive southern revolutionaries. The sentiments of southern revolutionaries was based on long-standing mutual enmity and rivalry with the north; but in more concrete terms, the outward, international orientation of many southerners and their migration networks were also significant in shaping the generation that would overthrow the Qing.

So in Changtai village, Feng Baiju's father, Yunxi was a respected member of the community. He had some farmland, and so would be considered a subsistence farmer or peasant in the class distinctions that would become so important in the revolutionary era. But he was also a skilled stonecutter, and his revenue from this work and from his fields allowed him the income to educate his eldest son, Feng Baiju, born June 7, 1903.

Little Feng's given name was Yuqiu, meaning "Abundant World"; and his study name was Jizhou, meaning roughly "Constantly Attentive"; and it was only when he was establishing himself as a revolutionary leader on Hainan as a young man that he took on the name he is known by today, Baiju, meaning "White Colt."

In 1911 the Qing dynasty crumbled on the mainland into province-sized chunks. In that same year, eight-year-old Feng Baiju (then Yuqiu) began to make the daily trip from Changtai to be tutored in the Chinese classics in neighboring Lingjiao village, about a mile to the northeast. Six years earlier, the imperial examination system had been abolished, and Chinese elites already enjoyed access to a modern curriculum including mathematics, science, foreign languages, and other subjects. And yet, for the son of a stonecutter in a sleepy Hainan village, Feng's studies began with five years steeped in the Five Classics and Four Books, the Confucian canon that constituted the basis of the imperial examination system from 605 to 1905. For Hainanese, remote as they were from the northern capital of Beijing, success of their native sons on the imperial examination had long been a point of pride. Indeed the Hainanese boast of their intelligent sons with good reason, since their proportion of exam candidates succeeding at the highest level (*jinshi*, or "presented scholar") is five times higher than the national per capita average.[56]

And so Feng Baiju's family nurtured the old-world hopes that their son would make the most of his classical education and become a great minister, bringing wealth and prestige to the Feng name. Indeed the early republic saw many old Qing officials continuing in their posts and maintaining positions of prominence. But the rising class, as would soon become clear on Hainan, was the military rulers, some of whom had been educated in new military schools or abroad in Japan. By 1916, with the failure of imperial restoration attempts, it was clear to most that the new republic, fragmented as it was, would remain. With the imperial order overthrown and twice rejected in failed restoration attempts, intellectuals like Hu Shih, Chen Duxiu, and others went further and challenged the old order's underlying philosophy and educational system.

In 1916, these iconoclastic trends had rippled out even to Hainan, and in that year, Feng began an education in the equivalent of a modern junior high and high school. For this he traveled to the market town of Yunlong, about two miles to the north, which meant also two miles to Hainan's only major city of Haikou. One of Feng's classmates, Li Aichun (1901–1927), was two years his elder and by all accounts a brilliant student and inspiring presence. Li, Feng, and others formed a student union or "comrades' mutual aid society" during their time at school in Yunlong. They were steeped in the anti-imperialism of Sun Yat-sen's revolutionary thought, including his broad ideas encapsulated in his "Three People's Principles" (*san min zhuyi*). These have been translated as nationalism (*minzu*), democracy (*minquan*, literally, "people's power"), and the people's livelihood (*minsheng*). Those who see in Sun an ally of the early Chinese Communist Party sometimes choose to translate this last term as "socialism," because it certainly entailed a degree of economic justice.

In 1920, Li Aichun went on to attend Guangdong Province's Sixth Teaching College, and then in 1924, Guangdong University (later renamed Sun Yat-sen University) in Guangzhou (Canton). While there, his radical views led him to join the Chinese Communist Party (CCP) in 1925. The CCP was then only four years old, and membership in the CCP for many members meant that they were also members of the larger Nationalist Party (Guomindang/Kuomintang, KMT). This "bloc within" was an arrangement of the early 1920s that allowed the Communists to operate under the Nationalist umbrella, while the Nationalists enjoyed material and personnel assistance from the Soviet Union and the Comintern. By the spring of 1927 this alliance would collapse in a violent purge, but for Li and Feng, in the late 1910s and early 1920s, the teachings of Sun Yat-sen aligned with their passions and their yearning for revolutionary action.

CHAPTER 3

FROM GLOBETROTTERS TO GUERRILLAS

Hainan's Early Communists

Feng Baiju (1903–1973) was one of the earliest Hainanese members of the Chinese Communist Party (CCP). On September 5, 1926, with the introduction of his former Qiongshan classmate, Li Aichun, Feng joined the CCP in Haikou. Li had long been an inspiration to Feng, as the brightest student in his school who had gone on to attend university in Guangzhou (Canton) when Feng was still finishing his studies in the town of Yunlong. As students they had worked together, and Feng had also excelled in his studies in the small Hainan town. The anti-imperialism and nationalism of the May Fourth Movement of 1919 had reached Hainan after German concessions in northern China were to be handed over to the Japanese forces as determined at the Versailles treaty conference. Li and Feng had been imbued with the righteous rage that was expressed in passionate declarations, speeches, essays, and boycotts of Japanese goods, and Li had left for Guangzhou during the high tide of the movement.

While Feng's family was not wealthy, his family continued to pay his school fees through these years, and Feng remained diligent in his studies through the years to come. He continued to help his father with his stone cutting business, as he had as a small child, and also helped the family during harvests. Every day, as class was dismissed in Yunlong, Feng walked home to Changtai village to help his mother with her work. At school, as he later recalled, he acquired the progressivism of the modern intellectual spirit and at home he lived the life of a peasant son. In these early years, Feng also made the acquaintance of Hainan's earliest CCP member, Xu Chengzhang.

In 1924 he completed his high school studies and graduated. He returned home to Changtai village, but did not stay long. The example of Li Aichun had lit a fire in him, and he also longed to attend a great university on the mainland, where the intellectual ferment and revolutionary organization seemed to be most urgent. Before he had even submitted an application, Feng was gone, on his way to Nanjing, about halfway up the eastern coast of the mainland. Once there he applied to Southeastern University (*Dongnan daxue*), but before hearing whether he was accepted, he continued on to Shanghai where he was accepted into Daxia University. He studied for one term there and became politically energized through his involvement in the May 30th Movement in the spring of 1925. The anti-imperialist movement involved a series of protests after British police fired upon an unarmed crowd of Chinese students and workers. The crowd had been protesting a previous killing of a Chinese worker by a Japanese factory supervisor, and this poured fuel on the flames.

Feng was far from home, but he was swept up in the kind of excitement that he had dreamed of as a boy. Throughout the protests, he did not abandon his studies but continued to read and work, steeped in the political climate of 1925 Shanghai. Then, later that year, a letter came from his father, Feng Yunxi.

> Dear Jizhou, my son,
>
> Because of difficulties here at home, I must write to you. This past fall and winter, we have lost the income from our rice paddies, the quarry is closed, we have begun to rack up debt, and life is difficult for the entire family. There is truly no way for me to support your continued studies. I hope that once you receive this letter, you will immediately withdraw from school and return home to find another livelihood.
>
> Your father, Feng Yunxi[1]

Feng did not linger in Shanghai, but began to make his way home almost immediately. Passing through Guangzhou he reconnected with old classmates there, some of whom had joined the CCP. Among them was Li Aichun, who told Feng in a letter that he could best serve the revolution by returning to Hainan and helping to build a Communist organization there. Already on his way home, Feng's spirits rose as he imagined a revolutionary role on his home island. He had left Shanghai with regret, but a new path had appeared.

The Case of Li Shuoxun

On Hainan, and in some Hainanese history books (as in history books of American and other world leaders), Feng Baiju's path to the leadership of the island's Communist movement sometimes seems predestined in a way that encourages the historical fallacy of "retrospective determinism" and teleology. In this way, according to the idea developed by the French philosopher, Henri Berson, the history of Communism on Hainan might consist merely of tracing Feng's path to greatness. Stephen C. Averill rightly counseled China historians to avoid this kind of "star-centered" history, now that local archives have opened to scholars and a vibrant new historiography of alternatives is emerging.[2] Indeed, looking closely at the ideological and political conflicts that Averill examines on the mainland in the 1920s and 1930s, it becomes immediately clear that the fate of the CCP was far from predestined to rule China, or even to agree on a unified platform. There were other voices and other views that would shape the Party as much through conflicts and paths not taken as through triumphant unity. On Hainan, one mainlander in particular can be taken as an example of an alternative path that the Communist movement on the island might have taken.

Li Shuoxun (1903–1931) was born in the same year as Feng Baiju, but far away, in landlocked Sichuan in mainland China's central-western region. His roots were far from the South China Sea and Hainan where he would be killed, aged twenty-eight. As a member of the early Chinese Communist movement, his credentials were impeccable. He had joined the Socialist Youth League in 1921, the year of the CCP founding. He attended Shanghai University and joined the Party in 1924. He was an active student leader in the May 30th Movement in Shanghai in 1925, which connected the anti-imperialism of students and Shanghai factory workers in anti-Japanese and anti-British protests, and in which Feng Baiju was also involved. Li then took part in the Nanchang Uprising of August 1927, the first trial of the fledgling Communist military against their new Nationalist Party enemies. In the following years, young Li held a series of high posts in the CCP leadership of Jiangsu, Zhejiang, and Guangdong Provinces. In the summer of 1931 the Party's leadership sent him to Hainan to help organize the Communists there. Li arrived in Hainan in July of 1931, and the Hainan Party organization seemed to be in disarray. Less than two months later, Li Shuoxun was dead, captured by Nationalist authorities and quickly executed.[3]

Today, Li Shuoxun is known best as a martyr of the revolution, but also as the father of Li Peng (1928–), who was less than three years old at the time of his father's death. After Li Shuoxun's death, Li Peng was adopted and raised in part by Party luminaries, Zhou Enlai and his wife, Deng Yingchao. Like his adoptive father, Li Peng became premier of the People's Republic of China (PRC). Li Shuoxun was a rising star in the CCP in 1931, and like so many revolutionary martyrs, we can only speculate as to where his trajectory might have taken him in the pages of Chinese history. His career was abruptly cut short after he took up his post on Hainan and prepared to lead the Communist movement there. Today, a mighty tomb near Haikou honors Li Shuoxun, and the questions surrounding his death cut to the bone of the problematic Hainan-mainland relationship in the Party's early years.

Was this simply a question of Hainanese nativist (*paiwai*) tendencies enduring into the modern era? Had Li's status as unwelcome mainland advisor been the root cause of his death? Did Hainanese Communists perceive him as a kind of officious revolutionary carpetbagger, arriving from the mainland to dictate policy and teach the islanders how to make revolution? Lin Wenying, Xu Chengzhang, and others had worked to pull Hainan out of what they perceived as its parochial backwardness and into the modern international world. They had hoped to make Hainan a national priority based on its strategic and economic potential. But this attempt to make the island a cosmopolitan and revolutionary center off the southeast coast of the Asian continent was largely unsuccessful.

Li Shuoxun's death seemed to represent the impossibility of bringing together mainland and Hainanese Communist revolutionary itineraries. In some current accounts of Li Shuoxun's death, it is noted that he was betrayed by one of his comrades on Hainan. It seems impossible that there is any documentary evidence of this, but today, the placard near his mausoleum implies that a fellow Communist betrayed him to the Nationalist authorities. The genesis of this accusation is not clear, though the swift capture and death of Li following his arrival on Hainan suggests at least that he and his hosts did not take appropriate precautions in getting to a safe location on the island. Based on his long experience with military and political organizations including underground work, it seems unlikely that Li was simply careless. Some Chinese historians imply that Li's death seemed to be a result of either nativist treachery or the work of resentful local Communist leaders who had heard enough instruction from the mainland and decided to take their fate into their own hands.

If Li Shuoxun was indeed betrayed by local Communist leaders who were resentful of his presence on the island, what greater lessons could we surmise? Was it a victory for small-minded, treacherous, and short-sighted islanders who would wind up with little more than a dozen partisan guerrillas by the mid-1930s, sitting around a campfire somewhere off the map in the island's interior or huddling in the family home of their leader? Or was Li's death the inevitable result of a shift in local revolutionary priorities that had moved away from the tactics of conventional positional warfare and ideological orthodoxy; for their own survival, had the local Communists foregone the costly protection of quixotic urban revolutionary organizers like Li Shuoxun? Perhaps there is a middle ground.

Foundations of the Local Party

Chinese Communist Party members set up a branch in Hainan in June of 1926, nearly five years after the Party was founded in Shanghai. In its early years on the mainland, the Communists and Nationalists were united in fighting southern, and later northern, militarists. After the death of the Nationalist unifier, Sun Yat-sen (Sun Zhongshan) in March 1925, and then the May 30th Movement only weeks later, political divisions within the Nationalist Party grew significantly. Conservative and radical elements moved apart ideologically, and grew increasingly suspicious of each other's activities. Less than a year after the 1926 founding of the CCP branch on Hainan, the Nationalist leadership would launch a violent purge of Communists and leftist elements in its midst, first on the mainland, and then on Hainan a few days later.

Thus the 1926 founding of the Hainan Communist movement took place in an extremely tense political moment. The island's close quarters made this tension an enduring element of the Party's history for the next twenty-three years. It was from its 1926 founding that the Hainan Party's slogan would eventually become "for twenty-three years, the red flag never fell."[4] Separation from the Party's Central command made the Hainanese Communist struggle distinct from the mainland narrative of the revolution that has become part of the national mythology of China. CCP history on the mainland has become known for its iconic episodes like the Nanchang Uprising in August 1927, the Long March from 1934 to 1936, and the Yan'an years spent regrouping in northwestern China.

The earliest developments of the Chinese Communist Party on Hainan were closely connected with the Party on the mainland. The top leaders in the Hainan Party had been studying and working on the mainland and they returned to Hainan to launch the Party at its first representative meeting in Haikou in June 1926. Some of the major figures in the early years of the CCP, like Li Shuoxun, were not Hainanese, but had been posted to the island to begin organization work there. Others, like Xu Chengzhang, introduced in the previous chapter, were Hainan natives but had spent much of their formative careers as organizers and revolutionaries on the mainland or abroad. Xu was the bridge between the new Communist presence on Hainan and the generation of merchants, newspapermen, and aspiring politicians who had tried to incorporate Hainan into the national and international realm of the revolution. This group of early revolutionaries on Hainan definitely saw the island's political interests as the same as the national priorities of the CCP prior to the Party's split with the Nationalists in April 1927. In the violence that followed 1927, the Hainan Communist movement turned inward and focused on survival on their home island over all other priorities.

Prior to this inward turn, Xu Chengzhang had worked and given his life to keep the Hainan revolution connected to the mainland Party. Xu had been an excellent student in the final years of the Qing, and had been inspired by the efforts of Lin Wenying to bring about a revolution and a new national consciousness. Lin's imprisonment and secret execution had proven to Xu that on Hainan the new regime was just as oppressive as the last one. He took part in doomed uprisings against Yuan Shikai and his allies, but the island proved too stifling for his ambition and desire for radical change. Xu left Hainan, and spent his formative years on the mainland, first in a Yunnan military academy, where he experienced the political and cultural upheaval of the May Fourth Movement. Factional fighting throughout the south prevented Sun Yat-sen's revolutionary government from gaining political traction, and in the early 1920s, Xu returned to Hainan to work organizing laborers and publishing newspapers that opposed warlordism, imperialism, and the persistent factionalism in the south. Like Lin Wenying before him, he targeted local figures as well, including the local strongman, Deng Benyin.

By 1925, as southern factional fighting was nearing a frenzy, Xu returned to the mainland and Guangzhou (Canton) where he began work as a drill instructor at the new Nationalist military school, the legendary Whampoa Academy (pinyin, Huangpu). His training in Yunnan and his battlefield experience qualified him to serve as an instructor and he worked closely with the Nationalists in 1925, during the "bloc within" period. This policy stipulated that Communist Party members were permitted and encouraged to also join the Nationalist party, though the CCP was clearly the junior partner within the Nationalist Party. Zhou Enlai also served on the faculty of the Whampoa Academy in this period, and Xu became well acquainted with the man who would become the second most prominent member of Party in the decades to come.[5]

Most importantly, back on Hainan, the Communists had built support among farmers' associations. After April 1927, the Hainanese leaders of the Communist Party evacuated the cities and withdrew to their rural support base. In the main history of the CCP, April 12, 1927, is remembered as the day that started the "White Terror," which led to summary imprisonment and execution of Communists and leftists, beginning in Shanghai. In Haikou, April 22 (a day many Hainanese refer to as "Four-Two-Two," and not "Four-One-Two" as mainlanders refer to the events) is the day remembered as the betrayal of the Communists by their erstwhile Nationalist allies. Hours before the Nationalists raided the headquarters and homes of Communists and their sympathizers, the Party's local secretary, Wang Wenming (1894–1930), received a message that warned all Communist operatives to leave the cities.[6] The weeks that followed were obviously chaotic. Less than one year earlier, the founding Party Representative Assembly in June of 1926 had established the CCP's official presence on Hainan, representing 240 Hainanese members.[7] Though the Party had grown in that year, its members that were not captured or killed were scattered throughout the countryside.

On the mainland, there were still enough leftists and Communists to give the Party a coherent platform and leadership. More importantly, once the dust of the White Terror had settled, the Communist leadership on the mainland courted and won important allies, especially in the military. By August 1, they had launched a civil war on their own terms with the Nanchang Uprising. On Hainan, and in other provincial CCP branches, the way forward was not as clear. Consolidation of the Hainan Communist Party was one option, for the wide-reaching activities of the Party that had developed under the umbrella of the Nationalist Party seemed to no longer be sustainable. But the question of what losses should be cut remained unclear. For several months after the April 1927 purge and executions, the Communist Party leadership remained on the run and hidden among their rural supporters.

Again, Hainan's island geography influenced the nature of the choices for the Communist movement there. The limits of the surrounding seas prevented the Party leaders from moving into the neighboring province, or the provincial borderlands, and rallying their forces there. A leadership meeting was arranged in June in Lehui, near the central eastern coast, and the Hainanese Party members Wang Wenming and Yang Shanji were elected to lead. Their decision was to move immediately in counterattack, and to expand the Party, to seek new recruits and supporters across the island, rather than consolidating their loyal adherents and taking stock of their losses. In the case of the Communist leader, Feng Baiju, it was his family's local prominence, their education, and their capacity to lead that won them support. Feng returned to Changtai village and established contact with his friend and comrade, Wang Wenming. Both of them had narrowly escaped capture and certain execution in Haikou.[8]

The results were surprisingly quite successful, and in six months, Party membership had swelled to fifteen thousand on Hainan.[9] Military forces sprang up in the form of local militias, armed farmers, and regular forces. Some of Hainan's Communist leaders returned to their hometowns where they were able to rally forces. By August 1927, at the same time as the mainland Communists launched their Nanchang Uprising, the separate Communist forces across Hainan, along with their partisan supporters, were sufficiently strong to launch pitched battles with the Nationalists and their own adherent militias.

The Coconut Stockades and Fast-Changing Fortunes

One noted battle in September revealed both the strength and the inexperience of the Communist forces on Hainan. The battle of the Coconut Stockades (*Yezi sai*), south of Jiaji on the island's central eastern coast involved hundreds of Communist forces, and some of the notable leaders, including Wang Wenming and Yang Shanji.[10] On September 23, 1927, the Communist forces stormed the stockades and routed the Nationalists, sending them into retreat. Following this speedy victory, the main part of the Communist forces withdrew, leaving a small force to mop up the straggling Nationalists. Among those who stayed was Yang Shanji, and when the Nationalists regrouped and counterattacked, he was killed along with the small force that was left to hold the stockade.[11] To many, this was a cautionary lesson against positional warfare waged by inexperienced forces. The coming year, however, would see the catastrophic results of the Communists' attempt to take Hainan's urban centers and wage positional warfare across the island. But before this destructive strategy was fully implemented, the end of 1927 and the beginning of 1928 saw a period of explosive growth for the Hainan Communists and their support base.

By January of 1928, the leadership of the Hainan Communist Party filed six reports to the CCP Provincial Committee of Guangdong, explaining their current situation. The sixth is extant, and it explains that they had recently sent one Feng Zenghua with the fifth report several days earlier, hoping that it had arrived safely. The sixth report reflects uneven stability across the Hainanese Communist movement.[12] The report cites Communist strength around the cities of Fucheng, Haikou, and Jiaji, and generally in the north of the island. The Communist strength in these cities resulted from the support of workers' movements there.

Lingshui, in the far south, was an early soviet base of the Communist movement on Hainan, and the report notes that things had settled enough for the soviet government there to begin combing through its ranks and counterpurging reactionary elements. Yaxian, neighboring Lingshui, was also strongly consolidated, and the report confidently relates that they could be on the verge of overthrowing the Nationalist authorities there, as they had in the Lingshui region. In most other regions, the report lists a series of military struggles that are either in progress, or on the verge of breaking out. But this unrest is not strictly credited to the Hainan Communist leadership and those who are writing this report. Further, it is likely that reports of progress were exaggerated for propaganda purposes, and while the documents reflect early ambitions, they must be read with skepticism.

As in the reference to the workers' unrest in the northern cities and the peasants' unrest in the south, the report does not claim that these are regular Communist fighters who might respond to the leadership of those who are writing the report. The tone of the report is both optimistic and chaotic, almost giddy. The unrest was positive as long as it was directed at the Nationalist regime, who no longer shared the burden of power with the Communists they had just purged. The violence of the purge had further alienated the Nationalist leadership from the workers and peasants of Hainan, although it may have temporarily strengthened their position as rulers of Hainan and China.[13]

By June of 1928, however, the optimism of the January report had faded. This change of tone came as a result of the first Nationalist extermination campaigns launched against Communist military and political organizations on Hainan. In March of 1928, the Nationalist 10th division of the 11th army arrived on Hainan from Guangdong under the proven leadership of their commanding officer, Cai Tingkai (1892–1968). Cai (also rendered as Ts'ai T'ing-k'ai) had earned a national reputation in Shanghai in 1931, resisting a short-lived Japanese offensive there. Cai's 10th division was more than four thousand men, and it far outnumbered the entire Communist fighting force, which was just over fourteen hundred in early 1928.[14] Nine trying years later, the Hainan Communist leadership remembered this as the end of one of their ebullient high tides, as they were "smashed to pieces" (*da de qilingbaluo*) by the better trained, better supplied, and better led Nationalist forces.[15] At this early stage, losing contact with the mainland Communist authorities, particularly the Guangdong Provincial and

Southern Regional Bureaus, was seen as a major challenge to the Hainan Communists' ability to operate and grow. Still, a few communications remain extant from this period.

A report was filed in June from the northern city of Haikou, the island's governmental center and the founding site of the Hainan Communist movement.[16] This report begins with a complaint that the writers, who call themselves the Haikou Military Committee, have not received a response from their Guangdong provincial leadership, their "elder brothers," in more than a month. They diligently sent weekly reports on their progress, but have received no instructions in response, and it is not clear if this is a result of difficult or dangerous communication channels, or apathy on the part of the Guangdong leadership. The implicit criticism leveled at the Guangdong leadership may have been a swipe at the newest leader of the Hainan Communist movement, Huang Xuezeng (1900–1929), a mainlander fresh from the Guangdong Provincial Committee CCP headquarters who was on his way to Haikou.

According to the June 1928 report, the Haikou Military Committee had ordered Party members underground, and to temporarily cease any expression of revolutionary views. This was meant to protect those of their supporters who were prominent members of the overseas Hainanese community or schoolteachers, but it was possibly a countermeasure in anticipation of the brash urban strategy orders that Huang was bringing from the mainland. Still, the committee reported that it was making progress with an increasingly disaffected workforce, among which was a wave of unemployed laborers migrating to Hainan from the mainland. In the Committee's report on the activities of the enemy, they note that the Nationalist authorities had established wireless radio contact with Nanjing, the new national capital and center of the Nationalist republican government. The only note of optimism in the Committee's report on the Nationalist activities was that they were possibly moving a military division off the island and to the north, and thus loosening what seemed to be a stranglehold on the Communist activities on Hainan.

In the Committee's self-appraisal, they were blunt in relating their own recent difficulties. "At the moment, the Military Committee is responsible for five persons. In the previous meeting we decided to leave three members operating in Haikou, assigning others to work as appropriate. (Due to financial constraints, we are unable to communicate with [and report the progress of] all other cities and counties.)"[17] The reports of fighting in southern Lingshui had made their way north to Haikou, and the Military Committee reported this, in sketchy detail: a hundred or so of the Communist organized peasant soldiers had routed four hundred or so government troops, but with no information on casualties or territory held. There was also fighting in Qiongdong, and the report refers to another account of that, without providing detail here. In Wenchang and Qiongshan, however, the report cites the terrible impact on the Communist organization in these regions following the "White Terror" of the previous year, concluding that little information was available from these regions and any kind of organizational work there was not feasible at this time.

The weakness and scattered nature of the Communist organizational structure on Hainan is also evident to the Military Committee in the recent upsurge in reactionary militias within various townships across the island. (The report notes the arrival of weapons from Guangdong as the only bright spot in military developments.) It is not clear whether the reactionary militias the report is referring to are militias that are supportive of the Nationalists against the Communists, or if they are essentially loosely organized bandits who were not cooperating with the Communists. But in either case, they presented a turn for the worse in the Hainan Communists' fortunes after the relatively positive developments of the previous years in growing Communist support in militias and peasant organizations across the island. Compared to the report of only six months earlier, this June 1928 account of Communist activity on Hainan is much less optimistic. The report even gives vent to some of the frustrations of the Haikou Military Committee when it doggedly explains the failures, referring to other reports that should have been answered by the Guangdong Provincial Committee but apparently were not, and finally ends with an exasperated exclamation to the Provincial Committee to please reply with instructions for moving forward.[18] Also at the time of the June 1928 report, the Military Committee officially put forward the local Hainan leader, Wang Wenming as its leader and secretary. Within the month, Huang Xuezeng's arrival as emissary of the Guangdong provincial Communist authorities meant that Wang would be replaced. There are few documents extant from the Hainan group in this time, and none of them express any protest of Wang's replacement by the newly arrived Huang, but the change of strategy that Huang brought with him—to return to an urban strategy—must have been received with some skepticism by the battered Hainan cohort.

If the earlier June 1928 report conveyed any coherent message about the Communist movement on Hainan, it was that any attempt to hold the island's cities and towns was impossible under the current conditions. Still, with Huang Xuezeng's arrival, a renewed urban strategy was attempted, and the Guangdong native urged coalescence of the Communist forces on the island and general assaults on the cities, beginning with the capital of Haikou. Huang reported these plans to the Guangdong Provincial Committee immediately after his arrival in Hainan in July of 1928, most likely as a demonstration that he was attempting to implement the marching orders he had been given for the island.[19] These orders came, in turn, from the Shanghai Party center that was also reluctant to fully abandon the urban strategy.

Wang Wenming and others in the Hainan command took a secondary role in the following year, but Huang had little success in his attempts to retake the urban centers, especially the northern Haikou where he concentrated his efforts. With Cai Tingkai and the Nationalist forces' arrival from Guangdong in the spring of 1928, Huang's urban strategy was especially destructive. In pitched battle, the partisans and militias under Communist leadership had little hope of holding their own villages and towns, let alone trying to take the island's urban centers.[20] Almost exactly a year after Huang Xuezeng's arrival on Hainan, he was dead, captured and executed by the Nationalists in Haikou in July of 1929. The official Party history declares that Huang was betrayed to the Nationalist authorities, and his death led to the collapse of the urban workers' movement on Hainan.[21] Judging from the 1928 reports from the Haikou Military Commission and the arrival of Nationalist forces under Cai Tingkai's leadership, it seems the urban movement had already crumbled at least a year before Huang's death, and that the twenty-nine-year-old Guangdong native's life had been lost in a lost cause.

In September of 1929, another report was written and submitted to the Central Party leadership by Luo Wenyan (1904–1961), a Wenchang native and early member of the CCP.[22] Luo had joined the CCP in 1924, and he was a leader in the Hainan Party since its founding in June of 1926.[23] Luo's report notes similar problems to the 1928 report, and also the new problem of infighting within the Hainan Communist leadership. The violence of 1927 and 1928 led to a scrambling chaos among the Hainan Communist leadership, according to Luo, further complicated by conflicting views between the urban and rural strategies of different leaders. Some promising leaders sought refuge in Shanghai, Hong Kong, Guangzhou, and Southeast Asia. Among those who remained, all of the leaders thought of themselves as "great men," and entitled to lead the Party.[24]

Luo's bitterness reflected the conflict and struggles for power that were underway among the mainland as well as the Hainan Communist leadership. In this dark period, frustrations within the Party were manifested both on Hainan and on the mainland. Betrayal became a political tactic amongst rivals within the Communist Party, with Nationalist executioners ever ready to oblige and clean up the mess. This is not a fondly remembered chapter in national history, but as in any underground movement or civil war, it was a constant danger.

The early 1930s were trying years for the Communists of Hainan, as they were for the Communists on the mainland. The Communist movement was all but snuffed out by the arrests, executions, and battles with the Nationalists. On the mainland, the Communists were able to find some degree of safety and civilian support in the border regions between provinces, the traditional refuge of bandits. And finally when the Nationalist military offensives threatened to completely wipe out the Communists on the mainland, they were able to escape the encirclement and make their way through the western frontier and beyond the reach of Chiang Kai-shek. There was no chance for a Long March on Hainan, of course, bounded as they were by the ocean. Instead of borderlands and frontiers, there was the ocean and emigration on a junk or raft, or retreat into the island's unknown mountainous forests and jungles.

The Long March brought the Communists of the mainland to the fabled caves of Yan'an, and those who had made the trek were now fiercely loyal to the cause, though nearly nine in ten marchers did not reach this destination. On Hainan, according to most accounts, the common or unchanging theoretical or political foundation of Communism in the early 1930s is only the finest of threads. There were times when the main force of the Communists of Hainan could gather around a single fire in the wilderness, listening to Feng Baiju tell stories and his wife sing arias from Hainan operas.[25]

Following on the work of Lin Wenying and Xu Chengzhang, the Hainan Communists increasingly took on the local priorities of the island. For the guerrillas, the first priority was survival. From the cosmopolitan newspapermen and Tongmenghui members, through the united front with the Nationalists, the Hainan Communists had been an urban group that moved easily between the mainland cities of Guangzhou and Hong Kong. On Hainan, the split with the Nationalists left the Communist leadership with almost nowhere to run. No foreign concessions, no far-flung frontiers, no bandit lairs. The result, for the Hainan Communists, was devastating. Of the eleven main founders of the Communist movement on Hainan in 1926, seven were dead at the end of 1929, and four more were dead by 1932, all but one of them killed in battle or executed. One of them lived past the age of forty.[26]

Following the death of Huang Xuezeng, there was nothing holding the Hainan Communists in the cities, and Wang Wenming shifted the political center to the rural, mountainous Muruishan soviet. This period saw continued growth of the Party, and relative calm. In October of 1929, the Hainan Communist Special Committee filed a report on their recent conference in Neidongshan, near the site of their inaugural battle at the Coconut Stockades.[27] The report was a sober and measured reflection on the disastrous and formative years that had just passed. The urban strategy, which would still hold some sway on the mainland for several years, was completely discredited, and the prospect of positional warfare was likewise blamed for much of the failure. The sacrifices had been great, and as Wang Wenming resumed the Hainan Communist leadership, he led the Party center to the mountains. Smaller bases here had met with greater success in repelling Nationalist assaults earlier in 1929, punishing enemy attempts to eliminate their bases there.[28]

Reviewing the original ranks of the leadership of the later 1920s, Wang Wenming was one of the few leaders who had survived Nationalist purges and battles until that point. But by late 1929, Wang had become very sick. Among his final decisions were two crucial ones that would shape the Hainan Communist movement for the following two decades. First, he designated Feng Baiju as the movement's next leader, and second, he determined that the urban strategy must be abandoned, and the Party should seek refuge, rehabilitation, and reorganization in rural base areas.

By May of 1930, the first stage of this consolidation effort was complete and the Hainan Communists were back on the attack, launching the "Red May" offensive across the eastern coast. At the end of the year, military and political success had rebuilt the Red Army on the island, and its ranks swelled to thirteen hundred fighting men and women. This was a major increase from the fighting force of about five hundred that had remained in the Muruishan base area after the assaults by Cai Tingkai's Nationalist fighters in the early days of 1930.[29] One portion of these forces established in Hainan's Lehui County in this period was a unit of women fighters, formed by the Hainan Communist leadership. The leadership formed the group to establish a framework for women to contribute to the revolutionary effort in a more substantial way than they had until that point. According to some accounts, as many as seven hundred women volunteered to join the all-female fighting force. Ultimately, on May 1, 1931, 103 women would form the Women's Special Services Company of the Hainan Independent Second Division of the Chinese Red Army. This company would later become immortalized in films and ballets as the "Red Detachment of Women," and they would stand in for most mainlanders' understanding of the Hainan Communist movement. During the Cultural Revolution, even U.S. President Richard Nixon would be treated to a viewing of the ballet based loosely on the "Red Detachment." The artists responsible for the numerous dramatic endeavors related to this group took many liberties. Surprisingly, the artists disregarded the most obvious dimension of triumphant feminism within the historical reality of this group, which was that the group consisted both of women fighters and women officers. The company's real authority figure was Feng Zengmin (1912–1971), and a photograph of her with filmmaker, Xie Jin, confirms that the two at least met, and yet amazingly, the commander of the company in the film and ballet versions is a man.[30]

The growth in Communist numbers gained the attention of Nationalists on the mainland, who sent Chen Hanguang to lead the encirclement and annihilation campaigns on the island. Chen was far more efficient than his mainland counterparts in Jiangxi, and by 1932, the Hainan Communist movement was again battered and reduced to only a handful of adherents.[31]

The rule of Chen Jitang in Guangdong (1931–1936) saw an increase in the province's autonomy from the Nanjing government. With the help of General Chen Hanguang, Chen Jitang almost completely wiped out the Communist presence on Hainan. But other than anti-Communism, Chen did not share many of Chiang Kai-shek's political views for China's future. The rift between Chen Jitang and Chiang Kai-shek would develop into open conflict, but in the early 1930s, Chen's rule in Guangdong and on Hainan was effective in containing the Communists' development there. Communist base areas saw their fluctuating fortunes take another turn for the worse after 1931, and the next five years would nearly see the complete annihilation of the Hainan Communist movement. The ties between the mainland Communist movement and the Hainan Communists were tenuously maintained through much of this period, but the small nucleus that remained of the Hainan movement was learning to function without the material assistance of the mainlanders. Rather than broadening their channels of support and communication from the mainland, the Hainan Communists turned inward once more to an alliance with indigenous Li people of the island's interior. More precisely, the Li and the Communist leadership found a shared cause of resisting the Japanese, and even more immediately, fighting the Nationalists.

Of course, on the mainland, Chiang Kai-shek's Nanjing government was also attempting to eradicate the Communists, and by the end of 1934, they had nearly succeeded after a change in tactics that saw the main Communist base areas ominously surrounded. After a series of annihilation campaigns, the Nationalists succeeded in driving the main Communist force out of central and southern China, and on the Long March. This Communist defeat and retreat has been celebrated as a triumphant crucible of the Party, but had it not been for the imminent Japanese invasion, it seems likely that this would have been the end of the Chinese Communists. The

Long March of 1934–1936 led the Communists to the caves of Yan'an in China's remote northwestern region.

These efforts at domestic repression of the Communists—both by Chiang Kai-shek and the Nationalists on the mainland and by Chen Jitang in Guangdong and on Hainan—while effective, also served to sap some of the leaders' popularity among the country's patriotic students, merchants, and increasingly broader portions of the population. Another greater threat was looming. In September of 1931 the Japanese military had begun to seize portions of northeastern China, and a stream of Japanese colonists followed. In January of 1932, bombing and fighting broke out in the "Paris of the Orient," Shanghai, as Japanese designs on greater China became more and more obvious. By 1935, an anti-Japanese movement had spread and perhaps by default, the Communists earned windfall support as the Nationalists continued to focus on repressing the Communist movement instead of confronting the Japanese threat. In late 1936, amid an international scandal, Chiang Kai-shek was kidnapped and forced to stop campaigns against the Communists by one of his most loyal generals. Locked in a tense alliance, the Communists and Nationalists faced the full-scale Japanese invasion in the following year. While Taiwan had been secured as a Japanese colony in 1895, in the 1930s it was far from clear where Hainan would figure in the emerging titanic struggle that would envelope the forces of China, the United States, Great Britain, France, and of course the Japanese empire, among other regional forces.

In September 1937, with Feng Baiju as the clear leader of the Communist Party on Hainan, he and his wife, Zeng Huiyu, were captured by Nationalist forces and detained until November. While in prison, Feng was interrogated but repeatedly reminded his captors that they had no cause to hold him or interrogate him, since their two parties were in alliance.

Feng's captivity was the subject of another interrogation, this one coming in the late 1960s, during the Cultural Revolution when his interrogators implied that he had struck a secret deal with the Nationalists. Indeed, as noted, there was no need for any *secret* agreement, since the two parties were already in alliance. Imprisoned for years during the tumult of the Cultural Revolution, Feng acknowledged only one mistake during his prison stay. When asked about his views of Sun Yat-sen, whom both parties view as their political forbear, Feng acknowledged the correctness of Sun's "Three People's Principles" of nationalism, socialism, and democracy, and affirmed his "lifelong commitment to struggle" for these teachings.

But in this, Feng was walking the narrow tightrope of the united front. His Red Guard persecutors thirty years later were aware of this overzealous statement of loyalty to Sun Yat-sen whose legacy was one of moderation and conciliation between the two parties. Feng had pledged his "lifelong" (*zhongsheng*) support for Sun's ideals, and he knew that this was overstepping the invisible lines that still existed between the parties. During the Cultural Revolution, the Red Guards' used this as irrefutable proof of his capitulation to the Nationalists. Feng responded that they only had this proof of his commitment to Sun Yat-sen because Feng himself had submitted a report to the party headquarters in Guangzhou immediately upon his release, already pointing out at that time his own mistaken statement about "lifelong" support for Sun's principles. He requested and received clarification of party policy regarding the united front.

But Feng's release was not a foregone conclusion in September of 1937. Hundreds of Communist cadres of even higher rank had died on the execution grounds of Hainan in the past ten years, and Feng believed that he might be another one of them. Of the top leaders of the Hainan movement, Feng was one of the only ones remaining alive after a decade of devastating struggle. As he sat in prison, separated from his wife, he tried to reason with his captors and contemplated the fate of the revolution, wondering if he would be a part of its future.

Following the deaths of Huang Xuezeng then Li Shuoxun, and the rise of Wang Wenming followed by Feng Baiju, the local turn of the Hainan Communist movement was perhaps irreversible. Though the goal of national victory in the Chinese Communist revolution was shared by the Hainan Communists, Hainan's path would be a lonely one, with little communication and less assistance from the mainland. After the deaths of Huang and Li, Party Central on the mainland only sent cadres like Long March veterans, Zhuang Tian and Li Zhenya, the former a native son of Hainan and the latter deeply familiar with the island, to propagate mainland policy and take part in the island's Communist movement. As for the international dimension of the Hainan Communist movement, that, too, would take on a new form in which Hainanese abroad returned to the island to join the Communist movement, but fewer and fewer islanders looked outward to flee or seek assistance in Southeast Asia. The Japanese invasion of Hainan in 1939 would shape the next phase in the continuing localization of the Communist movement, which would see six years of grinding conflict and isolation from the mainland command, as well as an alliance with the indigenous Li people of Hainan's interior forested mountains.[32]

CHAPTER 4

AN OUTRAGE OF LITTLE CONSEQUENCE

The Japanese Invasion and Occupation of Hainan

On February 10, 1939, forces of the Imperial Japanese South China Naval Fleet, also known as the Fifth Fleet, landed along the northern coast of Hainan with army support, and overran the island in a matter of days. The immediate diplomatic explanation that the Japanese government provided was that the action was carried out with the goal of exterminating the Chinese military presence on Hainan.[1] This began over six years of Japanese occupation of the island. Two days after the beginning of the landing on Hainan, a group of foreign journalists asked the Nationalist leader and ruler of China, Generalissimo Chiang Kai-shek (1887–1975) about its implications. Chiang's response was perhaps paradoxical and contradictory, not unlike the nature of Hainan's historical relationship with the Chinese mainland. Addressing a question about the influence of the Japanese action on peace in the region, Chiang said, "The attempt of the Japanese to occupy Hainan Island on February 10 is similar to their occupation of Mukden on September 18, 1931. In other words, by attacking the Island Japan has committed another Mukden outrage in the Pacific. The effect of this is the same irrespective of the fact that one outrage was committed on land and the other on the sea."[2]

Chiang's comparison seemed to have dire implications, but it was also perhaps a performance for an international audience. The Mukden (Shenyang) Incident of 1931 had been unheeded as a prelude to wider Japanese aggression, and it came about six years before the full-scale invasion of China. Chiang reminded his listeners that the failure in 1931 of foreign powers to realize the extent of Japanese territorial ambition had allowed Japanese expansion and aggrandizement to its current extent. With relatively little European and American attention in the Pacific theater still in 1939, Chiang was using the example of Hainan to echo this earlier missed opportunity to check Japanese expansion, and to encourage a more muscular confrontation of the current Japanese threat. Chiang was comparing the Japanese landing on Hainan to the infamous September 18, 1931, Mukden incident in Manchuria, clearly in an attempt to sound an alarm that had not been heard the first time.

The Hainan landing was part of a grand triangular plan, said Chiang, for Japan to control the Pacific between Guam in the ocean's east, Sakhalin in the north, and Hainan in the west. If the Japanese accomplished this aim, Chiang warned that any action by the French, British, or Americans in the region would be rendered impossible by the resulting Japanese naval strength. This was indeed a grand framework in which to characterize the Japanese occupation of Hainan. In terms of the failed defense of Hainan, the lack of Chinese naval force and organized beach positions had prevented any substantial protection of the island's coastline. The Japanese occupation of the island already seemed to be a foregone conclusion by February 12, 1939, only two days after the initial action.

It is almost impossible to imagine a grander way to cast the events of February 1939 than by linking the Japanese landing on Hainan to a total Pacific strategy, and comparing the event to the infamous Mukden Incident. But significantly in the final question of the interview, a journalist asked Chiang about how great an effect the Japanese landing would ultimately have on the Chinese-Japanese hostilities. Chiang responded flatly, "Very little. The issue between China and Japan will be fought out on the mainland. The occupation of one island is not of serious consequence to us."[3] The Japanese seizure of Hainan, ever the island of paradox in the eyes of the mainland, was both "another Mukden outrage" and, at the same time, "not of serious consequence to us."

An Uneasy United Front

More than a year and a half passed from the July 7, 1937, outbreak of full-scale war with Japan until the Japanese invasion of Hainan in February of 1939. Several events on Hainan in that eighteen-month interim reflect the degree of autonomy of both the governing authorities and the Communist movement there. Ever since the beginning of the decade, Chiang Kai-shek and the Nanjing government had been unable to realize broad national unity. Regional militarists blocked these attempts, reluctant to surrender their autonomy, or to commit their troops to aiding in conflicts in distant parts of the fragile republic. As the Japanese encroachment in Manchuria increased, and incidents between Chinese and Japanese troops in the northeast became more frequent, some became frustrated with the Nanjing government's reluctance to confront Japan. On December 9, 1935, student-led protests erupted in the streets of Beiping (Beijing), giving a public voice to the calls on the Nanjing government to take a stronger stand against Japan, and stop the piecemeal concessions that were being surrendered in the northeast. The students clashed with police, and they received support around the country. Chiang Kai-shek was vulnerable to criticism that he was more concerned with internal pacification than resistance of the Japanese threat. While this broad statement reflected reality to an extent, recent mainstream scholarship has also urged a reconsideration of the Nanjing-Chongqing Nationalist regime and its challenges and endurance in the face of impossible adversity during the 1930s.[4]

In the summer of 1936, southern leaders including Chen Jitang moved again to assert their autonomy from Nanjing. In 1931, it was Japanese action in the northeast that had brought the southern militarists and the Nanjing regime back together when the southerners had been on the verge of open war with Nanjing; but by 1936, so profoundly had the political landscape changed, that the southerners were able to now use the Japanese threat as part of the reason not for closing ranks, but instead for escalating their opposition to Nanjing. In May of 1936, a succession crisis had followed the death of one of the prominent southern leaders, Hu Hanmin, and in the confusion, other southerners from the "New Guangxi Clique" moved to capitalize on both defending their autonomy and attacking Chiang's reluctance to confront the Japanese threat. The plan quickly backfired, and massive defections within the southern military gave Chiang an easy victory in reasserting his control over the south.[5]

The divisions within the Nationalist regime, and among its regional leaders seemed to present a possible weakness to be exploited by the Communists, and perhaps the most spectacular example came with the detention of Chiang Kai-shek in December of 1936 by Zhang Xueliang, one of his top generals who had been the most powerful figure in Manchuria. Zhang demanded that Chiang cease his attempt to eradicate the Chinese Communists, and instead turn to face the Japanese threat. After all it was Zhang's Manchuria that had already been turned into a Japanese puppet state, and it had been his troops that Chiang ordered to strike a final blow against the Communists in Yan'an. The detention, or kidnapping, became world headlines, and Chiang was finally released with the understanding that a Chinese united front would face the Japanese threat together.

But the alliance was an uneasy one, and both parties soon retreated to separate inland corners of China proper. The Communists' central authority was based in northwestern Yan'an, and the Nationalists as leaders of the internationally recognized Chinese government retreated to western Chongqing (Chungking), following the long-awaited Japanese invasion of the coast in 1937–1938. Among the leadership of both parties, there was disagreement as to how committed they should be to this united front, and the party line shifted occasionally in both camps. The last alliance between the two parties had been shattered by the violence of 1927. In 1937, with the Japanese invasion, alliance was crucial, but both parties included a spectrum of opinion on the degree of investment in the alliance, and the degree to which they hedged their bets. Whereas one leader may declare enthusiastically that he believed in "total commitment to the united front," another within the same camp might privately or openly criticize the alliance as shortsighted and foolish, since, in his view, one party was simply waiting for the right moment to annihilate the other. Wariness and mistrust was common among both parties, as well as frustration that the other was not fully committed to resisting the Japanese invasion.

From the perspective of Hainanese leaders, it was sometimes difficult to keep abreast of the latest parsing on the mainland by the two parties, who seemed to be quibbling over troop commitments, uniform insignia, military unit titles, and command appointments. Mutual mistrust continued after December 1936, while military and political leaders sometimes improvised as to how they should respond to local conditions that brought up questions of the degree to which they should obey or disobey a command from one of the two parties. Differing political and military directives from the two parties eventually led to conflict, leaving field commanders in increasingly dangerous situations. The quibbling of political leaders in Party headquarters would lead to confusion and sometimes disaster, especially far from Yan'an and Chongqing, in areas like south China, including Hainan.[6]

Between the July 1937 beginning of full-scale war on the mainland, and the February 1939 landing of Japanese forces on Hainan, interaction between the Nationalists and Communists on the island was tense. Foreign observers noted the bandit-like violence of the "Reds" as well as the heavy-handed suppression campaigns launched by the Nationalists. The American Presbyterian Reverend David Stanton Tappan II (1880–1968) was one of the most prominent foreign figures on Hainan from the 1920s through the end of the 1940s. Tappan and other Americans on Hainan maintained official relations with the Nationalist authorities, and then later with the Japanese occupiers until the Japanese attack on Pearl Harbor in December of 1941, but they expressed little sympathy for the island's other aspiring rulers, the Communists. In their letters and diaries from this period, the American mission community referred to the misguided and godless Reds as little more than bandits. Vulnerable as the mission community was, often located in the island's smaller towns, their fears of bandits were not baseless. One Reverend Byers was killed in a botched attempt to kidnap and ransom him by a group of brigands in 1925.[7]

And so, considering this aversion to sympathy with the Communists, one example of Reverend Tappan's writing on the subject is striking. He wrote the following in the *Hainan Newsletter* of the American Presbyterian Mission, after observing a group of suspected Communists captured by the Nationalists near Jiaji (Kacheck) in 1937:

> During a Sunday morning service came the notes of the bugle that strike terror to one's heart for they mean an execution. Shortly out of the military headquarters across from the church came four or five soldiers pushing three women and three men with shackled feet and hands tied behind their backs.
>
> The procession with a quickly gathering crowd marched through the long wide streets of the market and back past the church. Then out beyond to the execution field where these six young people were shot for attending a Communist meeting.
>
> Supposedly the authorities feel that is one way of keeping people from being Communists. But that was not this writer's reaction as he saw a twenty year old girl being pushed along to her execution with hundreds of men, women and children following. I thought of one such misguided girl who, when she was being taken to her execution, turned to the crowd and cried,
> "I am dying for my faith! What are you doing for yours?"
>
> In other parts of China they have a better way of putting such young offenders, misguided youth, in prison schools where they are shown their mistakes and their visionary ideals are directed in more constructive channels.[8]

I include this entire passage from Tappan's writing to capture the ambivalence felt by an observer of the ongoing Chinese civil war in 1937, as it unfolded on Hainan. The title of Tappan's piece quoted above is "Communist Echoes: Dreaded Reds Still Taking Their Toll," and it seems, more than the article's content, to reflect the anti-Communist perspective that a mainstream American readership might have had at that time. But American voices like Joseph Stilwell, Edgar Snow, Theodore White, and others were complicating the simple narrative of support for the Nationalists' attempts to eradicate the Chinese Communists. Stilwell, Snow, White, and here, Tappan, gave the American reader a human face to the distant civil war, and soon also the Chinese war of resistance, which the Americans would not join until the end of 1941. In the above article, Tappan, a foreign observer on the ground in the interior of Hainan, voices a perspective that captures the complexity of China's civil war on the eve of the Japanese invasion.

In the summer of 1937, Feng Baiju and the Communist movement on Hainan had been reduced greatly to only a handful of fighters, and their contact with the central mainland Communist authorities, now based in northwestern Yan'an, had been severed. There were still Communist operatives in Hong Kong and Shanghai, and they did maintain connections with the Yan'an authorities. Feng knew that if he could make his way there, he would be able to receive updated instructions and know how to best proceed.

Shortly after Feng's return, he dutifully approached the local Nationalist authorities with the aim to arrange a framework for cooperation. It is noteworthy that this was not something that automatically followed the lead of the mainland Nationalists and Communists. While the lack of communication between the Hainan and mainland Communists explains the lag in directives and awareness, there was naturally a communication flow between the Hainan Nationalist governing authorities and their mainland counterparts. When Feng traveled to Haikou with the intention of arranging an alliance with the Nationalist authorities, however, he and his wife were captured by Nationalist soldiers, and he was imprisoned.

This detention would lead to a host of political problems for Feng in later years, because he was accused of collaborating with the Nationalists and betraying his comrades in order to ensure his release. These accusations, while potent and perhaps fatal to Feng during the chaotic years of the Cultural Revolution (1966–1976) were not considered seriously at the time. There was little question as to Feng's absolute loyalty among any who knew him well, and his release was secured not by any brokering between Feng and his captors, but rather by a combination of pressure from Zhou Enlai, Ye Jianying and the mainland Communist authorities, and vociferous complaints from the overseas Chinese community in Southeast Asia that had come to see Feng as the bearer of the torch of anti-Japanese resistance.

The awkward captivity and release of the Communist leader, Feng Baiju, also reflected this complex interaction. Hainan's remoteness added to the confusion and complexity of the battle lines, alliances, and revolutionary itineraries of China, and it seems from both Feng's captivity and the frequent executions of suspected Communists, that the Nationalist authorities on Hainan tended toward an even more brutal and oppressive anti-Communist policy than Chiang Kai-shek on the mainland. The Xi'an Incident in December 1936 and the outbreak of full-scale war with Japan in July 1937 had an impact on the Hainan situation, and probably saved Feng Baiju's life.

Violence and confusion had prevailed on Hainan as a result of both the sporadic communications between the Hainan Communists and their mainland counterparts, along with the hostile relationship between the Hainan governing authorities and Chiang Kai-shek's government on the mainland. The Liang-Guang Incident of June 1936 had exposed one of the many major cracks in the Chinese ruling Nationalist Party's foundation, and the Xi'an Incident of December 1936 exposed another. The divisions between China's regional rulers and the Nanjing government in the lead-up to the July 1937 outbreak of full-scale war meant that channels of communication and command were shaky at best, broken and not to be trusted at worst. Sometimes the Communists benefited from this alliance, as when regional leaders allowed the mainland Long Marchers to move through their territories quickly to avoid a confrontation that would mean casualties on both sides.

Yunlong Reorganization

It was late in 1938 that the Hainan Nationalist military authorities, then under General Wang Yi (1900–1948) accepted the Communist fighters into an alliance at what became known as the "Yunlong Reorganization" (*Yunlong gaibian*). The reorganization was named for the northern town where the talks took place, near Haikou and near Feng Baiju's hometown of Changtai village. In the first year of the Japanese invasion, as the Nanjing government retreated first to Hankou and then to its wartime capital of Chongqing, Japanese forces had not yet landed on Hainan. Some bombing missions terrorized the population, and demonstrated the destructive capacity of the Japanese air power, but no troops had arrived in force. In September of 1938, the bombing of the island's northern city of Haikou intensified, and representative of the Nationalist and Communist forces met to discuss a formal alliance in resistance to the Japanese. Following an initial exchange of communications, the commander of the Guangdong Twenty-First Regiment, General Wang Yi met with Feng Baiju and other representatives of the small Communist fighting force.

Now the United Front would officially come to Hainan, almost two years late. The Communists on Hainan had been reduced by fatigue and suppression to a guerrilla fighting force of about one hundred. The agreement framed by Wang Yi and Feng Baiju in October of 1938 established the legitimate operation of these forces, and an anti-Japanese alliance between Wang's Nationalists and Feng's Communists on Hainan. The basic points of the "Yunlong Reorganization" established first that the Nationalists and Communists would ally to fight the Japanese; second, that the Communist forces would be reorganized and renamed the Guangdong People's Anti-Japanese Independent Regiment of the 14th District; third, that leaders of the units within this force would be chosen in consultation between Nationalist and Communist representatives; fourth, that the new force would construct its own training and education facilities; and fifth, that Nationalist authorities would contribute a monthly stipend of 8,000 yuan to the new force. The changes that followed were rapid. Less than a month after the November 1938 signing of the Yunlong agreement, the immediate legitimacy of the Communist movement brought its recruiters into the daylight. Visibility of the movement tripled the fighting force from one hundred to three hundred by December, with more than two hundred firearms purchased and acquired through aid from the Nationalists.[9]

Feng Baiju carried on as the Hainan Communists' leader. Little more than a year after his imprisonment, he was now a rising star and rallying symbol of the movement to resist the Japanese invasion. With the fall of major southern Chinese mainland cities, most Hainanese believed that the Hainanese resistance would be called on soon to fight the Japanese on the beaches, in the forests, and in the streets of Hainan. Overseas Hainanese also became involved, and sent aid to any on the island who would resist the Japanese. In December of 1938, while the Communists and Nationalists of Hainan were setting the terms for their cooperation at Yunlong, the Reverend and Mrs. Tappan traveled across the water to Hong Kong to celebrate a "real 'homeside' Christmas away from home." While there, as Mrs. Luella Tappan recalled in a narrative written for her grandchildren, "Some wealthy Hainanese merchants from Singapore . . . invited the head of our family [Reverend Tappan] to a feast. . . . They had a fund to send down to their friends cut off behind the Japanese lines in Hainan." The merchants gave the Tappans $20,000 and 100,000 quinine pills, with the promise of more to follow. The Tappans accepted the money and medicine, and thus joined the Chinese resistance to the Japanese more than two years before the bombing of Pearl Harbor.[10] But it was only a matter of months before the Japanese occupation of Hainan.

"War Shadows"

In December of 1938, to Reverend Tappan and the mission community on Hainan, Japan's invasion of the island seemed imminent. It had been a year and a half since the July 1937 start of the full-scale conflict in Beijing, and now most of the Chinese coast had fallen to the Japanese onslaught. Most recently, Japan took Guangzhou (Canton), and the Japanese forces that sought to completely subdue China saw in Hainan a hole in the east coast firmament that they hoped could be sealed off as a route of supplying the fighting forces of China. Some American aid flowed to Chiang Kai-shek's Nationalists, but to the confusion of the Hainanese who spoke with Americans on the island, the United States also continued to trade with Japan. American munitions and fuel allowed the bombing and violence perpetrated in China by the Japanese forces. In his Christmas contribution titled "War Shadows" in the American Presbyterian Mission's 1938 *Hainan Newsletter*, Tappan wrote:

> The Chinese are more than friendly to foreign missionaries and Christian workers. They flock to our mission compounds for refuge in times of bombing. But they still hold on to their ancient superstitions as we were reminded by the way the crowds have swarmed to the large idol fair which has been held the past three days in the temple over the wall from our compound. The fact that Christian nations are selling war planes, gasoline and shrapnel to enable Japan to bomb defenseless Chinese does not help the cause of the Prince of Peace. After a bombing it is hard to answer Chinese viewing the ruins when they ask why America helps Japan to do this? We find it difficult to say that American sells war materials to anyone who pays the price. When will Christian nations practice Christianity at home as well as send missionaries to China to preach it? Then only will there be peace on earth and good will toward men.[11]

Tappan's position, and that of other Americans who agreed with him, were caught up in the paradoxes of their position, and his frustration is palpable even in a Christmas message to his countrymen, his flock, and his colleagues. Beyond monetary aid and refuge, the Tappans and other foreign observers could not stem the inevitable and impending arrival of the Japanese landing forces. Sealing off the coast from foreign aid to Chiang Kai-shek's Nationalists and establishing airfields and naval stations on

Hainan led the Japanese to invade the island. Tapping into Hainan's natural resources and quelling anti-Japanese resistance there also drove the Japanese plans for occupation. The task was to be carried out largely by the Japanese navy, following some probing actions along Hainan's southern beaches and a brief bombing campaign.

The landing of Japanese naval and army forces on Hainan in mid-February was a very quick action considering the ample size of the island. According to Japanese news outlets, the initial action resulted in the loss of three Japanese lives.[12] After some probing activity on the southern coast, near the natural harbors of Sanya and Yulin, the first major landing took place around the northern settlements of Haikou and Qiongzhou, and was conducted by a Taiwan (Formosa) Mixed Brigade, combined with Japanese special naval and army forces. Within a matter of days, the Nationalist authorities in the major coastal towns from Haikou in the north to Sanya in the south had either surrendered or fled, and the Japanese were in complete control of the island. By February 14, Sanya harbor had been seized by Japanese naval authorities, and work was underway to develop the great military potential of the port.

In the months and years to come, during hostilities with the Japanese, Hainanese would occasionally be surprised to find that some of the occupying Japanese soldiers were actually Taiwanese. One Hainan historian noted that over a short period, twenty Taiwanese soldiers deserted from the First and Second Taiwanese Infantry Regiments with which they arrived on the island, going on to ally with local Chinese guerrilla forces. They brought with them much-needed guns and munitions.

In this account, shortly after the Japanese occupation began, one of the Taiwanese soldiers began frequenting a village shop for his meals, and confided his grief with the local landlady. He called her "auntie" and bemoaned his fate as a soldier in the Japanese imperial forces. When his hostess asked why he had joined the Japanese military in the first place, he said that his family had always been poor, and that this was his only way to provide for them. In this account, local Communist guerrillas contacted the young Taiwanese soldier, Li Shuihang, and offered him the opportunity to prove his loyalty to China. He did so by delivering pistols and communication equipment, and then was accepted as a defector under Ma Baishan's (1907–1992) command.[13]

But this anecdotal success of the resistance forces on the island was certainly not the norm, and the Japanese conquest of the island's major northern and southern ports was completed in a matter of days, and all coastal towns under Japanese control by April. In the early days of the occupation, Japanese geologists were escorted around the island, surveying the soil's mineral content. Finding iron in the island's southwestern interior, this became one of the crucial reasons for the Japanese occupation. Besides its strong position as a naval and air base for the blockade and continued assaults on the Chinese and Southeast Asian mainland, Hainan's mineral potential was again touted as reason to make inroads to the inaccessible interior and find a way to tap its rich resources.

According to a November 1940 International News Service story out of Hong Kong, the Japanese authorities also sought precious metals on Hainan, including gold and silver. "The pot of gold exists, well informed circles here insist, and pointed out that the Japanese simply cannot find it because only the coastal regions of the island are in Japanese hands, while the hinterland has remained under Chinese control. Guerrilla warfare is going on in many parts of Hainan, to which smaller Japanese units dare not venture."[14]

By late 1940, according to this report, salt was the main resource being sent to Japan from Hainan, but in the coming years, Japanese forces would begin to venture inland, finding iron and building light rail links to the coast. Sugar and cattle were also the most immediately available resources that the Japanese authorities sent from Hainan to their forces on the Chinese mainland and back to Japan. The quest for precious metals on Hainan seems to reflect a continuation of the narrative of Hainan as a potential treasure island, and the ongoing perception of the great possibilities and wealth that might be realized through development and investment. In this way the Japanese occupiers continued a centuries-old tradition of ambitious but ultimately failed plans to develop Hainan's perceived potential.

In December of 1940, the alliance between the Communists and Nationalists on Hainan erupted in violence. Since the Yunlong reorganization of December 1938, and then the Japanese invasion of February 1939, Communist regular forces on the island had increased steadily as a result of effective propaganda, broad land reform policy appeal, and efficient organization. That organization came in part as a result of renewed contact with the mainland Communist central command at Yan'an. In the summer of 1940, Zhou Enlai ordered the native Hainanese and Long March veteran, Zhuang Tian, to return to Hainan and help with organization there. When Zhuang left for Hainan, Zhou was clear about how he and the Party envisioned the narrow command structure on Hainan: "Comrade Feng Baiju is the banner of the people of Hainan. The view of Party Central is that he should serve as Hainan Party secretary, the leader of the anti-Japanese guerrilla military forces, and the chief political representative. This will implement a unified leadership in the revolutionary struggle of Hainan. Take this directive to the Special Committee on Hainan. When you arrive in Hainan, you will support the work of Comrade Feng Baiju, respect him, and carry out the revolutionary work under this unified leadership."[15] Zhou's words, as promulgated by Zhuang Tian, reinforced Feng's authority, which some including Li Ming had challenged during and after Feng's captivity. After the summer of 1940, Feng was known as "the banner of the people of Hainan" to those who supported him, and Zhou Enlai's endorsement settled any question as to who spoke for the CCP on the island.

As the leadership question was being settled, the Communist presence on Hainan grew to three thousand fighting men and women with the Hainan Independent Column. The expanded, strengthened, and stabilized ranks of the Communists spread across the island, establishing guerrilla bases with the confidence that the Nationalist authorities had sanctioned their growth, and the Japanese forces were not adequate to track and quash them. Beyond the fighting force, civilian support for the Communists was also growing. The overseas Hainanese, many of whom had alerted the public to Feng's imprisonment, now rallied to his banner in increasing numbers. They sent funds, supplies, and their youth to support the Hainan Communists. In Hong Kong the Singapore Hainanese merchants had given the Tappans money and medicine to distribute on Hainan, and Feng Baiju maintained these contacts as well. In his public and private record of these days, Reverend Tappan makes no suggestions that the guerrillas he is supplying are Communists. But under the agreement of the "Yunlong reorganization," the Hainan Communists had been folded into the resistance forces of the island, and it is unlikely that the partisan fighters would have been brazen or foolish enough to wear insignia. Indeed it seems likely that the overseas Hainanese were using Tappan to supply the Hainan Communist forces because the historical record shows extensive contact between Feng personally and the extensive network of Hainanese communities throughout the region. In the year from November of 1939 until October of 1940, there are only three extant documents from Feng's hand, and all three of them are directed to the overseas Hainanese community in the region. They include matters like requests for aid and updates on the situation in Hainan. In the communications, Feng explains that a lack of medicine is causing wounded fighters to die when they might have lived with the help of basic supplies.[16]

In these communications, Feng also requests winter clothes, which might sound unusual to one familiar only with the image of Hainan as a tropical island. In the rainy winter months, high in the interior mountains, the temperatures drop, and the insidious, damp chill made the partisan fighters miserable. In one of Feng Baiju's recollections, during the darkest days of the guerrilla struggle, he walked among the thin ranks of supporters, checking on their health and morale. He recalled a young man of nineteen who was unaccustomed to the bitter cold of the island's mountains. Still he put on a brave face for his commander, though he was soaked to the bone and cold. Feng asked him how he was doing and the boy replied, "I'm not cold if you're not cold." Feng smiled and replied, "Well, I'm freezing!"[17]

Collaboration on Hainan

In the early days of the Japanese occupation, the Japanese imperial naval authorities took control of the island under Vice Admiral Nobutake Kondo (1886–1953), commander of the Fifth Fleet, and appointed a "puppet government" of Chinese officials, led by Zhao Shihuan. According to a 1945 report sent by the Hainan Communist leadership to the mainland Communist headquarters in Yan'an, the "puppet army" of Chinese who served the Japanese numbered more than five thousand, and was scattered throughout the island. By 1945, there were puppet forces in every county of the island, usually garrisoned with the Japanese forces. But the report notes that no prominent Hainanese had joined the puppet army. The leadership was neither famous nor infamous on the island.[18]

Zhao Shihuan (1903–1960) was from Hainan's northeastern town of Wenchang, like many of the island's elites. As an excellent student, he was sent to the mainland for his schooling, and eventually to France where he earned a doctoral degree, according to several sources, though it is not clear in what subject. He returned to China to teach, and at the outbreak of the war with Japan in 1937, he returned to Hainan. According to one of the few biographical treatments of Zhao Shihuan, he had returned to his hometown to teach because he had lost confidence in both of the two major Chinese political options. His personal experience trying to work within the Nationalist government on the mainland had left him disillusioned with its corruption, and the Communists seemed to have little hope of success. When Japanese forces arrived in Wenchang, they heard that there was a foreign-educated teacher in the area, and sought him out. Zhao was "invited" to serve in the puppet government that was being hastily assembled, and it seems that he had little choice but to accept the post.[19]

Zhao, and others who served in the collaborationist regime of Hainan, are generally deemed *Hanjian*, or traitors, in historical accounts of the Japanese occupation, but it is worth noting that Zhao and many others were effectively forced into this service. In the Hainanese historical record as well as the later accounts, there is little invective and disgust with those who served in the collaborationist, or "puppet" government. This is a significant difference from the kind of tropes that pervade much of Chinese writing about those who served the Japanese, whether they did so willingly or not.[20]

Brutality

Examining the Japanese invasion and occupation of portions of China during the 1930s and 1940s is a challenge to the human psyche, and often the writing about the horrors of the conflict are justifiably charged with emotion. Often in China, at the time of writing, the generations that are once or even twice removed from the events of the war in China continue to nurse resentment and even fury at the inhumanity of Japanese actions in China and throughout the region. Wartime memory as a political football in the region unfortunately further complicates the issue, as some politicians and pundits aim to harness nationalism or racism in order to bolster their platform. Still, in spite of these challenges, and sometimes because of them, inspiring examples of stellar and indefatigable scholarship emerge from the archives, and more often from the excavated fields and the oral histories of Hainan. During my archival work and travel in Hainan, I had the privilege of working with one such historian, Sato Shojin, whose aim it is, in a very real sense, to dig up and lay bare the evidence of atrocities on the island.[21] Sato publishes his work in newsletters and journals, and curates historical museum exhibits. In museums, he told me that he sometimes encounters resistance from sponsoring Japanese entities that seem less relentless than he is in their determination to catalog these horrors. He also makes and screens documentary films, including interviews with former comfort women and other victims of Japanese atrocities. He catalogs mass graves across the island, including Japanese iron works and other work sites where workers were executed. In a 2012 interview, Sato did not mince words about his aims. The atrocities, including enslavement of women and men, the mass killings, must be documented. The subjects of his studies who survived the intervening years are naturally reaching the end of their lives, and Sato's work has taken on a renewed urgency. In more than two dozen trips to Hainan, Sato's work has been singularly driven. He aims to achieve a direct apology from the Japanese government, and have that apology substantiated with reparations to the living victims and the families of the victims who suffered.[22]

The Japanese legacy of institutional rape and murder continues to live on Hainan.[23] Nearly twelve thousand Japanese marines and more than four thousand men in the police force kept the forces of resistance firmly in check.

In 1944, the Japanese estimates of the Chinese resistance were more than seven thousand troops loyal to the Chongqing Nationalist government, or the *Bao'an* forces (literally, "Peace-keeping" forces), more than four thousand Communist troops, and almost six thousand local irregular forces who did not seem to have any larger cause to identify with except resistance to the Japanese and defense of the island.[24]

In one 1945 telegram sent to the Communist headquarters in Yan'an (most likely sent from Guangzhou or Hong Kong, since the Hainan Communists had no access to wireless radio until the following year) the Hainan Communists were gaining in strength and cohesion three months before the Japanese defeat. More than five thousand Communist regulars were divided into four units operating in separate areas of the island. Their command had become clearly centralized, with Feng Baiju as the military and political leader of the Communist movement. The telegram claims that the Communist regulars on Hainan were well supported by the villagers of Hainan in terms of their food requirements, but their medical needs were great, and at the time of sending the message, more Hainan Communist soldiers were dying of diseases and complications from wounds than deaths in battle. The Japanese navy surrounded and ruled the island, but the complete lack of Communist sea power was not a problem for the Communist soldiers and guerrillas who mainly restricted their movements to the jungle interior.[25]

While the regular forces were based mainly in the mountains, the plains of northern Hainan also had Communist allies in underground militias and other irregular forces. According to the May 1945 message to the Communist military headquarters, the Hainan Communist presence was widely felt.[26] While its regular forces conducted asymmetrical warfare against Nationalist and Japanese forces, their ranks increased during the Japanese occupation, and they grew in popularity. In villages where the Nationalists and the Japanese were rarely seen, it was not a risk to proclaim one's sympathy for the Communists and their leader, Feng Baiju. There was always the risk of being reported to the Nationalist or Japanese authorities in a nearby town, but the long reach of the Communists was growing, and Communist supporters walked tall in remote villages during the late days of the Japanese occupation. These were the underground militia members who bided their time, and contented themselves, for the moment, to proclaim their support for their comrades in the mountain forests. Their chance to kill and die for Hainan's red flag would come in 1950.[27]

But the Japanese reputation of cruelty and collective punishment extended beyond the regions where they held direct power, and this could counteract the recruiters and propaganda workers of the Hainan Communists. Soon after Japanese learned of the guerrillas' leader, Feng Baiju and his Qiongshan county roots, either through rumors of heroism or "wanted, dead or alive" notices in Japanese and Nationalist papers, Japanese marines paid a visit to his hometown of Changtai, then again, and again. Ten times Japanese and Chinese soldiers in the service of the Japanese authority raided the village, looking for Feng Baiju or anyone they could find with the surname Feng, terrorizing the village, the county, and the island.[28] A young girl was returning from the forest and she hid and watched as, on the final Japanese visit, a Chinese officer led one hundred Chinese and Japanese soldiers into the town. Seven women were publicly gang-raped by the soldiers. All of the villagers that the soldiers could find were then herded into a house, including the girl's parents. The house was doused in gasoline and burned. In remembering this horror sixty-eight years later, she muttered that her family name was not even Feng.[29]

There was a late attempt, in the early spring of 1945, by the Japanese to bolster its presence on Hainan, but it was soon reversed as the island's aircraft were withdrawn to the Japanese homeland in May of 1945. Desperation in the Japanese military administration also led to increasingly harsh treatment of the prisoners that they held on Hainan. According to one American military observer who arrived on the island in the weeks following the Japanese surrender, the prison camps on the island were "every bit as cruel as Buchenwald or Dachau."[30] Six years of Japanese occupation on the island escalated to a bloody finale under the authority of the Japanese Navy who worked in concert with zaibatsu like the Mitsui Corporation, to enslave Chinese workers, hold captives in demonstrably unlivable conditions, and massacre military prisoners and civilians in orgies of beheading and bayoneting, "to provide a diversion for the Japanese officers." Allied servicemen from Australia, Great Britain, Holland, India, and the United States suffered and hundreds died in Japanese captivity, some executed, some perishing in forced labor, some dying of disease or starvation, and some killed by Hainanese bandits when they were out on work parties.[31]

But the Hainanese bore most of the brutality, with some accounts putting the death toll at fully one third of the adult male population, which would mean nearly half a million dead, and thousands of women. The most recent authoritative Chinese study on the Japanese occupation of Hainan puts the number of violent deaths under the Japanese at more than four hundred thousand.[32] This figure is about one in five of the Hainanese population, including men and women of all ages, killed under the Japanese occupation. The work of the Japanese historian and documentarian, Sato Shojin, confirms these figures, while emphasizing the human toll through his tireless interviewing among the elderly witnesses and survivors of the Japanese occupation of Hainan.

Beyond the Hainanese and prisoners of war, tens of thousands of Chinese and Korean detainees were brought to Hainan to augment the slave labor force that also consisted of Han and Li Hainanese. Recently, Sato successfully lobbied the Hainanese provincial government to honor the Korean dead whose mass graves were recently discovered near the southern city of Sanya. The Korean dead had been captured and transported to Hainan to work in the island's southern region building docks and shipyards, and the light-gauge railroad that connected Hainan's iron mines to the southern coast.[33]

The same American military observer cited earlier noted that of one hundred thousand Hong Kong civilian internees who had been brought by the Japanese to work on a Hainan mining project, only twenty thousand had survived to see the end of the war with Japan.[34] This figure is astounding in itself, and if it can be extended to the rest of Japanese rule of Hainanese slaves and internees, the astronomical figures that are used by most Chinese historians about the death toll of the Japanese occupation of Hainan are probably accurate.[35]

Like most of the information collected by the Hainan Communist leadership, news of the Japanese surrender of August 15, 1945, came late—on the 23rd of August—and through a Nationalist source.[36] At the time of the Japanese surrender in August and September of 1945, the Hainan Communist statistics that have since been compiled by Chinese historians stood as follows. The Communists controlled territories inhabited by over one million people—roughly a third of the island's population at that time. Much of the Communists' holdings in this period were inland mountainous hideouts that had been secured with the help of the Li people who hosted them there.

In the ensuing civil war, these inland bases would be the main operating region of the Hainan Communists, but immediately following the Japanese surrender and withdrawal, the five active detachments of Communist forces were holding or fighting for significant territories throughout the island.[37] This was one of the high tides of their regional control of Hainan, which might account in part for the negative reaction to the orders from the northern Communist headquarters to send their best leaders and fighters to the north less than a year later. As is explained in the following chapter, the Communist alliance with the Li people following the Li Baisha Uprising in 1943 brought a renewed vitality to the Communist movement, including substantial territorial gains.

Following the Japanese defeat, the Hainan Communist leadership expected to build on these gains, not to forfeit them to the Nationalists, who were also reduced to guerrilla tactics in the island's interior. The Nationalists, while enjoying far broader international recognition, most importantly including the support of the Americans and support of a kind from the Soviets, did not have a promising future on Hainan unless the hostile Communist and Li threats could be neutralized. The Nationalist leadership on Hainan, as under Chen Jitang, had established a precedent for relatively autonomous governance from the mainland over the "fiefdom" of Hainan, so that even with nominal control over the island, the Nationalist regime could not necessarily dictate policy on the island as well as in the mainland provinces or Taiwan after the Japanese withdrawal. Following the Japanese defeat, regional peace talks were attempted between the Nationalists and a delegate of the Communist leadership of Hainan in the northern capital of Haikou. While the Nationalists were recognized internationally as the legitimate government on the island, they were not in control of large regions that were under Communist and militia control, and the Communists entered these negotiations with a strong hand to bargain for power. Military victories through the 1940s had reinforced these claims, especially following the 1943 Baisha Uprising. After 1943, Communist strength grew steadily in Li territory through the Li-Communist alliance. The undeclared civil war continued between the Nationalists and Communists, and by early 1946, the Communists were able to claim a series of counterattack victories as they claimed that the Nationalists violated the armistice that followed the Japanese withdrawal.[38]

The Communist claim to occupying territories that accounted for nearly a third of the island's inhabitants is explained by their hold on the populous northeastern region of the island. The territory the Communists held did not include the important cities of northeastern Wenchang or northern Haikou, but many of the northern towns that were slightly inland of these cities were under Communist control at the time of the Japanese retreat. These cities were turned over to the Nationalist government as the Japanese evacuated.

By 1943, a foreign observer noted in the *Far Eastern Survey* that Hainan and the southern Chinese coast had "recently been very quiet, since its [Japanese] garrison is barely sufficient for defense."[39] Japanese forces were drawn to the mainland and out to the Pacific, leaving Hainan fortifications relatively sparse. Guerrilla forces on the island for the most part continued to frustrate inland Japanese activities, and held their mountain strongholds rather than engaging the Japanese forces in pitched battle. This was the time of the formation of a crucial alliance between the island's indigenous Li people and the Communist forces on the island.

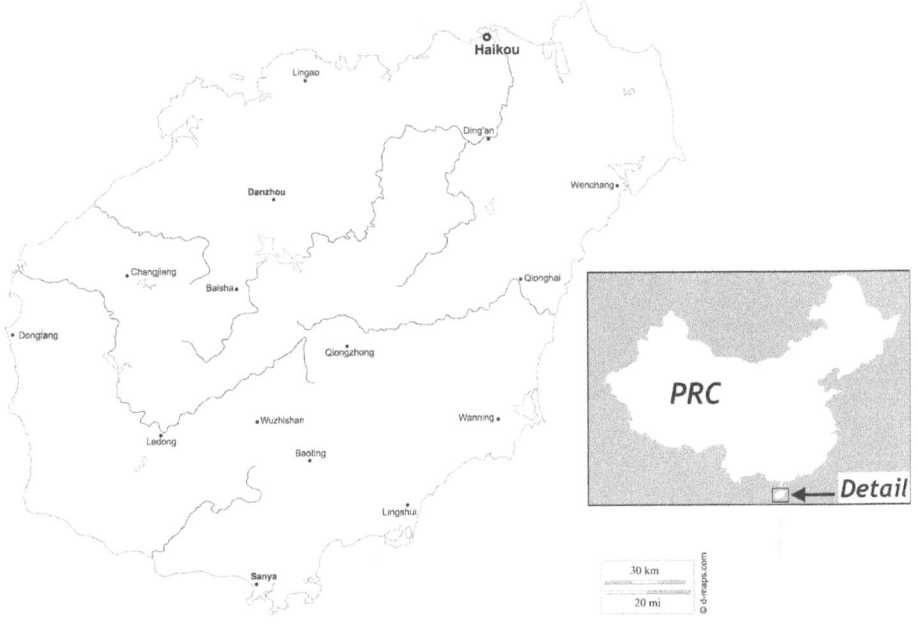

This map indicates the major cities and towns of Hainan island, with an inset of the People's Republic of China (PRC) indicated to show Hainan's location off China's southern coast (source: D-Maps.com, used with permission. http://www.d-maps.com/carte.php?num_car=21221&lang=en; http://www.d-maps.com/m/asia/china/chine/chine49.pdf).

Feng Baiju (1903–1973) in 1950, shortly after the Communist victory on Hainan (author's collection).

Feng Baiju Memorial Pavilion in Haikou, Hainan on the Qingming Festival, 2008 (author's collection).

Feng Baiju Memorial Pavilion in Haikou, Hainan on the Qingming Festival, 2008, with paper money burned at graveside (author's collection).

Feng Baiju Memorial Pavilion in Haikou, Hainan (author's collection).

Feng Baiju pictured with his wife, Zeng Huiyu, in 1956 (author's collection).

The monument commemorating the Yunlong Reorganization (*gaibian*) of 1938, which established the Second United Front between the Nationalists and Communists on Hainan (author's collection).

A 2008 billboard commemorating the twentieth anniversary of Hainan becoming a province in 1988, featuring former paramount leader of China, Deng Xiaoping, and a quote reading, "Hainan's development is extraordinary" (author's collection).

Rice paddies in a northern Hainan coastal village (author's collection).

A country road in northern coastal Hainan (author's collection).

Shrine at the "Five Ministers Temple" or "Temple of the Five Lords" in Haikou, Hainan. The shrine honors five officials who were banished to the island in different periods of Chinese imperial history, and include Li Yude (787–850) of the Tang; and Li Gang (1083–1140), Li Guang (1078–1159), Zhao Ding (1085–1147), and Hu Quan (1102–1180) of the Song. While their banishment was a result of perceived crimes against the realm, in Hainan they have been celebrated as heroes, and essentially adopted as local sons. Su Dongpo (Su Shi) is a sixth very prominent official who was also banished to Hainan. He is remembered for his poetry and other writings (author's collection).

A banyan tree makes its way over the wall of the "Five Ministers Temple" in Haikou, Hainan (author's collection).

Feng Baiju's writing desk, at his ancestral home in Changtai Village, Hainan (author's collection).

An ancient *Antiaris toxicaria* tree at the ancestral home of Feng Baiju in Changtai Village, Hainan. The tree is said to possess poisonous qualities, and its sap is used on poisoned weapons in hunting and warfare (author's collection).

Xue Yue (Hsueh Yueh, 1896–1998), tasked with the last ditch defense of Hainan by the Nationalists in 1949–1950 (author's collection).

Li Shuoxun (1903–1931) pictured with his wife, Zhao Juntao (author's collection).

Vegetable vendors on the street in Haikou, Hainan. Hainan's economy is still more agriculturally driven than any other Chinese province (author's collection).

The memorial placard at Feng Baiju's ancestral home, featuring commemorative calligraphy by General Xu Xiangqian, installed in May of 1989. Xu was one of China's storied "Ten Marshalls" (author's collection).

Some of Haikou's architecture from the early twentieth century was influenced by colonial styles found in French Indochina, British Burma and Malaysia, and the US-dominated Philippines. Hainanese workers traveled to these regions and returned home to build houses in the styles that they encountered in these colonies (author's collection).

A fishing boat in Wenchang, Hainan. Fishing has long been a livelihood of thousands of coastal Hainanese, and today the waters of the region have taken on major geopolitical importance through conflicting maritime sovereignty claims, adding risk and complication to their work (author's collection).

Li men pose for a photograph published in *The Li Tribes of Hainan Island* (Die Listämme der insel Hainan) by Hans Stübel (Berlin: Klinkhardt and Beirmann, 1937. Reprinted with permission from publisher Klinkhardt and Biermann).

A Li man poses for a photograph published in *The Li Tribes of Hainan Island* (Die Li-stämme der insel Hainan) by Hans Stübel (Berlin: Klinkhardt and Beirmann, 1937). This image shows a Li man who has assimilated into the local Han Chinese community, at least in dress (reprinted with permission from publisher Klinkhardt and Biermann).

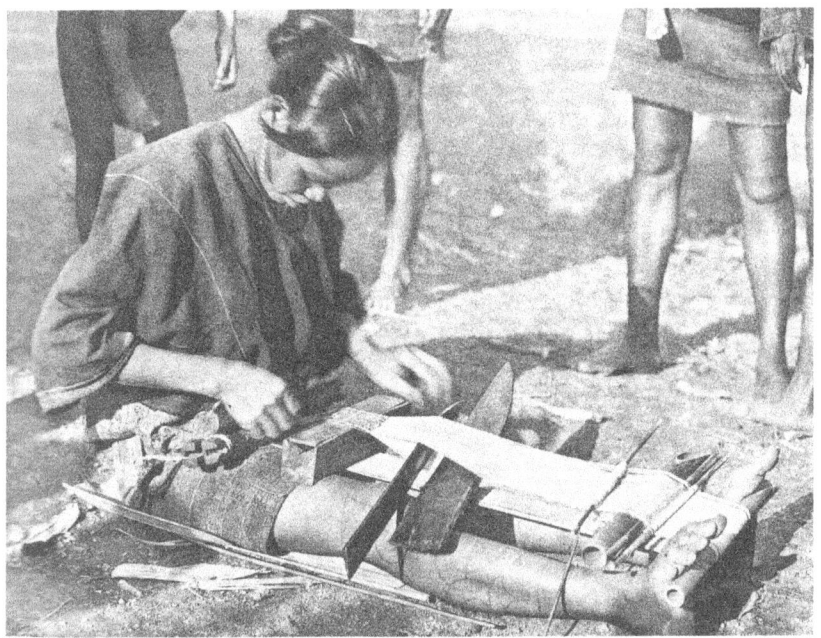

A Li woman weaves in a photograph published in *The Li Tribes of Hainan Island* (Die Li-stämme der insel Hainan) by Hans Stübel (Berlin: Klinkhardt and Beirmann, 1937. Reprinted with permission from publisher Klinkhardt and Biermann).

An example of Li weavings, published in *The Li Tribes of Hainan Island* (Die Listämme der insel Hainan) by Hans Stübel (Berlin: Klinkhardt and Beirmann, 1937. Reprinted with permission from publisher Klinkhardt and Biermann).

An example of Li weavings, published in *The Li Tribes of Hainan Island* (Die Listämme der insel Hainan) by Hans Stübel (Berlin: Klinkhardt and Beirmann, 1937. Reprinted with permission from publisher Klinkhardt and Biermann).

A Li man poses for a photograph published in *The Li Tribes of Hainan Island* (Die Li-stämme der insel Hainan) by Hans Stübel (Berlin: Klinkhardt and Beirmann, 1937. Reprinted with permission from publisher Klinkhardt and Biermann).

Wang Guoxing (1894–1975), a prominent Li leader and main organizer of the Baisha Uprising, 1943 (author's collection).

Tianya Haijiao or "the ends of the earth" (literally, "edge of heaven, corner of the sea") is a popular tourist destination in southern Hainan representing both the remoteness and the natural beauty of the island (source: Wikimedia Commons, public domain, Accessed May 1, 2016. https://en.wikipedia.org/wiki/Tianya_Haijiao).

CHAPTER 5

NEW ALLIES

The Baisha Uprising and the Li-Communist Alliance, 1943

It was in the island's interior that Hainan's Communist movement found its salvation after the challenges of Nationalist extermination campaigns and Japanese invasion. Feng Baiju later wrote of the Communists on Hainan that while the movement began with little Li participation, by spring of 1950, one in five members of the Hainan Independent Column were members of the island's minority community.[1] The Japanese occupation was mainly restricted to the coast, and the headquarters of the Nationalist and Communist resistance to the occupation both moved to the island's interior for its relative safety. This shift paralleled the mainland retreat to the west by the Nationalists to Chongqing and the Communists to Yan'an. The Communists were at a low point in their Hainan activities under Nationalist extermination campaigns in the early 1930s, and the Japanese occupation beginning in February 1939 compounded their problems. The Nationalists and Communists had formed an uneasy alliance, but they did not completely integrate their military forces, and so with the Japanese occupation, they were forced to compete for space in the island's interior.

In the island's southern mountains, the Nationalists and Communists encountered the indigenous Li people in different ways. Nationalist forces tried to displace the Li, which led to resistance and sometimes violence from the Li. There are accounts of Nationalist forces carrying out massacres of entire Li villages either by way of example or simply in order to pacify and fortify a region without the unknown variable of the Li presence. In 1943, Li headmen, Wang Guoxing and Wang Yujin, led the largest Li uprising in recorded history. Shortly after the uprising, under the leadership of Wang Guoxing and Feng Baiju, a confederation of Li people and the Hainan Communists struck an alliance, and together they went on to fight both Nationalists and Japanese.

The Baisha Uprising is an important watershed in the island's history. The Japanese occupation of Hainan was one of enslavement, brutalization, and mass death, and the impact of the Japanese presence on Hainan was felt severely by the Li. And yet, in the midst of the Japanese occupation, the Baisha Uprising was aimed at the Nationalists, and not the Japanese. The Nationalist occupation of Li territory was unprecedented among mainlanders' political and military activity in the island's interior. The organization and scale of the violent Li response also had no precedent in their own history, though their ancestors had left a long legacy of violent uprisings against mainland regimes. Following the Japanese defeat in 1945, the Nationalists were able to return to the coasts and abandon the Li territory, but the newly allied forces of Li and Communists made that inland refuge their central base area for the next five years of civil war. The survival of the Communist movement on Hainan, and hence the ease of the 1950 takeover, is thus at least partially a result of the Li-Communist alliance that followed the Baisha Uprising.

The Li in China's Transitional Period

The surveyor from Beijing, Peng Chengwan, who came to Hainan in 1919, believed that establishing a solid, working relationship with the Li people was essential to any lasting development of the island. Like mainland emissaries to Hainan for centuries, Peng assumed that the Li would happily "Sinify" if given the chance; that is, they would become civilized in the Chinese image, if only they were shown the path to this progress. Sinification of the Li was a precondition for a working relationship with the republican regime.[2] For centuries, only a thin coastal ring and the northern plains of Hainan had been successfully settled and haltingly developed by Han Chinese people from the mainland, and the island's interior and southern highlands remained completely unsettled by Han people and undeveloped on mainland terms. Many of the Li people there continued to practice swidden agriculture well into the twentieth century. They used bows and arrows, spears, and flintlock rifles for hunting and inter-village warfare.[3] They also used these weapons in perennial uprisings that were sometimes sparked by the abuses of Han settlers, merchants, and officials.

For more than two thousand years, mainland regimes had claimed all of Hainan as their own, but in fact, it was only the Mongols, who ruled China during the Yuan dynasty (1279–1368), who had ever successfully conquered the entire island's territory including the interior. The Yuan instituted a policy called the "Li military 10,000 household government," in which a vertical command system incorporated the Li in the government of the Mongol regime on Hainan. This was similar to the system used in Yuan military organization on the mainland, and it was successful in preventing significant Li uprisings for much of the dynasty. But the precedent of combining central flexibility and the granting of autonomy was not followed by subsequent dynasties. Subsequent imperial outposts in Li territory were largely untenable and they served little economic benefit that could not be attained through enterprising Han merchants who visited the territory and sometimes married into Li villages.[4]

The Qing empire (1644–1911), according to Anne Csete, a scholar of the Li in imperial times, offered a qualified change in the mainland regimes' legacy of clumsy and brutal rule of Hainan and the Li.[5] This was especially true in the eighteenth century, known by historians as the high Qing, and a period of lasting domestic peace and prosperity.[6] A Qing official of the mid-eighteenth century left a record of what he experienced and learned as an official on Hainan. He wrote with regret, after the suppression of one of the more violent uprisings of the Li during his tenure. The Li once lived in peace, he wrote, and it was only the provocations of dishonest merchants, settlers, and officials that brought about the cycle of uprisings and suppressions, and resulted in a constant state of uneasy relations.[7] In this common lament by antimercantile Confucian officials, the exploitation and dishonest dealings at the hands of predatory merchants and local officials caused the suspicion and volatility among the Li that led them to rise up in violence in earlier dynasties as well.[8] Even after the fall of the Qing, Peng Chengwan agreed with this general assessment during his 1919 tour of the island. He added an element, however, that could not have been relevant to his Qing predecessor on the island. Peng wrote that there was an "anti-Han revolutionary movement" (*pai-Han geming yundong*) afoot on the island, and that it was not simply an issue of economic or political exploitation, or of brutal suppression. It was an animosity based in race and culture that drove the Li to violent resistance.[9]

This ethnic or racial distinction that Peng made simplified what was in fact a very complex set of problems. He did not fail to see the complexity of the situation, citing similar problems to what had been noted by the eighteenth-century Qing official—exploitation by merchants and also brutality at the hands of glory-seeking generals.[10] But in lumping all Li violence into an island-wide anti-Han revolution, Peng's anxieties may have been more a reflection of the Chinese political climate during which he visited Hainan and wrote the survey, than an accurate account of the motivations for Li violence and resistance. Han chauvinism had helped to topple the Qing dynasty in 1911, with the Manchu rulers depicted as alien invaders in revolutionary tracts. Histories filled with scenes of rapine and massacres of Han Chinese at the hands of the alien Manchus resurfaced in the revolution to overthrow the Qing, even though these atrocities of the Manchu conquest had occurred nearly three hundred years earlier. Peng was a product of a culture in which the line between Chinese patriotism and Han chauvinism was a thin one from Hainan's perspective, and this certainly influenced his perception of Li-Han relations on Hainan in the early republic.

From the perspective of the mainland or of coastal Hainanese Chinese, and also in the view of many foreign observers, the Li were divided into two distinct groups. In Chinese these groups were rather dramatically labeled as "raw" and "cooked" (*sheng* and *shu*, respectively). The former were the wild Li who lived in the island's interior with little or no contact between themselves and Han Chinese or foreigners. The latter, the "cooked" Li, engaged in trade and sometimes intermarriage with the Han Chinese, learned the Chinese language, and even served the mainland regimes as leaders of their village or of a network of villages.

By the fall of the Qing, an imperial system of giving Li village leaders official posts was at least 150 years old.[11] In the previous Ming dynasty (1368–1644), the mainland administration gave the Li a relatively free hand to govern their own affairs. The policy of allowing the Li to more or less govern themselves does not seem to have connected the Li to the Ming government with a credible command structure, as it had in the Mongol Yuan dynasty, but rather seems to have been a question of the Ming military being incapable of, or unconcerned with, the direct governance of significant portions of Li territory with any efficiency. The Qing was more successful than the Ming in governing the Li through the implementation of a system of accountable village headmen. Under the Qing system, these leaders took responsibility for the village or villages that they led.[12]

In March of 1872, a British consul posted to Ningbo traveled around Hainan and delivered an official report. This was twelve years after Haikou had officially been opened (but little used) as a treaty port following the Second Opium War. Robert Swinhoe's report, "The Aborigines of Hainan," is informed by racial supremacy, referring to the Li people as "deformed" and to some as being more "docile" than others.[13] But it is worth noting the cultural cross-sections that Swinhoe draws in his observations of the Li, especially in his use of the standard Han Chinese distinction between the *shu* and *sheng* indigenous peoples.

> At Nychow the natives were often referred to as the shuh Le [*shu*, or "cooked" Li], but they differed in no respect from the

wild tribes of their neighborhood except that their headmen acknowledged a kind of responsibility to the Chinese authorities which enabled the people of their tribe to seek labor in the Chinese towns.[14]

The distinction between the *shu* and *sheng* is usually one of culture in most orthodox Chinese accounts of nationalities within its borders. Those minorities who are said to "have culture" (*you wenhua*), traditionally meaning a Confucian or Han Chinese culture, are the *shu* or "cooked" savages. The civilizing projects of imperial China were directed at the marginal and cultural minorities as primarily a cultural endeavor.[15] But it seems that the distinctions between the two groups as observed by an outsider who did not share the mainland Chinese cultural bias (though Swinhoe had his own biases), seem to be more political than cultural. This is revealing about both the leadership structure and the political organization of the Li people in their relationship with mainland regimes.

The cultural dimension of categorization of the Li, as these groups are commonly defined from the perspective of mainland Chinese official and cultural biases, seems to have been less important than is supposed in most Chinese materials. It was not necessarily sinification, or the adoption of Chinese culture that distinguished Li leadership and participation. While there was a wide variation of Li costume, custom, and political participation, there was also a clear identity of being a Li person that straddled the artificially imposed *shu/sheng* cultural divide. The Li who had adopted Chinese dress—the ones who had abandoned the loincloth and bow-and-arrow for trousers, tunic, and a porter's pole—were not ultimately more malleable to the Han Chinese regime. On the contrary, it was precisely this type of Li individual, Wang Guoxing, who would lead his comrades in the Baisha Uprising of 1943. A peculiar preoccupation of ethnic studies is with those culturally distinct traits of a people that can be easily exoticized, feminized, or otherwise discursively "othered." Emphasizing the distinctive cultural practices that can be exploited in tourist parks or the pages of a magazine can neglect the crucial political questions of a group's struggle, and such is the case with the Li.

The Li people live primarily in the interior of Hainan island, and at the time of writing, number well over a million.[16] The word "Li" is a Chinese language word, and the origins of its application to these indigenous people of Hainan who now bear that label is murky. The most common etymology of the Chinese character for this particular *Li* (黎) is ironically a very early linguistic reference of Han Chinese to themselves, and its initial meaning was "black-haired people." Most Li call themselves *Sai* (賽), another Chinese word translated from the Li language, in which it is simply a word for the first-person plural pronoun. Most scholars agree, based on linguistics and ritual practices, that the Li originally came to Hainan thousands of years ago from what is today mainland Southeast Asia.[17] The Li language, like several of the regional Chinese dialects of Hainan, falls into the Tai-Kadai or Kra-Dai language group (in Chinese this is the Zhuang-Dong group), while some dialects of the island are also related to the Chaoshan and Minnan dialects of the mainland; these claims are not without some controversy related to cultural and historical narratives surrounding the region.[18] This sets Hainan apart from its Chinese island neighbor, Taiwan, which hosts an aboriginal culture that is much more strongly tied to Oceania and other islands of the South Pacific.

Ethnologists and anthropologist have also made much of Li hairstyling, jewelry, clothing, and tattooing. Different hair knots set apart the different groups of the Li across the island. Until the past few decades, Li women had their faces distinctively tattooed when they reached early adulthood, usually before taking a husband. This practice prepared them for recognition by their ancestors in the afterlife. The bare breasts of some Li women scandalized the Han Chinese visitors to Li territory, and some Li women wore many hoops of brass from their ears, often so large and heavy that they pulled down the earlobe, and they had to be tied over the head while they worked.[19] These and other cosmetic characteristics of the Li woman, such as their short skirts, later banned as pornographic in the puritanical atmosphere of the Cultural Revolution, drew the focus of the cameras of foreign visitors.[20] The convention of depicting a foreign culture or race as different through the appearance of the group's female attire and appearance is nearly universal, and gendering the ethnic frontier as female is common in Chinese civilizing practice.[21]

More substantially, early observations reveal the source of a mainland stereotype of gender relations on Hainan that is often heard today, in which the women work much harder than their male counterparts, who are reputed to lounge in hammocks through the long, hot afternoons. Among the Li, and much of the Hainanese population, it was common for men and women to work equally hard in farming duties, which may be the source of this stereotype. Early mainlander and foreign observers on Hainan were struck by the equal sharing of labor on Hainan. One French visitor noted that, indeed, it seemed that the most arduous tasks were reserved for the women.[22] It is difficult to take seriously the disdain of foreign observers as they sneer at the perceived laziness of their Hainan hosts, for in the next paragraph of their memoir, we watch them cheerfully cross little streams and brooks on the backs of their aging coolies.[23] Perhaps some of these American and British observers, including Protestant missionaries, felt a prick of conscience as they were carried around by their lazy Hainanese hosts. One made such a lame excuse in his popular 1925 travelogue that it bears mention as an indication of the relationship between host and guest: "We trotted on, dripping; *the old man* [my emphasis] carried me across a sliver of a river to save the time I should have lost with my shoes."[24] From either a Western Christian or a mainland Chinese Confucian perspective, the Hainanese people, including both Li and Han, were profoundly unequal.[25]

Wang Guoxing

In the orthodox jargon of Chinese empires, to "enter the map" (*ru bantu*) is the reward of ethnic minorities and border peoples who become tributaries or subjects of the realm.[26] During the Japanese occupation of Hainan, this construct was flipped on its head as Chinese Nationalist and Communist armies retreated into the island's central Li territories for survival, and it seemed that it would fall to the Li to decide their fate. First, in the face of the Japanese occupation of Hainan after 1939, the Nationalists' armies withdrew into the southern mountains of the island, which was historically the Li domain. Later, a Li alliance with the Communists made Li territory the main base area for the allied forces on the island. Wang Guoxing (1894–1975) led the Li people in seeking out an alliance with the Chinese Communists.

Wang's father had been a leader of several villages. According to Wang's biographies, his father was well respected in the Li community.[27] He served in the uncertain years that came after the fall of the Qing. The weakness of the central government in the first two decades of the Republic prevented any coherent and consistent relationship between Hainan's government and the Li people. Even during times of strong central Chinese governance, there were few exceptions to the prolonged conflicts between the Chinese military and the Li. The final century of the Qing, the 1800s, were rife with violence between the Li and government forces. In times of disunity and weakness, the Li felt heavier tax burdens, and this was also the case in the early republic.[28]

Wang Guoxing's father, Wang Zhenghe, felt that burden more than most as the leader of several villages scattered around his hometown of Hongmao. Under new Nationalist policies, it had appeared that the Li would be given an increase in their autonomy and their ability to choose their own fate in terms of economic and social activities. This shift toward self-rule echoed the Ming policies of allowing the Li to make their own way simply because the mountain-dwellers were beyond the reach of the central and provincial government. Work assignments and ritual observances were put in his hands, and social and economic organization seemed to be officially handed over to Li leaders like Wang Zhenghe.[29]

As Hainan officials began making their demands, however, they turned to Wang Zhenghe and other Li leaders again and again to implement burdensome policies of extraction. Cattle (water buffalo) were scarce in the highland Li community, but the Nationalist government made heavy demands on Li livestock, including their cattle, pigs, and chickens. The Li diet was generally low in meat, and slaughtering domestic animals of any kind was reserved for celebrations. An animal hierarchy reflected the value of animal flesh both in terms of nutrition and cultural and philosophical importance. Certain gatherings and minor celebrations warranted the slaughter of a chicken and the drinking of its blood. Slightly more important was the slaughter of a pig, and finally, reserved mostly for weddings and funerals, was the slaughter of water buffalo.[30] Hunting was also a common source of meat for the Li, but game was neither large nor plentiful.

> The meat they eat comes from little animals which they catch while they are at work [in their rice fields]. They bring them home in their little waist baskets and usually boil them. As for game (wild boar and deer) and fish, they are very seldom eaten.[31]

In another observation:

> After the [rice] harvest, the young men amuse themselves by getting up hunting parties, when spears, bows and arrows, and guns (the latter in surprising numbers) are brought out for use.[32]

It is noteworthy that this latter observer attributed a kind of ritual or sporting aspect to the hunt, which is consistent with other observations. The Li did not hunt every day, and when they did it was not always a task of subsistence. The scarcity of game meant that they could not count on hunting to sustain themselves. Taxation in kind by the Nationalist government that targeted livestock thus had a deleterious impact on both the rituals and the diet of the Li community. By the mid-1930s, the Nationalist government on Hainan was badly in need of supplies for the military that kept it in power. Beef was needed to feed the army, and it was taken without regard to the impact that this extraction would have on the community from whence it came. Graft and corruption within the government and the military wasted much of the supplies that would otherwise be used to build an efficient army that could keep the regime in power.[33] These leaks in the bureaucratic system that directed taxes away from their intended destination, from the perspective of the Li, only meant an ever-increasing need for their precious livestock. Soon, it became clear that livestock and other taxes would not be enough for the Nationalist regime on Hainan.

In 1934, Wang Zhenghe received requests to recommend Li youths to travel to Guangzhou to attend university on government scholarships.[34] He was asked to choose the most deserving of the people in his village and the surrounding area. There is no record of whether Wang was wary of this order. Old Li men in the village would have remembered Qing policies of sending youths to study in the relatively cosmopolitan Hainanese centers of Haikou and Wenchang. Some of them went on to achieve official degrees and serve in the imperial government. Wang Zhenghe might have considered this a continuation of a policy that provided a channel to official power for the Li youths who were inclined to follow it.

On behalf of the Nationalists, Wang promulgated this policy in the surrounding region, and soon several hundred men and women had been assembled for the purpose of traveling to Guangzhou to study. The Li youths were sent off from their villages with much fanfare in the fall of 1934. Months passed, and when the students did not return for the usual holidays, Wang realized that he had been deceived, and in fact had helped in sending off these young people to be conscripted into the military. Later it was learned that the youngest males and the females in the 1934 cohort actually became a part of an exhibition in Guangzhou on the savage races of China's margins.[35]

While the quaintness of the Li appearance and traditions were an exciting attraction in the bustling Chinese urban centers, the preservation of their culture does not seem to have been a priority.[36] While the Li were an amusing museum piece, the development of the island required their modernization, and improved communications and industrialization, which in turn demanded better relations with, or cooperation from, the Li. The Li territory had to be opened up to investment that would exploit the mining capacity and strategic importance of the island. For this, the Li would have to either do business on the terms of the newcomers to the island, or die in their unwillingness to cooperate. Either way, the culture of the Li was indeed nothing more than a relic for anthropologists to study, while it lasted.[37]

The "lack of adequate communication facilities," according to Nationalist China's most prominent financier, Song Ziwen (T.V. Soong), had been responsible for the past failures of all attempts to develop the island, and the primitive infrastructure continued to hamper development efforts.[38] Pushing forward with these development plans meant first crisscrossing the island with roads and communication lines, which would pull the Li out of their primitive existence. This was a continuation of earlier policy ambitions that had been favored by late Qing officials who turned their attention to southern China. Zhang Zhidong, for example, hoped to establish Hainan as a province separate from the authority of Guangdong Province on the mainland. Zhang believed that building roads around and across the island would be among the most important steps in this process, which would penetrate Li territory and elevate the island to deserving provincial status. In his view, the military development of the island also was essential in preparing it to be a province.[39]

Sinification of the Li was one consistent prerequisite for modernizing the island, as Peng Chengwan had called for in his 1919 survey.[40] During the Nationalist rule of the Nanijng Decade, this cultural assault became much more pronounced. By the middle of the 1930s, pressure was increasing from the Nationalist government on the Li to abandon their cultural practices. On the eve of the Japanese occupation of Hainan, one American visitor watched the frantic response to his small party being mistaken for Nationalist agents in a Li village:

> Before we reached Noh-Pong village, the people in the rice fields nearby ran in alarm at seeing my column. The village of 37 longhouses was practically deserted as we entered. A gong was being beaten frantically somewhere.
>
> Only an old naked man greeted us. He was too old to run, I guess. We learned that a ceremony had been in progress, and the people, afraid we were soldiers who had come to smash their gods, had fled in alarm.
>
> Soon the old man called them back, and in an hour, their shyness worn off, they continued with the ceremony. A man who had died three years before was being feted. Two gods about a foot high, and sitting on little chairs, were being "fed" rice balls while men played on flutes by exhaling through their nostrils, and the women wailed.[41]

No amount of idol-stomping by Nationalist soldiers would hasten the development of Hainan, nor improve the condition of the Li. The corruption and mismanagement of economic development on the island had led to the slow development of communication and transportation infrastructure.[42] But the backwardness of the island's inhabitants was also targeted, in part because tales of naked savages and their sorcery was more entertaining journalism, whether in America or mainland China.

In 1932, Nationalist commander, Chen Hanguang was tasked with suppression of the Li by the Nationalist governor of Hainan, Chen Jitang. Along with Wang Yi, Han Hanying, and other Nationalist officers and politicians, they implemented policies that led to the massacre and exploitation of thousands of Li, and also of the Miao minority. In the view of the Li leadership, it was Han chauvinism that fueled the merciless treatment of the Li and Miao.[43] Even in a recollection by one man who served under Chen Hanguang, his nickname was well-deserved: "the king of the Hainan murderers." Chen Hanguang's appointment was based on personal connections he had established while studying in Japan. His classmate in his military courses there was the younger brother of the Hainan governor, Chen Jitang. Chen Hanguang led a unit of guards that was not answerable to the command of the political or military leadership of the Hainan government. He was given free rein to deal with unrest throughout the island in any way that he saw fit.[44] From January through March of 1932, five hundred troops under Chen's command attacked Li fighters ten times, but the confrontations ended without a formal resolution, and Chen withdrew his troops from Li territory.[45] Massacres of Li villages were verified by foreign observers at the time, where the machine guns of Chen Hanguang's unit of guards answered any disturbance that was led by Li warriors armed with spears, bows and arrows, and flintlock rifles. By the end of the 1930s, the Nationalists on Hainan only had about six thousand uniformed soldiers, but their superior firepower made Li suppression through massacres and punitive expeditions a relatively easy task.[46] Collective punishment was the draconian policy of the Nationalists, as Leonard Clark observed the fate of a "luckless" target of Nationalist judgment in his *National Geographic* article on the Li.

> Throughout this Ha country the headmen insisted that I be supplied with bodyguards while camping near their villages. They feared that a neighboring village might send assassins to murder us so that the village would be held responsible and be made the object of attack from a Chinese punitive expedition.
>
> I saw the charred remains of one luckless village, punished for robbery. Hundreds of empty machine-gun shells still lay about in piles.[47]

Wang Guoxing's father, Wang Zhenghe, served as *zongguan*, head local official, to the Hongmao region of Li territory. His own village and several surrounding villages chose him to represent them in their relationship with the ruling Nationalists. Wang Zhenghe received no salary, but he shouldered the burden of his people's anger for conflicts with the government, including when the young Li cohort that he had recruited for the Nationalist education program never returned. Zhenghe became addicted to opium, though when this began is not clear from Wang Guoxing's biography. Following the 1935 conscription, Wang Zhenghe used his voice as *zongguan* to oppose the policy and demand its reversal and recompense. In response to these efforts, he was imprisoned. The combined fine and bail that was set for his release was 600 *yuan*, a fee that an entire Li village would have difficulty paying, let alone an individual or a family.

By the time of Zhenghe's imprisonment, Wang Guoxing had risen to a position of respect in the surrounding region. Unlike his father, he did not have any official position of authority, but he was renowned for his skill as a craftsman and leader of hunting parties. He helped plan harvests and food storage, and oversaw rituals and celebrations. From his teens, in the early republic, he had worked as a porter for Han merchants who did business in Li territory. His physical prowess also set him apart, gained carrying mighty loads of salt and kerosene on his back. For this work, he earned 2 *yuan* for three days' work. While his father had squandered money on opium, Wang Guoxing saved his earnings. In 1920, when Guoxing was twenty-six years old, he had saved up his wages to celebrate the wedding of his younger brother. On the day of the feast, Wang presented his brother with the lavish gifts he had purchased, bringing them out one by one: wine for the occasion, bags of rice, and finally, a pig. Before he could finish presenting the gifts, however, a local official who had gotten wind of the festivities, entered the village with his retinue for an inspection. He left with the wine, the rice, and the pig.[48]

Fifteen years later, in 1935, Wang Guoxing needed to raise 600 *yuan* for his father's freedom. By borrowing from acquaintances and selling all that he had, Wang raised the 600 in several months, and he paid the fee. But even after accepting the fee, the authorities would not release Wang Zhenghe. It was obvious that the astronomical fee had been intended to keep Zhenghe in prison and to prevent him from organizing the Li in protest. Finally, after languishing in prison for three years, Wang Zhenghe became gravely ill, and he was released in 1938. A few days later, he was dead. His wife, also aged at the time, died several days after him.

From the high Qing through the early Republican period, Li leadership positions were hereditary. Passing of leadership duties and privileges from father or mother to son or daughter (for it was not uncommon for Li women to hold prominent leadership roles) had been a characteristic of Li society for centuries, and it was in the Kangxi reign of the eighteenth century that the Qing state recognized this hereditary practice in its dealings with the Li.[49] During the Republican period, small local elections were encouraged by the Hainan and Guangzhou authorities, as an attempt to break with this old system. This new policy was promulgated as a modernizing break with traditional practices. Still, when Wang Zhenghe died shortly after his release from prison, the inhabitants of Hongmao and surrounding villages expected his son, Wang Guoxing to take over his father's position.[50]

Wang Guoxing's name was put forward for the position, but he was reluctant to accept it. His fellow villagers implored Wang to take the position, but before the matter was resolved, following a quick election, another Li headman of the same surname took Wang Zhenghe's vacant post. This man was not as popular, and the calls continued for Wang Guoxing to take over his father's post. Guoxing's popularity drew the interest of Nationalist authorities, and expecting to be similarly detained, a few months after his parents' death, Wang disappeared from the village. For an entire year, he stayed away from Hongmao, living alone in the mountain forests. While he was gone, an official election was held in the villages, and Wang Guoxing was chosen to represent them. Wang Guoxing had not communicated with the people of his village for a year, but they knew that he was living somewhere in the surrounding forests. The people of Hongmao then began walking into the forests each day, calling his name, imploring him to return to the village and take up his post. "Guoxing!" they called, while combing through the forest in groups, "Please come back and lead us! You are our leader!"[51]

By that time it was summer of 1941. During Wang's absence from the village, the Japanese had occupied the Hainanese coast, and they held strategic areas of the inland. The surviving Nationalist leaders and forces had retreated to the island's interior. Their weapons were their only significant assets, and these they used to extract their material needs from the Li people. While the Nationalists were far better armed than the Li, they were also desperate for food and shelter, and for this they relied on Li cooperation or at least nonconfrontation.

Nationalist reinforcements were not forthcoming, and Li scouts easily assessed their strengths in preliminary planning for an anti-Nationalist uprising. The Nationalists were also beset by hostile Communist guerrillas who had long held a position of some strength in the island's sparsely populated southeast, surrounding Lingshui. In the midst of hostile Li, Communist, and Japanese forces, the Nationalists in Hainan's southern interior still pursued a policy of ongoing suppression and exploitation of the Li. By the official count of the current Hainan government, as well as the authoritative history of the Li people by a leading scholar, the Nationalists killed more than ten thousand Li and Miao people in the region between 1940 and early 1943.[52]

Uprising

Wang Guoxing heard his fellow villagers calling his name as they walked through the forest, imploring him to return and lead them. He must have known that in the past year, the Nationalist numbers in the surrounding region had increased, and that any position of leadership had become far more treacherous for a Li headman. Still, he answered his neighbors, and returned to Hongmao to take up his father's position. Three days later, Wang received an order from the Nationalist authorities demanding that he turn over 120 *yuan* and nine men for conscription. He was also ordered to contribute an unspecified amount of livestock. This would be Hongmao's monthly obligation, and Wang Guoxing would be held personally responsible for delivering every month.[53]

Nationalist pressure on the people living in the Li territories had reached a breaking point. The Japanese occupation had led to execution, massacre, and mass conscription of the Li, but in Wang Guoxing's southern mountainous region of the island, the extractions and the massacres at the hands of the newly arrived Nationalist forces drew the most fury and resistance. In one record of early meetings in the planning of the Li uprising, one of the Li leaders even entertained the possibility of striking some kind of deal with the Japanese that would allow them to fight the Nationalists together. While the Japanese mining projects and harbor construction proceeded apace, their political priorities on Hainan had diminished.

There had been sporadic and spontaneous anti-Japanese uprisings among the Li, including one in April of 1939, just weeks after the Japanese arrival on Hainan. The leader of the thirty-man group of southern Li, Tang Tianxiang, was captured and executed, and the uprising was quelled.[54] Otherwise, Li resistance to the Japanese, while sometimes fierce, was limited to smaller uprisings, usually involving several dozen fighters from a single village. Involvement by dozens and sometimes hundreds of Li individuals in the Communist resistance to the Japanese was also common, notably in battles around the Zhongtianling base area on the island's southern coast.[55] But in the early years of the Japanese occupation of the island, and the Nationalist fortification of the southern highlands, there were no massive and coordinated Li uprisings against either occupying presence.

Up until this point in Hainan's history, the Li people had been involved in hundreds, perhaps thousands, of uprisings against the people who tried to control the island and dictate their policy. There were several major uprisings of the Li in the final years of the Qing dynasty. One of the largest of these came in 1897, and appears to have involved an alliance between the Han and Li peoples against Qing forces and involved more than four thousand Li fighters.[56] It is not evident that the Li people's uprisings were affiliated with any secret societies or piracy in this time, nor do the Li uprisings seem to have been sparked by nationalistic motives in concert with Han anti-Manchu revolutionary activities. There was occasionally an affiliation between the Li and Ming loyalists during the uprisings of the early Qing, but this seems to have been an alliance of convenience against the new Manchu rulers.

The Nationalist forces that operated on Hainan were not recruited or conscripted locally, but came to the island as fully formed units. It is not likely that any Li served with these forces except in noncombat roles. The same was obviously true of the Japanese forces, though their smaller numbers forced them to rely on local police forces. The Communist force on Hainan, however, was almost completely constituted of local Hainanese people. In regions where the Li made up a significant portion of the population, some of them had joined the Communists. The earliest and most important example of this before 1943 was in Lingshui county, very early in the development of the Hainan Communist movement. Lingshui is on the southern coast of the island, east of the harbors of Sanya and Yulin. During the late Qing, a British observer who was mapping the island's coast had noted that the Li people of this region were more reclusive than those of other regions, and that when Han or foreigners had come in contact with them, hostilities had been more frequent than with the Li of other regions.[57]

Half a century later, as noted in the previous chapter, Lingshui saw a growth of local rural autonomy among peasants, and local militias were influenced and sometimes controlled by the Hainan Communists. The Nationalist government sanctioned peasant associations in 1926, and in Lingshui these included a mixture of Li and Han, who had shared regional and economic interests.[58] After the spring 1927 purge of leftists and Communists within the Nationalist Party, Lingshui became an important destination of the Communists who survived the purge on Hainan. While the militias and guerrilla Communist forces around Lingshui included both Li and Han fighters, this was not a Li movement, organized by Li headmen or in the tradition of Li collective uprisings. It would, however, serve as a foundation for later cooperation between the Hainan Communists and the Li fighters, including one of the Baisha Uprising leaders referring to Lingshui as proof that the Communists were willing to work closely with the Li.[59]

In the late 1930s, a Li commander, Zhou Tangzhen, who was also a Communist Party member, helped to establish communications and spy networks that allowed the Communists to monitor Nationalists movements. Lingshui had initially been a relatively safe place for the growth of the Hainan Communist movement in cooperation with some of the local Li population, but in the 1930s it was too dangerous for anything other than underground organization. Lingshui was close to Yulin, which the Japanese authorities developed as a modern harbor under the Japanese occupation.

With the Nationalist retreat from the Japanese, the Li were faced with a new kind of total threat that was not avoidable by further retreat into the mountains. The healthiest and most able-bodied of the Li fighters could live in the mountain forests and survive for a time in a guerrilla existence, but it would not be possible to exist in their settled village communities until the Nationalists had withdrawn from their territory. Within days of taking up his position as a local leader, Wang Guoxing began to organize meetings. Arrowheads were circulated, as they had been for centuries, signaling that a council was to be held. There was no hierarchy in this process. There was no obedience to a great leader of the Li people that was demanded by this communication, but all knew that it indicated a communal desperation, and any who failed to answer this summons would have new mortal enemies—failure to appear at such a gathering was tantamount to a declaration of open hostility to the group assembled.[60]

Leaders of the Miao people were also invited to this meeting, and the fate of the two peoples was joined in their plans. The meeting was held in secret, high in the mountains. The leaders who were assembled swore mutual loyalty and sealed their oath in drinking wine mixed with the blood of a chicken. The meeting took place in June of 1942, and Wang Guoxing was still officially newly in the service of the Nationalist government.[61] The planning that took place for the Li uprising was slow and deliberate, though there is no written record of how it took place. Wang Guoxing sent written communications to leaders from other villages, including those of the Miao people, but these notes are no longer extant.

The numbers of participants and casualties in the Baisha Uprising vary throughout the sources that I have consulted. Taking the smallest of any set of figures, however, still makes the Baisha Uprising one of the most important events in Hainan's history, and an unprecedented Li movement that would play an important part in deciding the island's modern fate. Ultimately, it was between twenty- and thirty thousand Li fighters that joined the Baisha Uprising in the late summer of 1943. Kunio Odaka, a Japanese observer of the Li, visited the region bordering Baisha on the eve of the uprising, and estimated that the population of a single average Li village was about 155 men, women, and children.[62] Accounting for the elderly and children, and the fact that Li women were not traditionally involved in warfare, this means approximately 60 fighters might have joined the uprising from any given village. With these rough figures, it can be assumed that the Baisha Uprising involved an astounding 350 villages in Li territory, and coordinated their military efforts. Odaka's description of Baisha, observed in 1942, foreshadowed the events that would come in the following year.

> [Baisha], which is the gathering center for the Li of this area, is said to have a moat constructed behind its bamboo wall. It is also said that there are dirt walls with holes for rifles. However [the valley] does not have such formidable defense units; some units do not have fences, and some do not even have an entrance to the village. . . . On the whole the villagers were docile and showed no sign of enmity. They get along well with our soldiers too.[63]

Beginning simply with the smaller figure of twenty thousand Li fighters already makes the case for the unprecedented nature of this uprising in Li history, and in Hainan's history. The real significance is naturally in the way that this uprising was brought about, how it was planned, and what motivated participation. Wang Yujin, like Wang Guoxing, was a prominent Li leader, and he was one of Guoxing's earliest collaborators in the planning of a coordinated action against the Nationalist forces that had settled in Li territory. A native of the same Hongmao region, Yujin had been conscripted by the Nationalists as a young man and taken to fight on the mainland. He had later deserted and returned home to Hainan, and to Hongmao. In an early 1942 meeting between Wang Guoxing and Wang Yujin, they discussed the possibilities of an uprising in their home region of Hongmao, where there were relatively few Nationalist troops at that time. Wang Yujin said:

> If we deal with the traitors [*guozei*, meaning the Nationalist forces] in our home of Hongmao of course it would be easy. But the traitors' forces are all mutually connected, and in Baisha County

their military strength is several thousand. Our Hongmao forces would not be enough to defeat them all. The forces of all of our townships must also become mutually connected.[64]

Wang Yujin's observations suggest that any connectedness throughout the Li community would require active organization, and the Wangs could not count on broad participation without a significant summoning. The localized uprisings of previous periods were often prompted by individual incidents in which an aggressive official or a greedy merchant had caused some offense in a Li village or township. In such an instance, some Li fighters would be summoned to respond to this, often with a guerrilla attack on some government or merchant convoys, or, occasionally, with a direct attack on a neighboring Han village or official fortification. In 1942, Wang Yujin and the rest of the Baisha Li community were presented with a new challenge following the Japanese invasion, however, when the Nationalists retreated into their territory with a troop strength in the thousands and far superior weaponry including machine guns and artillery. While morale was perhaps low among the Nationalists, their military superiority was beyond question, and any Li attack that hoped to be successful would need a force that was far superior in numbers.

Wang Yujin's experience with the Nationalist military had taught him that it was not the loosely cobbled forces of the waning Qing or the early republic, and he shared this with Wang Guoxing. Vertical loyalty and a sense of the national mission infused the officer corps of the Nationalist military with an unprecedented nationalism, and Yujin knew that the forces that had arrived in Hongmao and the rest of Li territory would not simply try to hold a town on their own, but would react to any uprising as a single unit, retracting into an area of defensive strength and then counterattacking. It was this perception that led Wang Yujin to the conclusion that the Li would have to unite and similarly act as a disciplined military force.

It was this negative impetus of the Nationalists that led the Li people to unite and rise in response to the new threat to their people and territory. The threat was unprecedented, and the response would bring an unprecedented unity of purpose for the Li people. Even while Wang Guoxing and Wang Yujin planned their uprising, scattered preparations for smaller Li uprisings were already underway. The leadership of Wang Guoxing, Wang Yujin, and others would bring together at least twenty thousand fighters, and this figure was built on the widespread discontent and military preparedness that the Nationalist presence had already begun to fuel among the Li in the southern highlands. After a meeting of Li leaders in June of 1942, Wang

Guoxing personally walked around the region for two months, and found that in hundreds of other villages, weapons were being consolidated, and preliminary preparations had begun. Volunteers had already voiced their eagerness to join an uprising against the Nationalists, and even by his own account, Wang Guoxing did not personally conceive of and execute the uprising. By August of 1942, Wang hosted another meeting, this time with fifty representative leaders of the region. Reporting on progress that had taken place since the June meeting, they found that they had twelve thousand flintlock rifles, and thousands of spears and bows. Most importantly, Wang Guoxing received reports that thirty thousand fighters would join the fight against the Nationalist forces. As they toasted and sealed their alliance with rice wine and rooster blood, some of those present proclaimed that there was no way they could lose.[65]

The actual violence of the Baisha Uprising itself was brief, taking place mainly between July 12 and July 17, 1943. About seven major engagements took place throughout Baisha county, centered around the county seat of Baisha. Initially, following the surprise Li attacks, the Nationalist officers in the county seat abandoned their posts and fled. The early days of the uprising brought some optimism for the Li. Wang Guoxing was asked to attend an emergency meeting with a Baisha district leader who might offer his help. It was a trap and Wang was captured, leading Wang Yujin to assemble a squad of men to rescue him. Ten Nationalists were killed in the rescue, the first casualties of the uprising around Hongmao. According to Wang Guoxing's biography, of the one hundred or so Nationalist forces in the region surrounding Hongmao, all but a handful of deserters were killed.[66] The fighting continued throughout the region, but as the initial surprise wore off, the Nationalists were able to regroup. Within a matter of days, the superior weaponry of the Nationalist forces had them in control again.

Aftermath

In the aftermath of the initial action of the Baisha Uprising, the killing still continued. The Nationalists sent Li spies into the mountains to infiltrate the remnants of the forces that had taken part in the uprising. Before the groups could reconstitute themselves, the Nationalists had inserted their agents into several Li fighting units, and from there, espionage ensued, including assassination of the most prominent leaders using methods such as poisoned wine that was drunk, ironically, in honor of the dead. But the Li fighters that had retreated into the mountains also had their own agents among the Li villages. When they reported to their leaders in the mountains, they told them that the Nationalists had resettled the Li villages in force and in preparedness. Any attempt to return to their homes was too dangerous. Their one chance at an overwhelming surprise attack had been spent, and it had not eliminated the Nationalist threat. Now there seemed little hope of resuming the conflict without some kind of help.[67]

The Nationalists' efforts to mop up the Li threat to their presence in the island's interior were successful in many instances, as Li headmen fell one after another. Some fell to assassination or execution, the latter fate being brought upon dozens of fighters or suspected fighters in one day. In one instance, more than 150 Li men were executed in one day in a single town. Other Li leaders surrendered to the Nationalists, turning over valuable weapons and some of the fighters that had been under their command.[68] In Wang Guoxing's home township of Hongmao, the population before the uprising was nearly ten thousand. By the time of the 1947 census, less than four years later, the population had dropped to about two thousand. The elimination or displacement of nearly four fifths of the Hongmao population is attributed to the Nationalist response to the Baisha Uprising. Wang felt the effect and the viciousness of the response in his own family. Nationalist forces took his two daughters. One of them was drowned and the other sold to a man in another village, though she was reunited with her father following the Communist takeover of Hainan in 1950. Nine of his male cousins took part in the uprising, and three were killed.[69]

The prospect of Li extermination now was more real than ever to some of the leaders of the uprising. Under Wang Guoxing and Wang Yujin's leadership, the Li fighters continued to retreat farther and farther into the mountain wilderness. Many of the Li people had come to live by agriculture, and not simply by subsistence hunting and gathering. The scarcity of food to be hunted and foraged in the mountain forests along with the obvious danger of such an organized unit made it impossible for the Li fighters to remain together as a fighting force. While some villagers secretly made their way into the mountains to feed the fighters, only a minority of expert woodsmen were able to survive alone in the wild forests.

This contradicts the misnomer of "wild" that has been attributed to the Li of Hainan. Long hunting trips had given only some Li men the skills they needed to survive in the woods without returning to their home villages. This was a kind of sport that the men engaged in during the New Year's festival, and often with the added amusement and challenge of intoxication. But irrigated agriculture made up most of the Li diet, not wild vegetation and game. After less than two months in the mountain forests, Wang Guoxing watched the desperation of hunger take its toll on the fighters who had hoped to follow him to the end. Finally he announced that those who could not subsist in the woods were to return to their villages. He told them that their chances of survival were better if they could gradually and secretly return to their homes. The risk of discovery and execution by the Nationalists was great, but the alternative was certain starvation in the unwelcoming mountain forests. Reluctantly, most of the Li force returned to their homes, where, they were told, they would receive instructions once the leadership had decided on the next move of the uprising.

By October 1943, another meeting was held that brought together most of the remaining leaders of the movement. None of the fighters who had come this far entertained the possibility of surrender to the Nationalists. According to later accounts of the events, it was Wang Yujin who first put forth the decision to turn to the Hainan Communists at this point. Since the events, and since the Li uprising has been entered into the annals of Communist history, rather exotic versions of the decision to turn to the Communists for help have emerged.

You Qi, a mainland journalist who came to the island in the spring of 1950, did his part to build this magical tale of the Li people being led to the Communists by their own superstitions and omens. Wang Guoxing, in this version, had heard of the Red forces on Hainan, and he and others were entertaining the possibility of turning to them for help against the Nationalist forces. Early one morning, in a moment of introspection and meditation on the matter, a red mist came to him from over the hills, descending on his camp from the north, where the Communists were known to be operating with the greatest strength. At this point, in this retelling, there was no more doubt of what was the best course of action, and Wang sent out messengers to find the leaders of the Communists.[70]

Actually, in Wang Guoxing's own biographical account, which relies on the recollections and eye-witness accounts of participants in the events rather than the fanciful exoticism of a revolutionary travel journalist, it was Wang Yujin who suggested that the best decision for the embattled Li was to seek out the help of the Communists. Yujin remembered the popularity of the Communists during his time serving in the Nationalist military in the southern mainland. He recounted this to the other Li leaders, and he also told them what he knew of the Han-Li cooperation in the Communist revolutionary base that had been established in Lingshui. This southeastern base had since been greatly weakened, and the Baisha Li fighters could not simply make their way to Lingshui. They would have to seek out the Communists in the northern part of the island. But cooperation between the Communists and the Li was not unprecedented, Yujin urged, and for those with him it would be the best step for them to go to the Communists next.[71]

The alliance between the Li under the leadership of Wang Guoxing, Wang Yujin, and others, with the Hainan Communists was the most important political result of the Baisha Uprising. The statistics surrounding the events vary with some predictability, depending on the source. There are some localized accounts that are probably more accurate than the figures that are attributed to the entire uprising, but there is not a systematic compilation of local histories that might be cobbled together to provide an accurate set of statistics on the uprising. In terms of the participation of Li fighters, the two figures used most consistently are twenty- and thirty thousand. The significantly larger figure of thirty thousand is found in the accounts that rely on the recollections and eye-witness accounts of the Li participants. The figure of twenty thousand occurs more often on the whole, and it is found in the secondary accounts of Hainan's revolutionary history. It is notable that in the accounts where the Li struggle is central, the figure of thirty thousand is used, and where the Communist revolution is central, the twenty thousand figure is more common. Nationalist casualties are similarly divided between these two types of sources, and the figures most commonly used are three hundred and eight hundred, used together with the larger and smaller of the Li participation figures, respectively. These two sets of figures (twenty thousand Li fighters and three hundred Nationalist casualties, and thirty thousand Li fighters and eight hundred Nationalist casualties) appear together in all instances I have found.[72]

Another important variation in the many accounts of the Baisha Uprising is the treatment of the movement's preparation. In the accounts that do not take the Li as the center of the narrative, there is little or no attention to the early preparations and meetings of the Li and Miao headmen that began more than a year before the uprising was launched. This oversight may be explained by a general lack of attention to detail in these accounts of the uprising, but I believe that the discrepancy between these accounts and the Li accounts is more important than simply a lack of detail. There are two conclusions that must be drawn when accurately conveying the context and the extensive planning with more thorough attention than is generally allowed in mainland or Communist accounts. First, the fact that the uprising was planned for more than a year with dozens of village and township headmen involved, completely changes the mainland or Communist understanding of the Li as a primitive people who were simply prodded by Nationalist or Japanese injustice and rose in a reflexive response.

Second, the planning that was involved in the Li uprising sets it apart from the violent movements of the Li throughout imperial Chinese history and the early republican period.

In the Communist version of the Li uprising, it is the Li participation with another group—the Communists, themselves—that sets the movement apart from other Li disturbances. The Li sent messengers to establish contact with the Communist leadership in November and December of 1943, and by early 1944, the two groups had begun working together.

> The arrival of the military work unit [in early 1944] was extremely moving for Wang Guoxing and the other leaders of the uprising. Wang Guoxing and Wang Yujin . . . said, "After hoping day and night, our parental army (*fumu jun*) has finally arrived. The sun has risen over Wuzhishan!" The arrival of this work unit caused the Baisha Li people's resistance movement to come under the leadership and organization of the Chinese Communist revolutionary movement.[73]

It is correct in that the Li had never before collaborated with another force consistently in an attempt to expel a common enemy. The exception of the Ming loyalists in the early Qing dynasty is notable, but it is not well documented, and it does not seem to have been widespread within the Li community.[74] While the above description is perhaps overly dramatic in its propagandistic tone, the extensive Li-Communist cooperation was indeed the ultimate result of the Baisha Uprising. The initiative for the cooperation came from the Li themselves, and the resulting alliance was quickly welcomed by the Communists. Attempts had already been underway on the part of the Communists to establish good relations with the Li. A July 1940 directive from the mainland Communist Party headquarters instructed the Hainan Communist leadership to pursue an alliance with the Li.

> Conduct your work vigorously in establishing alliances with the 300,000 Li people. Respect their customs and rituals. Earn their trust, do not allow them to be used by the enemy, and bring them into our resistance movement. You must recognize that their ancestral home territory surrounding Wuzhishan is the last refuge that we might be able to use as a last resort in our resistance. . . . It is only with access to this region that we can carry out a long-term resistance.[75]

The Communist priority of establishing an alliance with the Li reflected their understanding of the importance of the Li dominance in the island's interior. In a sense, the Li uprising played perfectly into the hands of the Communists. There are some references to Communist influence in the planning of the uprising, but these come only in secondary sources that provide triumphalist accounts of the Communist struggle, and they are dubious and not verifiable. Zhan Lizhi was a Li member of the Communist movement and served under Wang Guoxing. He remembered his service with Wang after the initial violence of the Baisha Uprising had subsided, and after the alliance with the Hainan Communists. Zhan's work with Wang was to subvert the functioning of the Nationalist government that remained in power in the region. According to Zhan, Wang Guoxing knew of pathways and trails through the mountains around Wuzhishan that it seemed no other person ever knew about. To Zhan, it seemed that Wang could summon trails as if he were drawing them on a map with his own hand as he ran through the forest. During the Baisha Uprising, many Li men, women, and children had fled to the mountains to escape the violence. Following the uprising, the Nationalists returned to the area and began propaganda work, according to Zhan, which was sometimes successful in building mistrust of the Communists among the Li. Following the Nationalist propaganda campaign, there was some reluctance on the part of the Li who had fled, to return to their villages. Again, Wang is credited with much of the ideological work that was required to reestablish unity among the Li in the region, and encourage some of those who had fled to return to their villages.[76]

For two years, the Li continued to frustrate the Nationalist occupation of their territory, now with the guerrilla training and experience of the Communists. Ties to the Communist movement in the north became stronger, and the alliance of convenience would benefit the Communists most when the Nationalists withdrew from Li territory in August of 1945. The Japanese surrender and withdrawal from the island was followed by the Nationalists' return to the cities and an attempt to reestablish control. For the Communists, access to the refuge of the southern mountains allowed them to subsist beyond the Nationalists' reach for the next five years as they gradually expanded their bases throughout the rest of the island.

CHAPTER 6

HOLDING ALOFT HAINAN'S RED FLAG

Disobedience and Survival in the Civil War, 1946

In 1945, in the wake of the Japanese defeat and withdrawal, on the national scale, even during the halting negotiations between the Nationalists and the Communists, the Nationalist leader, Chiang Kai-shek (Jiang Jieshi) "seemed, at this time, to be absolutely sure of victory through force." There were some sticking points in the peace talks, however, and it was not certain that the Communists were ready or willing to make the concessions demanded of them by the Nationalists, and the Communist leadership seemed divided. Through the fall and winter of 1945–1946, the pantomime of peace brought hope to American observers and negotiators, including General George C. Marshall, who hoped to overcome the crucial step of joining all Chinese military bodies into a single national force. President Harry Truman declared the American position that would be Marshall's marching orders as negotiator: "autonomous armies should be eliminated as such and all armed forces in China integrated effectively in the Chinese National Army."[1] American policy was officially to withhold assistance that would be used by the Nationalist government against the Communists in a civil war, but that did not preclude logistical aid and extensive cooperation. Noncombat military and intelligence missions were carried out in cooperation between the Nationalists and the Americans. The complex and ultimately doomed process proceeded but with few moments of satisfaction for any of the players.

On Hainan, Feng Baiju and the Communists entertained the possibility of again working with the Nationalists, but they had cause to extend little trust toward the group that had opposed national directives for unity, from the capture of Feng in 1937 to the continual skirmishes. The blame for some of these clashes after 1937 could be traced to both Nationalist and Communist forces, but the Communist leadership would later be persecuted by the mainland Communist regime for being too cozy with their Nationalist neighbors, and too eager to support the united front. The shifting alliance was difficult to track on the mainland where communications were largely free flowing, but on Hainan it was impossible for Feng to keep up-to-date on the shifting nuance of the united front. Now at the time of the Japanese defeat, the Hainan Communists were out of contact with the mainland Communist authorities in Yan'an, and for months thereafter, they were unable to safely establish radio contact with the mainland. When an Australian official asked Zhou Enlai, for example, in early 1946, about the possibility that missing Australian servicemen might have escaped Japanese prisoner of war camps on Hainan and joined with the Communists guerrillas, Zhou could not give him a definitive response. Zhou's letter of May 14, 1946, is worth quoting in its entirety to reflect the CCP's awareness, or lack of awareness, of the Hainan Communists at that time:

Dear Mr. [Patrick] Shaw:

Your letter of April 27th was received. We have immediately taken necessary steps to obtain the report on the Australian prisoners of war in Hainan Island. However, since the recent conditions of the Communist-led forces in Hainan Island under General Fung Pak-kee [Feng Baiju] have close connection with the Australian prisoners of war in the area around [Danxian] as mentioned in your letter, we like to make the following statement:

1. General Fung Pak-kee's units have fought for eight years against the Japanese under extremely difficult circumstances, have done many meritorious deeds. But just because of the very fact that General Fung Pak-kee and his units have accepted the leadership of the Chinese Communist Party, they not only have been ill treated by Kuomintang [Guomindang, Nationalist Party] who have denied their achievement in these years and refused to recognize their due position, but also were openly branded as "bandits." Recently the Kuomintang has massed a force of an army with 4 divisions to besiege General Fung's units. Fighting is still going on.

2. Under the circumstances of civil war in Hainan Island the connection between us [the Communist leadership on the main-

land] and General Fung Pak-kee's units in [Danxian] becomes extremely difficult, since we never have any air communication with General Fung in ordinary times. So it is hard to estimate the time needed for informing General Fung to protect and send out the Australian prisoners of war; as to the safeguard for these prisoners of war in case they venture to break through the blockade of KMT troops, we hope that you, on behalf of your legation, can negotiate with Generalissimo's [Chiang Kai-shek] Canton Headquarters. Nevertheless we will try every possible effort we can to search for the whereabouts and other information of these prisoners of war. If we get any information from General Fung Pak-kee, we will let you know as soon as we can.

Faithfully yours,

Chou En-lai [Zhou Enlai][2]

The disconnection between the Hainan Communists and the mainland was such that even the mainland command could not portray themselves as being in control of all Communist base areas throughout China. Interacting with foreign government's with such an appeal as the one above, the Communist leadership frankly explained that the Hainan Communists were outside of their control. While they shared a common cause, they could not communicate with or command them. A small American unit of officers parachuted onto Hainan just a few days after the Japanese surrender. Their mission was an "OSS [Office of Strategic Services] Mercy Mission POW rescue."[3] The various Chinese missions of this sort were code-named: Magpie to Beijing, Sparrow to Shanghai, Flamingo to Harbin, and so on. Hainan's was Mission Pigeon. There were other missions throughout the region with similar tasks: Raven to Vientiane, Laos; Eagle to Korea; and Quail to Hanoi.[4] Even in the weeks after the Japanese surrender, these missions began to show the fissures that would lead to the monolithic blocks of Cold War alliances. Historian, Maochun Yu wrote about Mission Quail, in Vietnam, Hainan's neighboring country to the east, asserting that these OSS missions explicitly eschewed political ideology in their inception and objective. After working with archival sources on these missions, Yu believes that it is obvious that the OSS missions were not launched as a propaganda coup, though making political pawns of POWs was not unheard of. Still, Yu notes, Mission Quail ran into political trouble when picking up French POWS from a Japanese camp. These French servicemen "were not necessarily friendly toward the

Vietnamese Communists" prior to their internment by the Japanese, and Ho Chi Minh's followers did not welcome the American OSS working to evacuate them without a reckoning, which caused an international fracas among Japan's erstwhile enemies.[5]

The ongoing hostilities between the Chinese Communists and Nationalists amidst the Japanese occupation would cause some trouble on Hainan's OSS mission as well. The officer in charge of carrying out Hainan's Mission Pigeon, Captain John Singlaub, wrote, "Our orders were to make contact with Allied POWs in our respective areas, take the prisoners under our protection, and render all possible medical and humanitarian assistance to them."[6] Captain Singlaub (operating with the temporary rank of major), was concerned with non-Chinese "Allied" POWs, such as the Dutch, Indian (Sikhs from the Hong Kong-Singapore Royal Artillery), and Australians, as well as American airmen who had been shot down and were being held in Japanese camps on the island. Singlaub's observations and recollections from this mission provide a unique picture of a newcomer to the island in the late summer of 1945. (In 1981, after duty in the Korean and Vietnam Wars, Singlaub went on to become a founder of the American chapter of the World Anti-Communist League and the Victims of Communism Memorial Foundation. He was also an early member of the Central Intelligence Agency, and during the Reagan administration worked for the "Contras" against the Nicaraguan government. One should keep Singlaub's career in mind when reading his account of the situation between the Hainan Communists and Nationalists published in 1991.) He was the first American whose presence on Hainan is recorded in this period. The American Presbyterian missionaries who had made Hainan their home for decades earlier in the century were gone now, and had been for nearly four years.[7]

On August 27, 1945, the C-47 plane of Mission Pigeon left Kunming for Hainan to drop the squad of fewer than ten men, consisting of several Americans, including a medic, "a damn good weapons man" with a Thompson machine gun, and an intelligence officer, as well as a Chinese Nationalist lieutenant, and a young Japanese-American lieutenant as interpreter. Adding a Nationalist officer and no Communist representative to the group in this period was hardly unusual, and it reflected the ongoing and unbroken cooperation between Washington and the Nationalists.

Singlaub had his hands full leading a drop of inexperienced men into Japanese Hainan. Some of the men had never jumped from a plane before, and in the minutes after the drop they were still nursing bloody chins and concussions, and tending to broken supply crates when two Japanese army trucks approached them across the open field. Captain Singlaub quickly took charge of the situation, issuing orders to the small group of Japanese soldiers to defend his supplies and his men from a group of Chinese villagers who were watching the curious scene unfold. The uneasy relationship between Singlaub and the Japanese officers and prison guards, and the tricky negotiations with them that he undertook, are the focus of his recollection. But in the captain's observations as he drove across the island to the prison camps, he conveys a sense of the atmosphere of Hainan in the weeks after the Japanese surrender. He and his squad rode across the island in Japanese trucks.

Japanese soldiers protected Singlaub's men and their supplies from the onlooking Chinese villagers who, even according to Singlaub's own account, seemed to pose no threat whatsoever. Naturally, as a result of this arrangement and in order to carry out the directives, the Japanese soldiers were not disarmed, for they were now in that vague and uncertain limbo between war and peace, and at the service of a handful of Americans who had forced their empire's surrender on Hainan. Remarkably, the surrendered Japanese enemies of the Americans were thus dragooned and, in effect, trusted with armed military duties before any of the local Hainanese population was entrusted with such work. This striking detail is telling in how we should understand the isolation of the Hainanese conflict until this point, in which U.S. intelligence officers operating in that theater would sooner trust their Japanese enemy with armed guard duty rather than risk the uncertainty of local forces. Doubtless this command decision went far to alienate the Hainanese from the hasty Americans.

This little group reflected the political priorities of both the Americans and the Nationalist government at this time: the Japanese-American officer would interpret and ensure a smooth transition of power, the American military muscle and intelligence men reflected the importance Washington invested in China, and the Nationalist officer clearly reflected and anticipated the alliance that would attempt to isolate the Chinese Communists in this early postwar period. Before the Communists were able to capitalize on the gains that they had made under the Japanese occupation, it was essential to the Americans, the Chinese Nationalists, and also the Japanese, that the reins of power were passed off seamlessly to anyone but the Reds. It seemed that the entire postwar world was conspiring against the Chinese Communists, for on the mainland to the north even the Soviets were not as cooperative as Mao and the Communist leadership had hoped.[8]

In the example of Mission Pigeon, one ranking officer saw not only the Communists, but all Chinese, as less than worthy colleagues in the transition of power that followed the Japanese surrender. Captain Singlaub recalled with bilious relish, that this particular senior officer had carelessly crossed the line of protocol in warming up to the Japanese hosts on Hainan.

> ... Colonel Andrus had ordered all American officers to attend a formal dinner given by the senior Japanese staff ... an affair that clearly transcended the bounds of "fraternization" as outlined in our orders. During the banquet, Andrus—who had never heard a shot fired in anger—toasted the enemy and announced that the Japanese had proved to be "a worthy foe," and that the Americans were "deeply grateful for the cooperation" we'd received on Hainan, which was better, he added, than that he'd received from the Chinese, who were supposed to be our allies.[9]

When Singlaub confronted Andrus about the misguided affection he was showing to the perpetrators of such atrocities, the colonel retaliated by instructing the Japanese "to no longer obey orders from [Singlaub] or [his] officers."[10] While this petty behavior actually threatened the execution of a mission that was meant to save the lives of men, many of whom were desperately in the need of immediate medical attention, for our sake it shows the way in which Mission Pigeon reflected the larger political rifts that would develop into the Cold War. As one ascended the chain of command, political ideology tinted the decisions of military missions, and Colonel Andrus's cozy relationship with the Japanese officers of Hainan anticipated the broader relationship between the United States and Japan that was born in this takeover.

While the Communists throughout the Chinese mainland were isolated by the chilly treatment and sometimes open hostility from their neighbors and from the newly arrived peacekeepers from the north and across the ocean, the isolation of the Hainan Communists was even more extreme. Peace talks were planned between the Communist and Nationalist leaderships, and there was talk of a joint government. But it was painfully obvious, even at this early stage in post-Japan China, that the southern Communists were surrounded by an array of powerful and unfriendly forces. Further, the priorities of the Chinese Communist Party at the time of the Japanese defeat were clearly in the north. The aim of CCP policy was to "extend the CCP strongholds in Manchuria, defend the party's position in North China, and withdraw from indefensible areas in Central and South China."[11]

Captain Singlaub, though accompanied by a Nationalist officer, was not tasked with any reconciliation between the Hainan Nationalists and Communists. With the Japanese marines still firmly in control of their prison camps and military bases in the weeks following the empire's surrender, there would be no work to prevent the outbreak of the Chinese civil war on Hainan. After all, with both the Hainan Communists and Nationalists operating with guerrilla tactics across the island, it would not be easy to tell the difference between the two camps from Singlaub's perspective, let alone bring the two sides to the negotiating table.

Singlaub himself was ultimately willing to work with both the Nationalists and the Communists on Hainan. As it turned out, he would have to.

> Over the next few days we got definite word of several Allied evaders in the mountains. With [Nationalist Lieutenant] Peter Fong's help, I drew up some handbills in English and Chinese, requesting contact with Allied personnel still in hiding. We tied these handbills to bottles of Atabrine [an antimalarial drug], and each bottle was attached to a twelve-inch pilot parachute. Then we took a C-47 ride around the island, dropping the messages into the village markets in the highlands, where we knew the guerrillas were located.[12]

In the final days of his mission on Hainan, he received word that a large group of Allied prisoners—Indian, Dutch, Australian, and American—were being held in a Nationalist guerrilla camp. Taking his colonel's Jeep, Singlaub bounced up the mountain road to the camp, and made it through Communist territory without incident, to the amazement of Nationalist officers. Singlaub and his men spent the night in the Nationalist guerrilla camp, celebrating with liquor and song their victory over Japan. After bringing back the prisoners on the following day, Singlaub also received a note from an American pilot who was "holed up with the Communist guerrillas." Surprisingly, Nationalist Lieutenant Fong was delegated to escort the American out of Communist territory, and he did so without incident.[13] Japan's occupation of Hainan left the people of the island reeling as a result of the atrocities noted earlier, and the unsustainable economic steps taken by the military regime. As in the case of the Japanese occupation of South Korea and Taiwan, passionate debate rages over the economic benefits and the human cost of the Japanese occupation and colonization. For some who remember the Japanese occupation, or for those whose relatives or compatriots suffered and died at the hands of the Japanese, any discussion of economic infrastructural development for which the Japanese were responsible is tantamount to traitorous behavior.

While Japanese atrocities on Hainan island deservedly play a central role in any analysis of the occupation period, it is still worthwhile to examine some of the economic plans and efforts on the island in that period. Notably, while the Japanese purportedly planned for long-term occupation of Hainan, and eventually for the establishment of a full colonial governmental infrastructure, they never progressed past a military administration. And rather than moving toward a civilian colonial government, the reality of the Pacific War sapping the resources and administrative attention of the Japanese empire made the trend on Hainan toward a harsher and more draconian rule, as was noted during Captain Singlaub's OSS mission to Hainan following the Japanese defeat. Singlaub, a young but experienced officer at the time, with the firsthand military experience of the worst atrocities in both the European and Asian theaters of World War II, wrote that life for the Hainanese people under the Japanese occupation was "absolute hell."[14]

From February 1939 until August of 1945, the Japanese military mining and transportation developments had proceeded apace, but in a way that would not benefit the long-term growth of the local Hainanese economy. The two main developments—the southern naval ports and the inland iron mines—would not help Hainan's postwar recovery, even if it had not been for the ensuing chaotic civil war between the Communists and the Nationalists. The iron mines and the light rail that connected them to the southern ports were useless by 1945, for they had been largely mined out and their bounty sent to Japan for use in the development of the Japanese military and economy.[15]

As for the southern ports, no significant ship-building industry was developed here by the Japanese, and the harbor of Yulin was only useful for ships in transit, coming from Singapore to Hong Kong or Japan, or connecting to the Southeast Asian mainland. "Hainan had been a backwater in China, and Japan almost succeeded in drawing it fully into the economy of East Asia, where its geographical situation and rich resources should have earned it an important role." Ultimately, as a result of Japanese military priorities in the Pacific Ocean and broken communications that endangered shipping to and from the island, "Hainan could no longer serve its new master with the resources it had to offer and thus became another isolated part of a defeated empire."[16]

This role of being a neglected outpost of great potential at the margins of a crumbling regime was simply a return to Hainan's pigeonhole. As long as Hainan has been ruled from without, viewed from without, and exploited from without, it has always been labeled a backwater. And as the Japanese retreated, even the political calculus at the dawn of the Cold War did not prompt any representatives of the powers except for Singlaub's Mission Pigeon to visit Hainan. There were no Soviet advisers in Hainan to help with the takeover of the Japanese industry, as was the case in the Japanese colony of Manchukuo in northeastern China, and in North Korea. Figures on the forces of the Hainan Communists have generally been accepted by Chinese historians from a report that the Hainan Communist leadership sent to the mainland Communist headquarters, dated October 26, 1945. This message was carried by messenger to the mainland Party headquarters, because it was sent before the reestablishment of two-way radio contact. Lin Ping wrote to Zhou Enlai that there were about 5,000 Communist Party members on Hainan, a military force of more than 7,700 regulars in five detachments across the island and about 9,000 militia fighters throughout the counties.[17] This last figure seems to be used with some flexibility, probably for the purpose of expressing an enhanced viability of the Hainan Communist forces to the mainland Communist leadership. And yet, Japanese sources credited the Communist presence on Hainan with having provided them far more trouble than the Nationalists, and while they estimated a lower number of Communists in total, the Japanese occupiers also acknowledged an active but politically unaffiliated Communist resistance on Hainan.[18] It seems likely that Lin and the Hainan Communist leadership would claim these irregulars as their own, and probably it was a claim with some traction.

Two militia groups from different towns gave me some impression of their daily lives and interaction with the Hainan authorities. One militia member explained that he and his fellow supporters of the Communist movement were not constantly making trouble for the authorities in their hometown of Lincheng. Lincheng was a significant northwestern town, near enough to the coast for the Nationalists regime to occupy it solidly following the Japanese evacuation. As they were instructed, the Communist militia there operated underground, and did not engage in frequent and dangerous propaganda activity. The Communist militia members exchanged messages with various Communist agents throughout the island, and they would occasionally hold secret meetings. In the months following the Japanese retreat, a unit of Nationalist soldiers arrived in Lincheng with mainlander officers, making the work of the underground militia much more dangerous. But they went about their daily lives as best they could. Late in the afternoon they would stop working in the rice fields or tending to the mango, banana, and rubber trees, and gather to play volleyball late into the evening. Often the underground militia members would be on teams mixed with the handful of Nationalist soldiers and officers who were garrisoned in Lincheng.

The militia men I interviewed in another more remote village, Xianlai in Feng Baiju's native Qiongshan county, told me that the fear of retribution from the growing Communist forces on the island prevented the militia men from being sold out to the Nationalist authorities. In Xianlai, the militia veterans I spoke with explained that while the Nationalists claimed to administer their little town, they almost never saw any representative of the Nationalist military or civilian government. The Japanese had come through the town violently, burning houses and murdering civilians, but they had not stayed to govern, much like their sporadic and terrifying presence in Feng Baiju's hometown of Changtai.

Consolidation and the Civil War

In 1946, less than a year after the Japanese defeat, Hainan Communist fighters twice disobeyed orders from the mainland central Communist command to abandon their home island. In Hainanese Communist historical accounts, Feng Baiju and the Hainanese were proven correct in this decision, and Mao Zedong also retroactively approved of the decision to disobey the order to leave Hainan. From 1926 to 1946, the Hainanese Communist movement had turned from a group of students and newspapermen to hardened guerrilla fighters in the island's interior. While this quite neatly parallels the development of the mainland Communist movement through the end of the 1930s, by 1946, the Hainanese Communists were an anomaly in the Chinese Communist movement. The mainland forces were becoming a conventional fighting force, and they were preparing to abandon their northwestern bases for the pitched battle in northern and central China.

On the Chinese mainland, the Japanese withdrawal meant that the two armies were on the eve of a conventional military civil war. The mainland Communists had passed through the days of guerrilla struggle when they clung to minor gains, desperate escapes, rearguard actions, and partisan victories. By early 1946, they were marshaling their forces in the north for a conquest in the north-to-south traditional expedition that had successfully established most Chinese dynasties of the past. Military and political command was becoming increasingly centralized, and there was an effort at consolidating the scattered base areas that had characterized an early stage of the Communist movement.

According to an agreement with the Nationalists, the mainland Chinese Communist central command would abandon all of their bases and holdings south of the Yangzi River. Following the Japanese defeat in August 1945, the Communists and Nationalists briefly engaged in peace talks, in the winter and spring of 1945–1946. The southern holdings of the Communists were negligible compared to the northern bases that they had built up during the war with Japan, so this concession of southern territories to the

Nationalists was relatively easy for the Communist leadership. While there were some sticking points in the negotiations between the Communists and the Nationalists, there was no protest from the Communist negotiators over giving up their southern bases, which consisted mainly of the Dongjiang (East River) Column near the southern city of Guangzhou (Canton), and the Hainan Independent Column.

The Dongjiang Column followed their orders to abandon their former guerrilla territories, withdrawing to the Communist-held northern bases. When the civil war resumed in the summer of 1946, the Dongjiang Column continued to fight for the Communists from their new Shandong base area.[19] When the Hainan Communists received a similar order to leave their southern territory and retreat to Shandong, they responded that they could not safely comply with the order, and they would not attempt it. In the fall of 1946 they refused to obey another directive from Party Central to retreat to the Southeast Asian mainland and join forces with Communists forces in Indochina.

With the August 1945 defeat of the Japanese military and the end of the Pacific War, the Japanese occupiers of Hainan handed over the command of the island to the Chinese Nationalist regime that was internationally recognized. Since 1941, there had been a Japanese civilian population of more than ten thousand, many of whom were technicians who left their work in the mines, factories, fields, and harbors to the Nationalist authorities who would largely allow any developments to go to waste in the four years of civil war that would follow.[20]

The Japanese administration of Hainan had been almost completely military, a "Special Military Government" under the Navy. For some Hainanese, cooperation with the Japanese led to imprisonment, execution, or a hasty departure from the island. Zhao Shihuan (1903–1960), the most prominent collaborator on Hainan, left with Japanese forces, living in Japan for several years. According to one account, Zhao followed the trials of some Hainan collaborators from Japan, and when he saw that some were receiving light sentences and others were being released from prison early by the Nationalist authorities, he decided to return home in 1947. A brief imprisonment of less than a year by Hainanese Nationalist authorities followed, after which he left the island for good, this time for British Hong Kong where he lived for the rest of his life, working as a university professor.[21]

But life in most Chinese towns and villages continued as it had during the war years and the Japanese occupation, with unrest, violence, and underground activities shaping the political landscape for Communist guerrillas and the Nationalist forces who tried to wipe them out. The

Japanese departure allowed Nationalist forces to reassert themselves along the coast, and establish political control. Most larger towns saw an increase in Nationalist military presence, while villages continued to see relatively loose political control. The village of Xianlai is not far from the capital, Haikou. It was much smaller than the neighboring town of Lin'cheng, where the Nationalist presence was more obvious. On the mainland, peace talks were underway, but according to several of the Communist militia men of Xianlai that I spoke with, the news of the Japanese defeat did not bring hopes for a unified government with the Nationalists. Living a few villages away from the charred remains of Feng Baiju's hometown, the villagers of Xianlai remembered that before the Japanese had arrived and burned the village and gang-raped its women, the Nationalists had executed many of the villagers for suspected affiliation with Feng and the Communists. Then under the Japanese occupation, it had been difficult to tell the difference between regular Nationalist forces and those that were collaborating with the Japanese and doing their bidding.

While on the mainland, the titans of the political realm were discussing a unity government, in Xianlai, the Communist militia men already knew that there would be no peace with the Nationalist rulers of Hainan. This memory was clear for the men I spoke with in Xianlai, even though they did not hold a hatred for their former Nationalist enemies. For the militia men of Xianlai and Lincheng, there was no respite while the Nationalists were still the masters of Hainan island.[22]

Reconnecting with the Mainland

On the mainland, the way forward was not clear for China. Stalin was worried that the Soviets would be blamed for fomenting a civil war if he expressed enthusiastic support for the Chinese Communists, so instead he advised the continuation of the old and tattered United Front, and hastened to remove his own troops from China (laden with the spoils of Japanese industrialization—factory equipment that they brought back to Russia).[23] The Japanese defeat and withdrawal led to an awkward period in which the Nationalists and the Communists wobbled on the brink of total war. For most of two decades since 1927, the two parties had been in open military conflict with each other, with military engagements continuing even during the Japanese occupation.

The Communists emerged from the war with Japan in 1945 having become a military force that the Nationalists would have to take seriously. In Hainan, the guerrilla struggle had hardened the resolve of a core of partisan fighters who were loyal to their commander, Feng Baiju. While the Hainan Communists had operated for nearly five years without radio contact with the central Communist leadership in northwestern Yan'an, they had survived with the red flag held high. Theirs was, and would remain, an unbroken history of resistance to both the Japanese and the Nationalist governments of Hainan. This was essential to their identity, and in 1950, the slogan heard around the island was, "For twenty-three years, the red flag never fell." But in 1945, the Communists of Hainan were far from the masters of the island. Like their comrades on the mainland, the Hainan Communists had retreated to a relatively inaccessible region, in the mountainous forests and jungles of Hainan island. While the mountains of Hainan allowed the Hainan Independent Column to survive the war years with Japan, it also prevented regular contact with their mainland counterparts that might have been possible through closer interaction with the Nationalists. The Nationalist and Japanese military presence had isolated the Hainan Communists from any help from the mainland either in material or leadership.

The Communists and Nationalists on Hainan had been fighting since the Meihe Incident of December 1940, but with the Japanese surrender, there was nothing that would keep them from focusing all of their efforts on each other in an attempt to secure the strategic island for their respective camps. At the time of the Japanese surrender, both the Communists and the Nationalists had been forced to revert to guerrilla warfare. From most accounts, the stiffer resistance came from the Hainan Communists.[24]

The Hainan Communists had strengthened their hand during the Japanese occupation especially in their alliance with a confederation of Li villages following the Li Baisha Uprising of 1943. Feng Baiju and the Communist leadership felt that they were in a position to negotiate with the Nationalists as equals, and defeat them in battle if it came to that. This was the sentiment that prevailed in communications between the Hainanese Communist leadership and the mainland Party Central in the weeks and months following the Japanese defeat. Certainly the Japanese were a more efficient and deadly fighting force than the Chinese Nationalists, and the Communists had survived, in spite, or, more likely, because of, the Japanese occupation of the island. With 7,000 local cadres, 5,000 Communist Party members, 7,700 regular troops in the Hainan Communist military, and more than 9,000 militia fighters, the Hainan Communist movement was strong, and growing fast by 1946.[25]

American connections and support, both military and popular, were crucial to the Nationalists on Hainan and throughout the mainland. Incompetence and corruption in the political and military leadership of the Nationalists was part of the equation that made them rely heavily on U.S. aid. The Nationalists' military capability on Hainan reflected the larger reality of the Chinese mainland at the end of the war with Japan. Lloyd Eastman, in his authoritative account of the Nationalist failure summed up the state of the Nationalists on the eve of their final showdown with the Communists: "During the latter half of the eight-year war with the Japan, the Nationalist army was in an advanced state of disintegration. . . . This exhaustion and decrepitude were to be of supreme significance, for the army was soon called upon to fight a civil war with the Communists."[26]

On Hainan, there were peace talks held between the Communist and Nationalist forces in December of 1945 and again in January of 1946. Their expressed intention was to implement, at the local level, the fragile peace between the Nationalists and the Communists on mainland China, to halt any obvious preparations for civil war, and to implement a policy of a single, unified national military. This final aim had been only partially successful during the Japanese invasion and occupation, because the forces were never integrated and hostilities continued, most notably in the Meihe Incident. The "Haikou Negotiations" of 1945–1946 were attempted twice, but they did not get far. While they were underway, the Nationalist 46th Army was landing on Hainan's shores and securing important cities and towns as the Japanese withdrew. The talks fell apart with little accomplished except an increased knowledge by each group of their opponent's leadership and capabilities.[27]

One colorful anecdote emerged from the talks, and was remembered by the Hainan Communist delegate to the peace talks, Shi Dan. A high-ranking Nationalist officer approached Shi on the sidelines of the talks with an offer of covert cooperation that sounded too good to be true. This was Han Liancheng (1909–1984), commander of the Nationalist 46th army. Han informed Shi that he was in command of the army, and that he had made a secret agreement with Zhou Enlai to continue in this post while serving as a Communist agent. The Hainan Communist delegation did not trust Han's appeal to be genuine, and feared it was a trap.[28] Because there was still no direct and secure radio contact between the Hainan Communists and Party Central on the mainland, and also because Han was in no position to verify his claim and was not about to offer up the 46th on a platter, both sides chose to bide their time in mistrust.[29] The lack of clear communication on this meant that Han Liancheng could not fully reveal himself as a Communist agent. In a December 1948 speech to the Hainan Communist military leadership, Feng Baiju still put Han Liancheng in the line of Nationalist militarists and dictators who had been defeated to date by the Hainan Communists.³⁰ Han and the 46th left Hainan to fight in Shandong in the northeast of the mainland, and the Hainan Communists claimed this as a successful repulsion of the Nationalist onslaught.³¹

This crucial failure in communication could have been averted had Party Central made more of a priority of communication with the Hainan Communists. Perhaps Han's overtures would have been met with an understanding of his personal history and his willingness to work with the Communists. This is merely speculation, but the intelligence and communication failure would lead to a resumption of hostilities on Hainan that paralleled developments in mid-1946 on the mainland. Before the Nationalist 46th Army of the Nationalists had left Hainan, the Hainan Column was badly outmatched by its force. February of 1946 brought news to Hainan that the Communist leadership had agreed to abandon all of their bases to the south of the Yangzi River, including the island.

When the Hainan peace talks broke down in January of 1946, hostilities had quickly resumed, with skirmishes erupting in February between the 46th and the Hainan Communists. Unofficially, though, hostilities had never truly ceased, at least beginning with the Meihe Incident of late 1940, which seems to closely reflect the New Fourth Army Incident of January 1941 in southern Anhui. Though the Nationalist military infrastructure was still staggering out of years of pounding from the Japanese military, their dominance over the Communists in the air and at sea was undeniable. The Nationalist authority on the island easily prevented the Hainanese Communists from moving significant numbers of troops or supplies across the Qiongzhou Strait. Secure contact between the Hainan Communists and Party Central was limited to messages carried by hand. The relief of Japanese defeat and withdrawal would not last long. Communist messengers would still have to travel carefully, always under assumed names and with false documents, to communicate with their mainland counterparts. After the winter of 1945–1946, the Hainan Communists were continuing to grow in strength and support. Their base areas were expanding, and with the help of the Li tribes, they were able to maintain strong bases beyond the reach of the other Nationalists.

When, in April of 1946, the central command of the Communist Party on the mainland issued an order for the Hainan Communist leadership and most of its political and military personnel to evacuate the island and make their way to the northern mainland, there was much confusion and resistance among the Hainan Communist leadership. From June of 1941 until September of 1946, the Communist leadership of Hainan had no radio communication with the mainland Chinese Communist headquarters in Yan'an. In that period, agents of the Hainan Communist movement attempted several times to procure the necessary instruments and operators to reestablish communications, but every effort ended in capture and execution.[32] After the Japanese withdrawal from China in late 1945, Party Central in Yan'an stepped up its efforts to establish contact with its bases that had been behind Japanese lines or scattered throughout the country without communication. The fragile peace in late 1945 and early 1946 between the Nationalists and Communists offered a brief window for more open attempts at communication between the Party's central command and its regional outposts. These base areas and underground militias proclaimed their loyalty to Yan'an, even if they had endured half a decade without hearing their commands in real time.

Party Central's order to leave Hainan was sent out in the fall of 1945 and into the winter that followed, waiting to be picked out of the air by anyone affiliated with the Hainan Communist force. A repetitive message was sent specifically to the Hainan headquarters, naming its leader: "Comrade Feng Baiju. . . . Please use XX wavelength and XX call sign to communicate with us."[33] But without a two-way radio, it was impossible for the Hainan leadership to respond.

Feng and the Hainan Communist leadership could not afford to trust the tentative truce that prevailed on the mainland. As it had for twenty years, pragmatism drove the will to survive of the Hainan island Communists, and they were neither reckless nor overly trusting. There are only passing references to the importance of the medium of radio contact between the columns of the Chinese Communist movement in this period, though it was a vital lifeline that was maintained by trained personnel and at the cost of many lives. Between 1938 and 1940, the Yan'an headquarters of the Communist Party and the Eighth Route Army sent about eight hundred radio technicians to work with the Communist New Fourth Army.[34] This was in a time of professed cooperation between the Communists and the Nationalists, and unified resistance to the Japanese. Following a series of military confrontations between the Communists and Nationalists in 1940 and 1941, logistics and technical aspects of the Communist military infrastructure suffered major setbacks.

Communist recruitment in technical schools was forced underground in the major cities. On Hainan, Huang Yunming, a radio technician, remembered a Nationalist raid in June of 1941 that ended the hope for Hainan's ability to contact the mainland Communist headquarters. The commander of his unit of radio technicians was killed, causing a chaotic retreat in which their radio equipment was lost. For the next five years they continued to try to rig up a functional radio. There were no desks, let alone sophisticated equipment, and two timbers were roped together for a makeshift workspace. Huang remembered the tropical conditions with some humor, saying that the mosquitoes incessantly buzzing around their ears while they worked interfered with their concentration and their ability to hear signals from the mainland.[35] Without help from Guangzhou or Hong Kong it was a hopeless task. So stripped was the island of functional communications that even the American OSS mission to Hainan, with the full cooperation from the Japanese occupation forces in the fall of 1945, had considerable difficulty establishing a wireless radio communication with their command.[36]

Hainan's ability to relay messages of its progress back to the mainland was cut off, except for the occasional messenger who made the precarious trip through hostile territories controlled by either the Japanese or the Nationalists. Not only were there no wireless radio communications between the Hainan and mainland Communist leadership, Feng Baiju, the military and political leader of the Hainan Communist movement wrote very few directives in this time of any kind, and none of his speeches from this interim are extant. The communications sent from Hainan to the mainland headquarters, often handwritten directives carried by messengers, requested that more trained Communist cadres be sent to Hainan to aid in political and military leadership. Survival became the first order of business of the guerrilla, not ideological purity, and in the example of Hainan, not obedience to the national Communist movement.

The lack of radio contact between Hainan and the mainland Communist Party center was either the result or cause of a historical southward and westward orientation of Hainanese culture and economy. Hainanese native-place associations were common throughout Southeast Asia and Oceania urban centers, with frequent movement between Hainan and cities like Singapore and Manila. Even throughout the Japanese occupation, merchant networks that had been established centuries earlier continued to operate and allow movement from Hainan to the Southeast Asian mainland and other islands throughout the region. With the end of the Japanese occupation and the resumption of the civil war between the Nationalists and the Communists, a new decision of alliance confronted many within the overseas Hainanese community.

Communication and networks of support remained active throughout this period between the Hainanese Communists and the Southeast Asian mainland and Oceania, especially Singapore. During the Japanese occupation of Hainan, coastal China, and Southeast Asia, Hainan native-place connections continued to flow throughout the region. In these groups there was often a kind of pilgrimage mentality in which the ultimate aim of

Hainanese in Southeast Asia was to return to their home island to fight the Japanese, or to support that fight monetarily. Throughout much of Southeast Asia there were opportunities to fight the Japanese on one's own doorstep, but the idea of fighting for Hainan, on Hainan, seemed to have a more hallowed meaning among the Hainanese abroad.[37]

Even while it was impossible to establish radio communication between Hainan and the mainland Communist headquarters, the southern and western orientation of the Hainan Communists allowed them to maintain frequent contact with their supporters throughout the region. One Hainanese Communist operative established a newspaper in Singapore that provided its readers with updates on the progress of the Hainanese "people's army." Readers learned of the Hainan Communists being forced to renew their fight against the Nationalists, even before they could fully recover from the Japanese occupation that so devastated the economy and morale of the Hainanese people. The paper, *Hainan Tide* [Qiongchao bao], was mainly the work of a Chen Xianguang, who had received directives from the Chinese Communist Party central command. As a paper that was only circulated among the Hainanese community in Singapore, the circulation of one thousand was significant. The British authorities closed the paper in the summer of 1948, again reflecting, as in the example of Mission Pigeon, the way that the Hainan Communists were besieged not only by the Nationalists, but by an array of international forces.[38] The British had returned to power in Singapore after the Japanese defeat, and they continued in their tradition of anti-Communist counterintelligence.[39]

Loyal Disobedience

In April 1946, the order came to shift the bulk of the Hainan Communists far north to Shandong province. The order reflected the disconnect between the northwestern mainland Communist movement, and that of Hainan. For five years there had been no radio contact between the two forces, and under Japanese occupation beginning in 1939, it was never easy for messages to travel in any other way either. The messenger who came in April of 1946 made his way to Feng Baiju via the Guangdong Communist movement, which also had maintained only poor and sporadic communications with the Yan'an base area during the war with Japan.

The winter of 1945–1946 had revealed the intentions of the Hainan Nationalist leadership to bend all its efforts to eliminating the Communist presence on Hainan once and for all. Feng and the Communists had resisted complete annihilation and now their numbers were growing with their inland territories, and their popular policies and resistance credentials won them favor not only among Hainan's population, but also throughout the overseas Hainanese community, especially in Southeast Asia.

Still, in spite of the Hainan Communists' growing popularity, there was no overcoming the Nationalists superiority at sea and in the air. This imbalance provided an effective blockade on the Communists in Hainan. There was no way for the Hainan Communists to obey the order to retreat north (*beiche*). They simply did not have the resources to get two thousand or more Communist officers and soldiers off the island and up the coast to Shandong. Sending the messenger back to Yan'an with this response—that it would be impossible for the Hainanese Communists to obey this order and that they would be forced to remain on the island—would have been sufficient explanation for why the northern Communists could forget about being joined by the southern guerrillas. But Feng went a step further, and emphasized the strength and vitality of the Communist movement on the island. He noted that indeed it was impossible for him to implement the order to retreat to the north because of the Nationalist sea power and the blockade that prevented any movement of significant forces to and from the island. But then he went on. He remarked that even if it were possible to move the bulk of the forces under his command, he did not see how they would be able to preserve their gains on the island. In Feng's view, this led him to wonder how the Communist forces might return to the island and take it without a friendly force there to coordinate the attack.

While the Hainan Communist movement had taken on a distinctly local character, by all accounts, the reestablishment of radio contact with Yan'an was celebrated by the Hainan leadership as the renewal of the guerrilla movement's sense of purpose, and vindication of decades of struggle. The Hainan Communists never avoided the tutelage or threatened to actively oppose their mainland commanders. And their activities over the past half-decade of radio silence were congratulated in 1946, and they were encouraged to keep on this path.[40]

The order to retreat south, to Vietnam, was a clear vindication of Hainan's valued and time-honored connections with the Southeast Asian mainland. And in explicit advice from the mainland, shortly after the resumption of radio contact, the Hainan Communists were encouraged to expand their connections with Southeast Asian overseas Chinese supporters. This reflected similar orders that they had received as early as 1940 from the mainland Party Central.[41] So the Hainan revolution was not willfully violating mainland Communist orders in its policies to connect to the Southeast Asian international community, or to move forward with improvisational plans in its economic and military policy. But there was precedent for the concerns of mainland Communist leaders that the Hainan Column and its leadership was becoming too focused on its local revolution, and that when the time came, the Hainan Communists might not be prepared to sacrifice for the new nation.

But as the final arrangements were being made, in the summer of 1946, for the resumption of radio contact between the Hainan and mainland Communist commands, the Hainan Communist leadership sent one of their highest officials, Zhuang Tian, up through Guangzhou, Hong Kong, and Shanghai to meet with local and provincial Party leaders, and finally to Nanjing, where he met with Zhou Enlai.[42] This was a strategic move by the Hainan Communists, if their aim was to convey a sense of loyalty and adherence to the mainland Communist Party even while gaining a sympathetic ear and increased autonomy in their local revolution. Zhuang Tian was a "Long Marcher" and a native son of Hainan, having returned to the island from Yan'an in 1940.

In Nanjing, among Zhou Enlai's retinue he met many old classmates from the "Japanese Resistance University" in Yan'an where he had been a student and instructor. Zhou gave Zhuang three days to prepare a report for him. While Zhuang had traveled aboard a British steamer from Hong Kong, he did not carry any documents that might compromise his mission. While Zhuang was preparing the extensive report, Zhou Enlai impressed his guerrilla guests—Zhuang and another native Hainanese—by presenting them with gifts of Western-style suits, leather shoes, and comfortable quarters.

Zhou listened with surprise as Zhuang finally made his extensive report, which emphasized the survival of the Hainan Column in spite of overwhelming odds. After more than twenty years the red flag had never fallen on Hainan, in spite of the best efforts of the Japanese and the Nationalists. Now, with the bulk of Nationalist forces removed from Hainan after a series of embarrassing defeats at the hands of the Communists, it would be easier than ever for the Hainan Column to continue its fight. "We can continue the fight indefinitely, and we trust that Party Central will not lightly discard this piece of South China's revolutionary base areas."[43]

Zhuang Tian received Zhou Enlai's support for continuing the resistance on Hainan. The ongoing struggle was a "struggle of self-defense."[44] Feng Baiju continued to be more assertive than Zhuang Tian in emphasizing the local nature of the Hainan struggle, often distinguishing it from the larger civil war on the mainland. In Feng's speeches and reports that are extant from and about the early civil war period immediately following the Japanese withdrawal, his emphasis is always on Hainan. His speeches and writings dealing specifically with the retreat orders are not openly defiant, but it is clear that the Qiongzhou Strait that separates Hainan from mainland China seemed far wider in that time to Feng. One phrase that he used in describing the mainland Chinese civil war context was *guonei*, which might be translated as "within the country," "domestically," "the interior." He uses this phrase in contrast to the Hainan revolution, even while he professes his loyalty to the cause of the greater Chinese Communist revolution. While the mainland Communist rallying cry became, "Fight to Nanjing, capture Chiang Kai-shek alive," Feng even changed that to suit his local purposes, invoking the chant, "Fight to Haikou, capture Han Hanying alive."[45]

Feng Baiju, as the unrivaled leader of the Hainan Communist movement, was beyond the reach of the mainland Communists. He was the authority on Hainan for the Communists, and he aimed to keep that movement alive. It is clear that Feng's priority was in Hainan. There is no indication in Hainan or in the mainland Communist leadership's assessment of Hainan's Communists of any concern about what would later be called "localism," or what in other regions of China was called "mountaintoppism." "'Mountaintoppism' is Chinese Communist jargon used to describe someone who suffers from 'mountain-stronghold mentality, a type of sectarianism,' that is, a tendency on the part of individuals or groups to stress their own importance and identity and to act independently of central Party authority."[46] Benton, in this study that narrated the foundational Communist entities that would later coalesce in the New Fourth Army, does not include the Hainan Communist movement because his focus is on those movements that did feed the later New Fourth Army. But Feng Baiju seems a likely candidate for the label of mountaintoppist. He would later be one of the main targets of the Anti-localism Campaigns of 1952 and 1957, and the characteristics of a localist in this period seem to be precisely those of a mountaintoppist who has made the transition from revolutionary to ruler.

Perhaps it was Hainan's distance from Yan'an, or its perceived irrelevance to the Communist leadership, or the impossibility of cracking the whip of discipline over the island's leadership, but in actuality, Feng's revolutionary *raison d'être* was always Hainan. Benton goes on, "Mountaintoppists are often accused in Party literature of wanting to set up 'independent kingdoms.'"[47] And this is precisely the same language that the Communist establishment would use in their later persecution of the "localists" who favored providing for their home province instead of sacrificing for the sake of the new national regime. Ezra Vogel, in his study of the first two decades of Communist rule in Canton, notes that "Hainan island had been the one place in [Guangdong] where localism was so firmly entrenched that the area was left alone during land reform. Gradually, the outside authorities attempted to infiltrate the 'independent kingdom of [Feng Baiju].'" While Vogel maintains the quotation marks for the *Nanfang ribao* editorial voice in labeling Feng the king of Hainan, he does not seem to take issue with the central Communist view that an essentially federated or provincialized perspective of state-building in a revolutionary regime might allow an alternative path.[48]

Although these labels of "mountaintoppist" and "localist" are taken from different times and places in the history of the Chinese Communist movement, it is clear that Feng would wear both of those labels. And his persistence in the type of leadership decisions that would earn him those labels, even being aware that other leaders throughout China were suffering persecution for similar behavior, seems to suggest that he would accept them without reservation or regret. Feng's treatment in the political campaigns of the 1950s are examined further in chapter 7, but the 1946 retreat orders should be understood as part of a pattern in an uncomfortable and asymmetrical disciplinary relationship between the Communist Party's central authority and the Hainan leadership. The perception of motives in Hainanese localism, on the part of the mainland Communists leadership, was that the zero-sum relationship of local and national loyalties and priorities was tipped in favor of the local in Hainan, and the leadership sought to ensconce itself as the local satraps.

If Feng had left Hainan as he was ordered to do by the Party authorities in 1946, or if he had tried to run the Nationalist blockade and make his way to the north, Feng claimed that the Hainan Nationalist movement would use the opportunity to crack down hard on those portions of the Hainan community that were expressly supporting the Communists. The Li people, the progressive students and intellectuals in the coastal towns and cities, the farmers and fishermen of the inland and coast who sent their sons and daughters to join Feng, they would all suffer for the support that they had provided Feng and the Hainan Communists.

Or at least this was the case that Feng made when he responded to the order to move his fighting force off the island and to the north. Feng's language combined an articulation of his obedience to the central command of the Party and an assertion of his position as Hainan's undisputed leader. The Hainanese Communists would stay put, and that was final. He was not able to implement an order from the central command, but he also did not waste the opportunity to assert his command of the Hainan Communist movement. He would be here, he said, when the time came for the final

Communist victory on Hainan. And he would be the leader who would protect the interests of the Communist movement on Hainan and the lives of its supporters until that final victory. Feng's desire to assert his strength on Hainan in relation to the central command is not clearly an asymmetrical power play. Throughout his communications with the mainland Communists during the 1930s and 1940s, he solicited orders and direction for the development of the Hainan Communist movement.

Still, Feng must have been aware that there was not simply a single revolutionary line that never changed with the times. Through improvisation during the early period of the civil war, before the Japanese invasion of Hainan in 1939, Feng had kept the Hainan movement afloat without any help from the mainland. The political and military lines of the Communist movement did not always dovetail into a coherent and single plan that all could easily follow throughout the massive country. For the guerrilla, the first order of business is survival.

Whether Feng sought to keep the Hainan movement alive and in Hainan for the sake of the national Communist movement, or whether his primary motivation was to keep his feet on his home soil, cannot be clearly known. What is known is that decisions like the disobedience of 1946 led to a perception on the part of the mainland Communists that the Hainanese were interested mainly in perpetuating their own leadership in their Hainan fiefdom rather than contributing to the national revolution. This became clear during the anti-localism campaigns of the 1950s. In the longer context of the Hainanese Communist movement, from its predecessors who helped bring about the fall of the Qing, straight through the victorious 1950 campaign, it is clear that we should challenge the zero-sum equation of national and local loyalty that developed in the campaigns of the 1950s. The dramatic campaign to take Hainan for the Chinese Communist cause in the spring of 1950 proved that victory could be won and shared between the locality and the nation.

CHAPTER 7

SHARING VICTORY

The Communist Conquest of Hainan Island

Histories of Hainan

With the successful Communist campaign to take Hainan in the spring of 1950, approximately half of the Nationalists' territory fell into Communist hands, the other half being Taiwan. Tibet also remained outside of the new regime's control, but plans and propaganda targeted both of these regions. The battle for Hainan was the last major conflict of the Chinese Civil War. The announcement from Beijing was triumphant but simple: "Our Guangdong vanguard of the People's Liberation Army overcame the resistance of the enemy's army, navy, and air force. With the assistance of the Hainan Column, they heroically landed on Hainan, and swiftly mopped up the remnants of the enemy forces, completely liberating the entire island." The declaration congratulated the victorious forces, citing the leadership of nine commanders. Eight of the commanders cited were with the mainland force and only one was Hainanese. In conclusion, it was noted that the success of the Hainan campaign was an example for the imminent liberation of Taiwan and Tibet.[1]

But this announcement conveyed none of the complexity that had made the Hainan conquest possible. So divergent were the mainland and Hainanese views of the island's conquest that, depending on one's perspective, the Chinese Communist fight for Hainan island had lasted either two short weeks or twenty-three long years. The final battle and decisive push in the victorious campaign during the spring of 1950 took only a few weeks, as People's Liberation Army (PLA) troops landed on the island's northern beaches and joined with the Hainan Column to defeat the Nationalist forces there. But the local guerrillas had been fighting the Nationalists on and off—mostly on—for twenty-three years, since the spring of 1927.

In historical memory, therefore, the Hainan campaign has at least two distinct narratives. One recounts a "people's flotilla" of wooden junks, some with motors hastily rigged to the stern, ferrying thousands of PLA soldiers through the famously dangerous eddies and shifting shoals of the narrow Qiongzhou Strait to liberate Hainan, enduring punishing fire from Nationalist warships and planes. In one recent history of the modern Chinese army, the case of Hainan is opened and closed with an especially laconic treatment: "The landing forces quickly overran the island."[2] Other accounts of the campaign, remembered from the perspective of the troops who crossed with the PLA Fourth Field Army's Fifteenth Corps, also emphasize crossing the treacherous strait as the most important part of the campaign, with the indelible image of wooden boats captained by fishermen volunteers taking on the Nationalists' modern warships and planes.

A 1998 Chinese history, *Liberating Hainan* (*Hainan jiefang*), begins with the winter planning on the mainland of 1949–1950 for the assault on Hainan. While the focus in that study is mainly a history of the Fourth Field Army, it is telling that the local Hainanese context of the campaign is not introduced until the fifth chapter, where five lines of text are apportioned for the twenty-three year struggle of the Hainan Communists.[3] The same text quotes a firsthand account of the events from the perspective of a soldier with the landing force, which reveals the precedent of this bias in praising the accomplishments of the preparations and the landing on Hainan over the coordination and cooperation with the local forces: "This miracle [of setting sail to take Hainan with soldiers who had never been to sea before] surprised many of the old seamen, and they praised the men saying, 'Chairman Mao's army is full of true warriors, true warriors.'"[4] Miraculous indeed, as one sailor cried out in relief after waiting in the doldrums of the Qiongzhou Strait, "Chairman Mao has called the east wind. Hurry and raise the sails."[5] As with the image of wooden boats taking on Nationalist destroyers, hyperbole and apparently even the supernatural characterized the retelling of the PLA crossing to take Hainan.

The other narrative of the Hainan conquest is summed up by the slogan, "For twenty-three years, the red flag never fell," recalling the long and difficult insurgency waged by the local Hainan Communist forces. A year after the campaign, in early 1951, the Hainanese Communist leader, Feng Baiju, wrote an article to commemorate the thirtieth anniversary of the 1921 founding of the Chinese Communist Party. In this piece, he recounted the long history of the Party on Hainan, enduring through "the endless, dark days, and finally joining in the great victory of the entire people's revolution." He noted that Hainan was just a "small example," but he went on to describe the "special circumstances" of being "blockaded, surrounded on four sides by counter-revolutionaries." He also reiterated that the Communists on the mainland had been unable to support the Hainan revolutionaries with instruction, troops, or materiel for much of their struggle, and that the Hainan Column had relied on the people of Hainan for their support. This was the victory of the Hainanese people.[6] During the Japanese occupation of Hainan as well, the Hainan Column had been heralded in song as the righteous defenders of the island:

> Who are the saviors of Hainan? The Hainan Column.
> Everyday they strike the Japanese devils, and protect Hainan.
> Protecting Hainan and saving the people, the Hainan Column.
> Who are the saviors of Hainan? The Hainan Column.[7]

I begin with an introduction to the campaign and its relevant context, then discuss two of the main figures in the Hainan Communist movement. Feng Baiju was the leader of the political and military Communist movement, and is recognized as the symbol of the revolution on Hainan. Ma Baishan was also a high-ranking political and military leader on Hainan, rising to the rank of general following the war. Ma traveled to Beijing several months before the Hainan conquest and met with the highest political and military commanders of the Chinese Communist Party. In this analysis, Feng represents the improvisational and pragmatic aspect of the Hainan revolution, and Ma represents the constant awareness of Hainan's connection to the larger Chinese Communist revolution. More than simply a trip to report Hainan's local conditions in Beijing and receive orders, Ma's mission to Beijing on the eve of the Communist takeover of Hainan was a kind of tributary journey—a promise of allegiance and dedication to the new Communist regime that he would actually witness being founded on the Gate of Heavenly Peace (Tiananmen).

There was never a plan for secession on Hainan, and never hope by the Communist forces there of making common cause with the Nationalists. Their commitment to the national Communist movement was never challenged from within the movement, and that unswerving loyalty is embodied by Ma Baishan. Feng's improvisational leadership was perceived as potentially subversive, and his local loyalties and priorities would obstruct his further advancement in the Party in the decade to come.

The central Chinese Communist perspective—that of Beijing, in the spring of 1950—will be most important in the concluding section, in an examination of the geopolitical importance of the Communist conquest of

Hainan, and how national, regional, and global politics shaped the historical narrative that emerged from the campaign. Cold War geopolitics put the Hainan campaign center stage, and the military performance of the PLA was important in establishing its global image and prestige. The heroics of a band of scrappy local revolutionaries like the Hainanese had already become an old story seven months after the founding of the PRC. This type of narrative had been important as propaganda during the war against Japan, and earlier in the Civil War with the Nationalists. It had been useful in strengthening national resolve years earlier, but in the spring of 1950, this type of "people's war" was not likely to intimidate the commanders of the new perceived enemy—Americans patrolling the Pacific with footholds in Japan and Taiwan.

So the history of the local origins of the Hainanese revolution, like many others that were not sanctioned in Beijing, has not been important to the geopolitical world of bluster and threats. But still the legacy of Hainan is wrapped tightly with that national narrative of the early Cold War. In May of 1950, half a year after the founding of the PRC and a month before the Korean War began, for Beijing's purposes, Hainan's debut on the global stage was to be seen most importantly as a triumph of the mighty PLA, not the local scrappers. This historical casting of these events parallels the propaganda emphasis on the Eight Route Army over the New Fourth Army on the mainland, another example of favoring the emergent power of the PRC, rather than its past as a "rabble in arms."[8] Therefore, the local context of the Hainan campaign was caught up in what Michael Szonyi calls "geopoliticization" in his study of Jinmen (Quemoy) in the Cold War. While Szonyi explains how the lives of the people of Nationalist Jinmen were affected by their precarious and unique Cold War situation, I will focus on how the global politics of the early 1950s affected the rewriting and forgetting of Hainan's history.[9]

Hainan Welcomes the PLA, and the PRC Welcomes Hainan

The speed of the Hainan conquest, and the Nationalist enemies' hasty retreat to Taiwan, amazed even the Communist victors. The Communist military expedition from north to south China had been carried out with exceptional speed on the mainland, surpassing even the ambitious plans announced by Party headquarters. Almost overnight, after more than two decades of struggle, the Hainan guerrillas were transformed from harried bandits, living in jungle and mountain hideouts, into masters and heroes of their homeland. And with victory came a welcome new contingent of political and military paragons who, they expected, would help them build their new Hainan, free of the corruption and incompetence of the Nationalist rulers.[10]

Deng Hua, a Hunan general, was the main tactical officer of the PLA landing force, leading the Fifteenth Corps of the Fourth Field Army. His recollection of the final campaign for Hainan is an unadorned account of the maneuvers of the battles. This source outlines the campaign itself, emphasizing the campaign as a successful conquest for the new PRC. Deng also tends to minimize the contribution of the Hainan Communists, and celebrates the unstoppable might and courage of the landing forces.

The planning for the campaign began in the winter of 1949–1950 on the mainland's Leizhou Peninsula of Guangdong Province, just over ten miles from the northern Hainan coast. By February 1, 1950, a final conference was held involving the leadership of both the Hainan Communists and the PLA officers, including Deng and Ye Jianying. In the first week of March, several vanguard units in thirteen junks were launched from Leizhou Peninsula, and after some fighting on the beaches of northwestern Hainan, they managed to join with the Hainan Communists and retreated to Communist bases inland.

While Communist strategy was an important factor in the takeover of Hainan, Nationalist disorganization and disunity also played an important role. Witnesses to the final days of Nationalist rule on Hainan, like *New York Times* correspondent, Seymour Topping, discussed the failings of the Nationalists authorities on the island in the early weeks and months of 1950. The disunity and frustration among the top Nationalist command reflected in Topping's writing could hardly have given the American public any confidence in the Nationalists on Taiwan as a stalwart and steady ally in the early rumblings of the Cold War. In his memoir years later, Topping remembered his conversations with Chen Jitang and Xue Yue, both of whom complained about Chiang Kai-shek's reluctance to reinforce them in the quantity and quality that they requested. In describing his meetings with Xue Yue and Chen Jitang, Topping later wrote:

> At the Nationalist military headquarters, I met with the top commander [Xue Yue] . . . , the former governor of [Guangdong] Province, who was known as the "Little Tiger." The general, an energetic man, dressed in a flashy tailored American-style uniform, complained he was receiving only meager aid from Chiang Kai-shek. He was frantically trying to organize a defense force out of some 140,000 troops, about 80,000 of them combat veterans,

evacuated from the mainland . . . [And on Chen Jitang, governor of Hainan . . .] The fifty-eight-year-old Cantonese marshal, a lively, outspoken man dressed in a brown tunic and white Panama hat, sat with me on the veranda of the [Haikou] airport's passenger shack gazing out to the Communist-held [Leizhou] coast. The governor complained angrily about the sparse assistance he was getting from Chiang Kai-shek. "We have not received the money or supplies we need . . ."[11]

The faltering and fractured defenses of the Nationalists still did not prevent them from punishing both the Hainanese Communists and the Fourth Field Army organizing on the Leizhou peninsula. Topping watched as Nationalists bombed both Feng's interior bases and those on the mainland with impunity. But the successes of secret landings of the early probing vessels along the northern and western coasts of Hainan in late February and early March led to a more substantial vanguard force of several dozen junks, deployed on March 10, 26, and 31, which followed the pattern of the first. Some of these units were scattered, and the Nationalist enemy was unable to track how many mainland Communist forces were now augmenting the Hainan Column. By mid-April, the full-scale attack was launched. On the night of April 16, the Communist junks began crossing the Qiongzhou Strait in waves, totaling 318 boats of various sizes. They landed after losing boats and taking casualties in the crossing, and were met and aided by the Hainan Communists in the early morning hours of April 17. After this landing, the conquest proceeded rapidly, with the Nationalists retreating to the south. Communist forces marched into Haikou in the north on April 23, and only seven days later, the southern towns of Sanya and Yulin had also fallen. The Nationalist commanders and thousands of the Nationalist forces fled to Taiwan, and on May 1, 1950, complete victory was announced in Beijing.[12]

The differences were stark between the PLA regulars and their Hainan guerrilla comrades. As they met on the palm-lined beaches of Hainan, in the towns and small cities, and in jungle hideouts across the island, both were surprised at the others' appearance. The Hainanese guerrillas wore sandals, shorts, and light collared shirts, if they chose to wear any shirt at all in the tropical heat. Their skin was copper, their faces gaunt, their muscles wire cables of strength from decades of warfare and jungle subsistence. Their clothes were worn and their packs were light. Among the few essential components of their kit were a rifle, a canteen, a few days' supply of food, and a hammock.[13]

Every day that military and weather conditions allowed, the guerrillas hung their hammocks and took long afternoon naps to avoid exhaustion during the hottest hours of the day. The PLA regulars, many of them northerners and not accustomed to the slower life of a tropical island, joked about this local custom. For some of the mainlander regulars, the custom of midday napping seemed to reflect Hainanese laziness, or worse, a lack of revolutionary zeal. The mainlanders had, after all, braved death and lost hundreds of their comrades in crossing the Qiongzhou Strait from Guangdong to Hainan to liberate these loafers.[14]

The PLA regulars had spent three months on the mainland coast of Guangdong, learning to swim and sail, and to operate their improvised motorboats. They were well-outfitted and well-fed compared to their guerrilla counterparts. The Hainan campaign was, after all, center stage in China's civil war in the spring of 1950.[15] The Fourth Field Army had been assigned the task of liberating Hainan, and posted to Guangdong Province's Leizhou Peninsula, which stretched south, close to the northern coast of Hainan. But not close enough for the PLA soldiers, many of whom had marched from their home provinces in the northeast. For them, it was a terrifying prospect to swim—or try to swim—after tumbling out of a crowded junk.

Han Xianchu (1913–1986), Fifteenth Corps Deputy Commander of the PLA's Fourth Field Army remembered the early days of the training. "Beginning the training at sea, a company boarded a boat, and 80 percent of them looked as if they wanted to throw up."[16] But crossing the narrow Qiongzhou Strait in April and May, after the most favorable winds of the winter had passed, was difficult for even an experienced sailor. The rough waters were an unwelcome introduction to life at sea for the northern soldiers, and the increasing heat would make the conquest even more difficult.

To celebrate the Communist victory on Hainan, Feng organized a banquet for the officers of both mainland and Hainan forces.[17] It would be an opportunity for speeches and celebration, and Feng chose to hold the event at the Five Ministers' Temple. The Temple stood close to the northern Hainan city of Haikou, and it had been commissioned half a century earlier by the Qing reformer, Zhang Zhidong, to honor five Tang and Song dynasty officials who had been banished to Hainan.[18] These officials, along with a sixth, Su Dongpo (also known as Su Shi, who shone brighter than all the luminaries in Hainan's pantheon) had risked all to criticize imperial excess or corruption, and they had been banished to this malarial and barbaric southern island. After arriving, the ministers made the most of their exile, reforming and building local infrastructure, educating candidates for the imperial examination, and becoming off-center heroes of China, and the pride of Hainan.[19] The Temple was a significant place to choose for the banquet, because it emphasized Hainan's distinct culture within China's imperial history. The Hainanese had welcomed the spirits of the imperial ministers who were honored and worshipped at the Temple, and their spirits are still summoned and soothed, as testified by heaping mounds of incense burned at their shrines. These old ministers might have anticipated the tension between the newly welcomed PLA guests and their Hainan hosts.

In Feng We Trust

The question of speed and urgency is a central one in *Dilemmas of Victory*, a recent volume of essays on the early years of PRC rule.[20] This revolutionary urgency was a radically different cultural construct than the Hainanese guerrilla struggle. For twenty-three years the Hainan Communists had met with varying success, sometimes with their ranks swelling to thousands of armed fighters, and at other times, having as few as twenty-six partisans camped in their commander's family home.[21] The Hainan Communist movement was characterized by improvisation and unusual allies throughout two decades of Feng Baiju's leadership. The geographic necessity of maintaining close ties with the civilian population led to Feng's popular maxim, "Mountains can't hide people; only people can hide people."[22] This meant political flexibility and patience. Both of these qualities of the Hainan revolution would be discarded in the urgency of the new regime that came to Hainan in the spring of 1950.

In late 1948 and early 1949, Feng took the initiative to organize political and military schools within Communist-controlled base areas. In an October 24, 1948, notice, "Chairman Feng" announced a planned Hainan Public School to be opened in March of the following year. The purpose, Feng proclaimed, was to "foster mass criticism," and to meet the educational needs of the island, or at least the parts of the island controlled by the Communists.[23] In January of the following year, Chairman Feng announced plans of the Hainan Interim Democratic Government to establish a military school as well.[24] On the eve of the Communist conquest of Hainan, Feng Baiju and the Hainan Communist leadership launched financial initiatives that were designed to succeed where the Nationalists had spectacularly failed. But telling aspects of the policy revealed that it was first in Feng Baiju that the Hainan revolution was to trust, perhaps vindicating mainland concerns about early strains of local interests trumping the national revolution.

For the most part, the Nationalists' handling of Hainan's financial sector ran parallel to the disastrous policies of the Nationalist mainland regime.²⁵ In late 1949 and early 1950, the Nationalist governor of Hainan, Chen Jitang undertook an effort to consolidate Hainan's banking system. In an attempt to unify and strengthen Nationalist control of the island's economy, Chen tried to summon prominent local bankers under a single "Hainan Cooperative Bank." Chen's gesture came very late, however, and it met with no success. It is easy to dismiss the effort as posturing for the Taiwan central authority, but Chen did not receive the Nationalists' endorsement in this effort. The failure of the Nationalists to support Chen's last-minute effort to shore up the island's apparatuses of governance was not an isolated incident, as became apparent in the military confrontation to come. Chen was given neither the titular endorsement nor the concrete support he needed to realize his efforts to save Hainan for the Nationalists. He received only ambivalent directives from Taiwan.²⁶ Apparently, Chiang Kai-shek felt that such an effort would have overstretched the Taiwan defensive capabilities.

The Hainan Communists had experimented several times with issuing currency in the territories under its control.²⁷ They met with limited success, but it was the issuance of "liberation bonds" (*jiefang gongzhai*) in the winter and spring of 1949–1950 that caught Chen Jitang's attention by strengthening the movement, and led to a final attempt by the popular Nationalist general, Xue Yue, to eradicate the Communist guerrillas on Hainan. In denominations of one *yuan*, 400,000 *yuan* in bonds were printed and issued, with the promise of an annual interest rate of 5 percent. The bonds were issued in exchange for supplies from villagers and other donors, in anticipation of the Communist takeover. According to the Hainan Communist records, by the end of 1951, all of the principal amount, plus interest on the bonds, was paid out in exchange for *renminbi*, the new currency of the People's Republic of China.²⁸

The policy was carried out by the Hainan Column under Feng Baiju, and at the behest of the Southern Branch Party Bureau as preparation for the imminent invasion.²⁹ While Feng had approval for the issuance of these bonds, one noteworthy characteristic in the isolated Hainan example was that the bonds were imprinted with a woodcut image of Chairman Feng Baiju and his signature, along with that of his vice chairman, He Dan.

Prior to the issuance of this Communist currency, the Nationalist currency issued on Hainan bore the image of Sun Yat-sen, not one of the local Hainanese leaders, nor even of Chiang Kai-shek. The infrastructural isolation of Hainan meant that the presses for liberation bonds used by the Communists on the mainland were not imitated or brought to Hainan to be used by the local revolutionaries. The Japanese occupiers of Hainan had also made unsuccessful attempts at implementing a currency policy that would work on Hainan. This and the Nationalist economic failures were the foundation for Feng's monetary policies.

The successful distribution of the Hainan Column's war bonds had broad implications for the transition to Communist rule. Each member of the amphibious force that arrived in mid-April carried three days' rations to sustain them on the march through the jungle to the Communist base areas. When this ran out, the distribution of war bonds allowed the Hainan Column to stock sufficient grain and other supplies in preparation to carry on the campaign with ranks that would be swollen by the arrival of the PLA regulars. Further, the Hainan war bonds allowed for a smooth transition to a centralized banking system. As late as the first week of May 1950, Feng was still managing the financial transition. Rather than wait for an appointment from Beijing or Guangzhou, Feng appointed his Hainan comrade Lin Keze to the task of consolidating the Haikou banks. Lin was trained on the mainland, but his knowledge of the local gold reserves and banks of the Nationalists allowed him to accomplish the task quickly.[30]

Where Chen Jitang had failed in his attempt to unify the banks of Hainan under a single authority, the Communists quickly succeeded. By May 28, 1950, the Hainan Civil and Military Administrative Committee had taken control of the six major banks on Hainan, and by June 9, had consolidated them into the Hainan Branch of the People's Bank of China.[31] Within weeks of the May 1 declaration of Communist victory on Hainan, the major financial apparatuses were solidly under CCP control. The work of the Hainan Column in preparing for the takeover made this an almost seamless transition.

Ma Baishan and Hainan's Tributary Revolution

Ma Baishan recalled the May 1950 celebration at the Five Ministers' Temple as a joyous occasion, with speeches, singing, dancing, and many toasts to the victory that was shared by the Hainan and mainland Communists.[32] As they first assembled in a small field under the walls of the temple, some of the officers and men and women who could not understand each other's dialects communicated by enthusiastically gesturing with their hands, or scratching the Chinese characters that they both understood in the sand.[33] Feng Baiju and Deng Hua entered the banquet together, and the crowd erupted in applause for the two most celebrated heroes of the campaign. There was a stage set up for them, with red flags hanging from each corner, and a banner hung across it that read, "Conference to celebrate Hainan's victorious liberation and joining forces." The outdoor banquet was an occasion for relatively lavish celebration. Though the food was simple, it filled the bellies of the guerrillas for the first time in what seemed like ages. Ma Baishan sat with Feng Baiju and looked on with pride. Ma noted the speeches of both Feng and the Hunan native, Deng Hua, who had landed on the beaches with the forces of the Fourth Field Army.

Just a few months earlier, Ma had seen a far grander celebration. He had traveled to Beijing with the commander of Hainan's Li people, Wang Guoxing. Their mission had been to report and receive orders for the final Hainan campaign.[34] Just as Feng Baiju was the leader of the Communist movement on Hainan, Wang Guoxing was the leader of the Li minority group that made up about 15 percent of the island's population.[35] For centuries of imperial Chinese rule of Hainan, the Li people had been an annoyance to attempts to control the island, at times rising in open rebellion, and consistently obstructing Han Chinese settlement of the island's interior.[36] Beginning in the 1920s, the Nationalists were clumsy and brutal in their attempts to negotiate with the Li people, leading to the latter's further estrangement from their mainland colonizers.

The Japanese were more efficient in suppressing and controlling the Li, beginning with their occupation of Hainan in February of 1939. Japanese enslavement of much of the Li population for mining operations in the central Li regions of the island led to violent and organized uprisings by the Li. Finally, in 1943, after the Japanese forced the Nationalists to seek an inland refuge, they massacred several Li villages, leading to the Li Baisha Uprising against them in July of 1943. This was shortly followed by Wang Guoxing's successful efforts to link the Li forces under his command with Feng Baiju and the Hainan Independent Column.[37] While the Li did not come to their alliance with the Hainanese Independent Column by the path of Communist ideology or even Chinese nationalism, the alliance resulted in the significant strengthening of the Hainan Communist forces. Wang's help was to be indispensable in the survival of the Communist presence on Hainan, for the Li maintained control of many of the nearly inaccessible reaches of the island's southern mountainous and jungle interior.

Wang's trip with Ma Baishan to Beijing in the fall of 1949 was a kind of tribute mission, in the tradition of the missions of imperial China that secured regional alliances and shored up the military, political, and cultural boundaries of China. Ostensibly, Ma was Hainan's representative at the Political Consultative Conference that was to be held there. In the summer of 1949, when Wang and Ma made the trip, much of southern China was still in Nationalist hands, so Ma and the rest of the Hainan delegation to the conference had to travel with fake documents and under assumed names, and separately. The traveling was dangerous and slow, and Ma bought his tickets under the name Li, his cover that of a businessman. He frequently changed trains, boats, and trucks when he thought that it was possible that he had aroused some suspicion. Ma reached the northern city of Qingdao by early September, and was safe within Communist territory. The Hainan delegation regrouped joyously, and in the surreal atmosphere of peace, the band of guerrillas was given two days to see the sights in Jinan.[38] Then they made their way on to Beiping ("Northern Peace"), the city that had long been China's imperial capital, but had been supplanted by the Nationalists' Nanjing ("Southern Capital") regime as capital of the republic. In a few days it would again be named Beijing ("Northern Capital").

On October 1, 1949, Ma was invited to a grand event to be held in the center of the city. Atop the Gate of Heavenly Peace (Tiananmen) Ma Baishan watched as Party Chairman Mao Zedong announced the founding of the Communist People's Republic of China. After meeting with the highest military officials of the new nation, and giving their report, Ma and Wang made their way back south. So fast had the Communist military conquest of the mainland progressed, that Ma did not need to travel under an assumed name with fake documents, moving through newly secured Communist territory. Arriving back in Guangdong, at the February 1950 meeting that established the final plans for the assault, Ma communicated Feng Baiju's assessment of the situation, and counseled against a direct assault on the north. Instead, he advised several pincer movements that would avoid a blunt battle of attrition to take Haikou.

Having observed the weakened state of the Nationalist forces that had retreated there in front of the southern Communist expedition, Ma and Feng realized that a frontal assault would most likely lead to a bloody and protracted battle for the city. This might have revitalized the morale of the Nationalists and turned the civilian population against the Communists.[39]

The examples of Jinmen and Dengbu were still fresh in the memory of all Communist military commanders, and doubtless remembered as a rare and proud victory for Nationalist leaders. While almost all of the news from China's military front in 1948–1949 was favorable to the Communists, the attempts in the fall of 1949 to take Jinmen and Dengbu were tactical blunders. When the Nationalists moved their political and military headquarters to Taiwan, and maintained significant, threatening island holdouts, amphibious warfare took on new urgency for the Communists. The Nationalists maintained massive fortifications on the Zhoushan archipelago, Jinmen, Hainan, and Taiwan. The Communists lacked any credible sea or air military force, though contemporary and historical bluster and propaganda suggested that was not the case, or that Soviet aid might soon change this.

In October of 1949, similar to the Hainan preparations that began three months later, Communist military commanders assembled a flotilla of junks to ferry soldiers across the narrow channel that separated the tiny island of Jinmen from the mainland. The momentum of the land war that had been so favorable to the Communists was drowned in the narrow waters, as communications failed, boats were scattered, and Nationalist fighters and warships obliterated the amphibious force. The Communist forces were repulsed, and Jinmen today is still administered by the Taipei government, in spite of its proximity to the mainland.

The lessons of Jinmen chastened the Communist high command, and far more preparations went into the Hainan campaign. Chairman Mao stated the obvious, as he had a tendency to do in military matters during the final stage of the civil war, when he remarked in a telegram that Hainan was not the same as Jinmen. He noted that the enemy force was relatively weak, and that on Hainan, there was Feng Baiju. While the first statement was self-evident in the fall of 1949, Mao perhaps was wrong when he said this in January of 1950. Hainan forces had been reinforced in the meantime, and the Nationalist General Xue Yue had been assigned to the defense of the island. Xue was universally respected as a tenacious and brilliant tactician, and he wasted no time in attempting to eradicate the Hainan Independent Column.

At the May 5 banquet, Feng Baiju gave one of the two main speeches that drew roars of approval from the assembled audience. Deng Hua gave the other speech. After the campaign, Deng briefly held the top post in the political and military authority on Hainan, with Feng as his second in command. Deng's speech acknowledged the help of the Communist forces, and he credited the local guerrillas with a major role in the victory. "Had it not been for the Hainan Independent Column, the liberation of Hainan would not have been accomplished in the manner that it was."[40] Feng, in turn, said that the Communist conquest of Hainan would have been impossible without the help of the "great army" (*dajun*), that arrived from the mainland.

While the speeches of both Deng and Feng paid compliments to each other's forces and their mutual roles in the Communist takeover of Hainan, there was some tension in apportioning credit. It seemed that there was immediately an awareness of the zero-sum perception of the mainland and local Communist forces. That is, there was only so much glory to go around. For those interested in the political stakes, that glory had to be carefully apportioned to the two clearly distinguished forces of Hainanese and mainlanders.

This reflected a concern with the divergent hopes of the mainland and local interests for Hainan's future. If the Hainan guerrillas gave all credit for the conquest to the mainland forces, or vice versa, the side that laid claim to that glory would be in a position to steer the political future of the island.

While the interests of the local guerrillas and the mainland regulars were different going into the campaign, and continuing in the wake of the victory, the military campaign itself was an unqualified success for both sides. The shared enemy of the Nationalists was the foundation of their cooperation. The Hainan Independent Column had relied heavily on the Li for its survival. Orders from the mainland to abandon the Hainan base had been flouted in 1946, albeit as deferentially as possible, by the Hainan Independent Column.[41] This perhaps reflected a consistent preference on Hainan for representing local interests over those of the mainland revolution, if and when the two diverged.

The banquet of May 5, 1950, was one of the first public moments of interaction between mainland and Hainan Communist leaders following the victory. The speeches represented both past conflict and cooperation between the Hainan and mainland Communists, and future hopes for the island. Feng's references to a "new Hainan" and the hopes for democratic change on the island reflected the interests of the Hainan revolution.

The Communist victory in the Hainan campaign, seen from the perspective of the island guerrillas, was a negotiation and a leap of faith. With victory came the greater Chinese Communist revolution, and naturally Hainan would become a part of the new Beijing regime. But the extent to which Hainan would maintain its leadership and autonomy was not clear. It was not clear that Beijing would endow Hainan island with provincial status, as had been long discussed in certain circles of Chinese politics in the far south. In the victorious ebullience of May 1950, leaders like Feng Baiju considered it to be the wrong moment for taking a stand on this question. Perhaps provincial status would come in time, but still, it was important that the local guerrillas were given their due, and Feng worked immediately to make sure that happened. As it happened, Hainan was not granted provincial status shortly after the Communist takeover. Only in 1988, almost fifteen years after Feng's death, did Hainan become a province, and, according to one Hainan author, finally "history proved that Feng's views and management had been correct."[42]

Feng's political acumen throughout his two decades of revolutionary leadership leaves no room for the possibility that the Hainanese revolutionary leadership was simply naive in its leap of faith into the arms of the Beijing regime. He had expectations for Hainan's treatment in the new PRC regime, most obviously, provincial status for the island. But he was realistic about Hainan's weak position in bargaining with a popular and powerful new Beijing government. The victorious conquest that brought the Communists to power on Hainan was a long fought struggle. The Communist leadership had allowed the Hainan leadership considerable leeway in its improvisational policy-making, and the flush of success perhaps masked the inevitable crackdown that would come with the rise of the Communists to power. Feng certainly realized this, judging from his writings. He often referred to the leadership of the Hainan Communists as being not adequately trained in matters of ideology.

In his speech at the Five Ministers' Temple that came years after his repeated requests for better instructors and cadres to be sent to Hainan from the mainland, he still explicitly referred to the need for the Hainanese revolutionary leadership and its ranks to learn from the correct example of the mainlanders. Like Ma, Feng sought to strengthen ties to the mainland revolution at every opportunity, but this did not necessarily mean sacrificing the experienced leadership—not least, himself—for the sake of political purity or unquestioning obedience to the central Communist authority. This, however, is what happened quickly on Hainan. The first casualty was the history of the Hainan revolution, followed shortly by the weakening of the Hainanese leadership.

Cold War Trophy

The insulated political and military situation on Hainan of the 1930s and 1940s was forever changed with the Communist victory there in the spring of 1950. The island became a prominent story throughout international headlines when the Communist victory meant that half of Nationalist-held territory had fallen into the hands of the Reds. While taking Taiwan presented far more logistical difficulties for the Communists, it was seen as the next step in the conquest. At the Five Ministers' Temple, on the night of May 5, 1950, no rambunctious toasts were offered about the imminent taking of Taiwan. The forces that were preparing for this campaign were hundreds of miles up the Chinese coast, and their preparations to cross a broader expanse with little hope of having sufficient naval support was more than daunting. It seemed it would require a miracle, unless the campaign preparations stretched on for another year.

The United States did not offer direct support for holding Hainan, the way that they would with the Seventh Fleet for Taiwan following the outbreak of the Korean War. At the time of the Hainan campaign, however, there was no promise that sufficient direct U.S. military aid would be forthcoming in the final battle of the civil war that many expected would be fought for Taiwan. While the ideological world of the Cold War had been far from Hainan, it became an immediate factor once the PLA troops landed on the shores of the island.

But even with the strength of the PLA, and the extensive preparations of the local Communist forces, the Beijing regime's posturing suggested insecurity in the volatile and uncertain early years of bluster and dissembling in the Cold War. What this meant on Hainan was that the victory must be swift and absolute. On the global stage, the Hainan campaign had not been a foregone conclusion. Outsiders saw this as a significant test of the young PRC, and its success or failure would be broadcast to the world by reporters in Hong Kong who were close enough to Hainan to bypass the propaganda reports from Beijing.

Feng Baiju and the leadership of the Communist movement had consistently built their revolution on improvisation and sensitivity in Hainan's specific political and cultural environment. They had welcomed all comers to their cause, needing all the support that they could get to strengthen their forces in the face of relentless Japanese and Nationalists attempts to wipe them out. This had allowed the survival of the revolution on Hainan, but on the national level, the transition from revolution to rule meant that there was no longer as much of a need for survival-based policies. The days of guerrilla warfare were over, as much as the propaganda emanating from Beijing and Moscow insisted that the revolution was still alive, and would remain the perpetual life force of the new regime.

Beijing aimed to solidify its holdings, and to appear strong and unified on the global stage. The weakness of the Nationalists was already apparent to the world, and the Cold War rhetoric of China having been lost to the Communists was prevalent, especially in the view of the Americans. The global realm of politics in this period left no room for nuance on the ground. The titans of the Cold War made Hainan nothing more than a pawn in the game, a trophy island. And so Hainan became again the treasure island of China. Its strategic importance now took the place of its natural beauty and its exotic resources as its regional importance, but still the Hainan revolution was not the narrative that emerged from the conquest. In the wake of the success, the Hainanese revolutionaries cast their lot in with the new Beijing regime, and the PRC history of the events became one of revolutionary fishermen volunteering their boats and their skills and knowledge of the region, and ruddy-faced northern peasants braving the dangerous waters of the Qiongzhou Strait to bring the revolution to Hainan.

So the ebullient atmosphere of the celebration was tempered perhaps by several factors. Tibet and Taiwan had not yet been incorporated into the PRC, and both presented the new regime with formidable challenges. Taiwan was much farther from the coast than Hainan, and would require a much more sophisticated naval assault. Tibet was to become another pawn in the Cold War clashes. Meanwhile, nearby Vietnam, and Korea to the north were also flashpoints in the titanic struggle for influence in the region. This was another important difference between the Hainan Communists and the mainland regulars. The interests in the revolutionary struggle were different in their connection to this larger political context.

Battle Lost and Won

Most of the forces of the Fourth Field Army were far from their homes in northeastern China. Many of them had never stepped on a boat, and had only a few weeks of training along the Guangdong coast to prepare. As noted earlier, the high-ranking PLA officer, Han Xianchu, remembered the preparations with a combination of humor and hyperbolic celebration. The constant seasickness of the once landlocked Fourth Field Army amused some of the local fishermen, who ribbed them even as they praised their determination and eagerness to learn. Han's account is full of Communist boilerplate and perhaps for this reason it has become one of the classic narratives about Hainan within the mythology of the Party's rise. But Han seems to have had little regard for the work of the Hainan Column. In reference to the conference in which Ma Baishan instructed the mainland forces on how they should execute their landing operations, Han seems to insert Mao Zedong, standing over maps consulting with Lin Biao. This is confusing because Mao Zedong was in Moscow at the time, and Lin Biao was in Beijing.[43] Ma Baishan does not appear in Han's account, nor is Feng Baiju's name mentioned. Still, Han's account is insightful and valuable for the perspective of a mainland commander arriving on Hainan with the main landing force in the spring of 1950.

The Hainan campaign has taken on mythic proportions both on the island and the mainland. In most official accounts of the campaign, narratives like Han Xianchu's version have come to prevail, recounting a spectacular, even miraculous battle at sea between wooden junks and Nationalist warships. Indeed, even with the lack of vigorous support from Taiwan, the Nationalists were far better equipped for the battle, with twenty-five warplanes, and more than fifty military vessels of various sizes and capacities.[44] Nationalist bombing campaigns went essentially unanswered over the

Communist troops on Guangdong's Leizhou Peninsula, while they were preparing for their assault on Hainan. Only when the Nationalist gun placements had been seized by the Communist forces could they be used against superior Nationalist vessels as well as planes.[45]

The Taiwanese Nationalist headquarters had not favored the task of holding Hainan Island with much aid. Taiwanese papers had accused the Nationalist head of Hainan, Chen Jitang, of harboring his own parochial views, in language that foreshadowed later Communist accusations leveled at Feng Baiju.[46] The same journal that criticized Chen for his localist views also encouraged the Nationalist fighters on Hainan to make "another Jinmen" of this battle and repel the Communist assault.[47] Although high-level pessimism on Taiwan meant that little more materiel would be committed there, some popular optimism remained.

In spite of the wide variance in statistics on military capabilities of both Communist and Nationalist forces, it is clear that the strategic advantage appeared to be with the Nationalists. Most observers agreed that Hainan could be held, but concerns had grown among advisors who had experience with Communist guerrillas. Yan Xishan presented a classified assessment of the situation on Hainan, advising an immediate adoption of policies that built support at the village level.[48] This was the only way the popularity of the Communists could be challenged. The policy answer to Yan Xishan's report was to put a Nationalist national hero in charge of the suppression campaigns on the island. Xue Yue, like Chen Jitang, was a Guangdong native.

Two months before the Communist assault was launched from the mainland, Xue launched a suppression campaign against the Hainan Column and any other resisters to Nationalist rule.[49] February 1950 was devastating to the Hainan Communists, but even after takeover of the island, Xue's reputation as a hero of the resistance precluded any denigration of his character by the Communists. Other Nationalist leaders like Chen Hanguang did not share Xue's credentials, and they became the villains of Hainan's local history, with oral histories remembering him as a ruthless butcher.[50] But even with the heroism or brutality of the various Nationalist leaders, it was indeed the "end of the line," as A. Doak Barnett reported.

Between local militia forces and army regulars there were still as many as 200,000 Nationalist troops on Hainan, and the highest concentration of them was in Haikou, on the northern coast. When Barnett visited Hainan in November of 1949, he reported on the pathetic state of the Nationalist forces in Haikou. Many of them had been fleeing before the Communist lines as the PLA marched more swiftly than they themselves had anticipated from the northeast to the south. The Nationalist forces in Haikou were demoralized and malnourished. They were also poorly armed, for Barnett reports witnessing some of the troops selling their rusted weapons for food or money that was not forthcoming from Taiwan. While the Nationalist central authorities horded munitions and the best-trained troops on Taiwan, Nationalist forces on Hainan languished in bitterness. Many of these troops were ripe for Communist recruitment, and desertion was endemic among those who were healthy enough to make their way to the Communist base areas.[51]

Though the final battle had not been as taxing on the PLA as some had predicted, it was still a great triumph on the international stage. And so the Hainan revolutionaries who had held aloft the red flag for twenty-three years were silenced in a matter of months, drowned out by the rhetoric of a new, unified China. The Korean War and the Taiwan Straits shelling of Jinmen in the 1950s reduced Hainan again to being a backwater of China, and a trophy island won in the final days of the civil war.

At least on the history of the Hainanese revolution, the past two decades have seen a flood of historical analyses and recollection volumes published. It is no longer possible to tell the history of Hainan as an island saved by a "people's flotilla" of volunteer fishermen and seasick PLA regulars. The essential role of the Hainan revolutionaries in the Communist success on the island complicates and enriches this narrative. But once the military campaign was won, a series of complex political issues needed attention. The success of the Hainan Communists, their endurance and their resilience, had often been achieved through improvisation, local resourcefulness, and independent action. With the transition from revolution to rule, assuming the burden of power on the island, the Hainan Communists were in for a jolting entry into the new People's Republic of China.

CHAPTER 8

BRINGING HAINAN TO THE NATION'S HEEL

Anti-localism in the Early PRC

The "Little Hungarian Incident"

In the fall of 1956, a revolution in Hungary broke out that challenged the rule and influence of the Soviet Union. It lasted several months, but Soviet troops finally crushed the movement and by early 1957 a new regime was in place, loyal to Moscow. While the uprising failed, the challenge it presented to the tiers of Communist hierarchy was cause for concern throughout the Communist world. Just as Khrushchev's de-Stalinization process had worried Mao about his own hold on power and his legacy, so, too, did Mao see possible Chinese parallels to incidents like the Hungarian Revolution of 1956. Within the PRC, the specter arose of local uprisings based on regional interest challenging Beijing's centralized rule, just as Hungary had challenged Moscow.

Political scientist Frederick C. Tiewes found in contemporary sources that throughout Guangdong Province (then still including Hainan) fully 80 percent of cadres at the county-level and higher rank were relieved of their duties during and immediately after the land reform campaign (1950–1953).[1] By December of 1956, a relatively small-scale uprising in Lingao County on Hainan island earned the nickname the "Little Hungarian Incident" (*xiao Xiongyali shijian*). Coinciding with the Hungarian movement, timing was obviously a factor in the nickname, but like the movement in Hungary, the Lingao uprising clearly articulated a regional frustration with central directives, and a shift in response, on the part of the central authorities, to increase rather than decrease their administrative penetration. A group made up mostly of disaffected Hainanese veterans had risen against the newly installed Party apparatchiks from the mainland.

For many of these troops, there was no life to which they felt that they could return. They had left their hometowns and fled to a life of guerrilla subsistence, and they had foregone their education and any professional training. A relatively high proportion of the Hainan fighting force was women, and they were expected to return to their homes and start families. This was hard to take, especially considering the self-proclaimed progressive New Democracy and professed gender parity of the Communist regime in Beijing, notably in the Marriage Law of 1950. The fighting women of Hainan protested the order to go from being Communist spies, soldiers, and field doctors one day, to housewives the next. Along with the rest of the demobilized Hainan forces, they watched as Hainan's leadership was also removed from high posts on Hainan and throughout the southern region. These and other factors combined to drive several hundreds of the former Hainan forces to rise against their new mainland political leaders.

Most official records of the incident note only briefly that a small uprising occurred and was quickly put down. Accounts of the incident were published in southern Chinese newspapers at the time, but the most remarkable accounts are found in recollections published in the *Wenshi ziliao* collections of Lingao County.[2] Other sources used here include interviews conducted by the author, recorded speeches of Party leaders, Hainan's provincial gazetteers, and official communications between the provincial and central leaderships during the 1950s.[3]

Casualties are not listed in the open official sources or the oral accounts, but the incident consisted of several hundred demobilized soldiers storming a government compound where local cadres had recently been disciplined and detained. The protests involved some violence, though none of the available sources are specific beyond citing the disruption of communications and the raiding of a jail to free the local cadres. Some sources clarify that there were no fatalities among the Hainanese cadres or the guards. The incident was quickly contained by all accounts. In the weeks that followed, the southbound cadres and their supporters held up the incident as an example of the kind of insidious localism that lurked beneath the surface in regions like Hainan.

The question of motivation, ideology, and the causes of Communist success must be asked repeatedly by successive generations because the Chinese Communist Party has shifted its priorities and perhaps even its reason for being. Sometimes this has been done deftly and brought the CCP great military victories, and at other times, the Party shifted its goals and identity with disastrous consequences. Observed from different levels of society, great successes and catastrophes could overlap. In the case of the early 1950s, as the Communist regime rapidly consolidated its rule, the groundwork was also established for the streamlining of command that would lead to the unchecked famine and social chaos of the two decades to follow. The political climate of the early PRC eschewed frank appraisal of failing policy. The pivot from revolution to rule in 1949–1950 represented a shift for the CCP from besieged insurgents to masters of China.

In the early twenty-first century, the CCP leadership has emphasized its role as standard-bearers of a patriotic and increasingly powerful nation, rather than as international leaders of Marxist revolution. Historically, this means that the nationalist identity of the CCP legacy is currently far more important than remembering class struggle, which has faded into the dubious academic realm of mandatory political-study classes in which students memorize and regurgitate Party boilerplate. In this current moment, the excesses and errors of revolutionary radicalism based on class struggle can perhaps be held at arm's length. An accounting of the events of the Great Leap Forward and its massive resulting famine has been published and banned in China, by a Party member, Yang Jisheng. While Yang's work has been banned in the PRC, he has not been expelled from the Party or publically punished for his groundbreaking scholarship, and his work reaches a wide audience through easily available downloads.[4]

A new generation of rulers in the twenty-first century does not shoulder the heavy mantle of the tragedies of Maoist policy. Indeed it is economic growth within a state-capitalist economy that undergirds the regime's legitimacy. The identity of nonideological modernizers and nation-builders is far more important today than the revolutionary class-struggle identity of radical Communists, some of whom remain, but only in the embattled fringe of the Party, at the time of writing.

The anti-localism campaigns were a convergence of the two perhaps contradictory identities of China in that era of the early PRC: patriotic nation-building on the one hand, and class struggle on the other. While this might be reconciled with a tidy label of "socialism within one country," the implications and implementation of this paradoxical confluence could potentially cause conflict and confusion among China's political players. The anti-localism campaigns were, on the one hand, a part of a larger project of nationalism and nation-building, for they sought to bring to heel those regional leaders and interests that threatened to spread power too thinly, and dilute the potency of Beijing's command over China. On the other hand, the anti-localism campaigns were part of a radical ideological program, which aimed to implement a zealous policy of class struggle that could shatter the residual networks and associations of traditional society and build a truly new culture in its place. So in the anti-localist campaigns, as well as in the "localist" or local movements that the campaigns opposed, ideologies of nationalism and communism were braided together inextricably as motivating factors. Contradictions abound in this type of conflict, as do constant incremental adjustments that can move the goalposts and puzzle the uninitiated observer.

One could use Marxist doctrine to defend both sides. Hainan's preeminent Communist leader, and a main target of the anti-localism campaigns, Feng Baiju, articulated this complexity when he remarked that in his reading of *Das Kapital* he had never come across anything about relying on the material welfare and greater wisdom of a "minority segment" of the population—in this case, Feng was referring to the anti-localist dictates to forgo perceived priorities of local peasants in order to rely on the southbound cadres and the mainland soldiers for ideological direction.[5] His bold statement was made retroactively in 1962, in defense of Feng's decisions and those of some of his Hainanese comrades in resisting some of the centralizing policies of the 1950s. There had been a brief period in the early 1950s during which the local Hainanese leadership was needed, and was therefore not immediately in conflict with the mainland cadres and soldiers. The early days following the military conquest saw a smooth transition, as Feng Baiju was left in power as the favorite son of the island. The work of accepting the surrender of bedraggled Nationalist soldiers and completing the takeover of power was done relatively smoothly, thanks to both the guerrilla and militia presence on the island, and thanks also to the initial reluctance to replace local cadres and demobilize the local fighting forces.

Following the successful Communist conquest of Hainan, and the end of the violence, came celebration for those who counted this as their victory. The guerrilla forces, along with their civilian support base, hosted the newly arrived "main army" (*da jun*) from the mainland. There were feasts for officers and joyful greetings between guerrillas and regular soldiers on the beaches and throughout the villages and cities of Hainan. But the celebration would be short-lived, and the relationship between the local Communists of Hainan and the "southbound cadres" of the mainland would be fractured within a few short years. On the national level, the beginning of the Korean War in June of 1950 heaped more doubt on the already unlikely Taiwan conquest, and the fervent momentum of the civil war turned to Korea and domestic campaigns of political consolidation.

In celebrations of the Hainan conquest in the spring of 1950, cries were raised to follow Chiang Kai-shek to Taiwan and finish him off. To the west, the conquest of Tibet was another major preoccupation, also with an international dimension that could complicate early ambitions of the People's Republic of China (PRC). And so, the Hainan conquest, within a matter of weeks, slipped into the new normalcy of the PRC's consolidation, making the pivot from revolution to rule on Hainan a very sharp turn. There was no period for acclimation, but rather an expectation from the mainland authorities that the nation-building project on Hainan would hit the ground running, and join the flow of national campaigns that had already been underway for months or even years in other regions of Communist territory.

The distance and communication difficulties during the revolutionary period had given the Hainan leadership some degree of de facto autonomy, but with the May 1950 incorporation of Hainan into the Communist regime, and the island's incorporation into the province of Guangdong, Hainan would be brought to the heel of the national government, and quickly. In official documents, there are no references to the mistakes of disobedience, improvisation, or moderation on the part of the Hainan leadership in the wartime period, but this was doubtless a factor in the early implementation of policy on the island.

The specter of "localism" (*difang zhuyi*) was raised early in PRC rule of the island, referring to any leadership that favored Hainan local interests over national priorities. Mainland cadres might perceive localism in the form of moderation of central policies, most importantly land reform and redistribution, blunted by local cadres for the sake of softening the impact of an otherwise harsh campaign. Localism could be nepotism more broadly defined; it could be any form of local heroism that transcended orthodox allowances; indeed it was such a catchall label that it could include anything at all that might detract from a commitment to the national revolutionary regime in favor of a local entity. In his study of the subject, Xiaorong Han develops the important difference between "localization" (*difanghua*), which was encouraged in Communist organization, and localism (*difang zhuyi*), which was not. They can be seen as two sides of the same coin in terms of engaging with the local population during revolutionary struggle. Whereas localization is a positive and productive way of engaging with a local population through familiarization with local customs and priorities, if carried into excessive advocacy or prioritization of local interests, similar activity could lead to localism. As Han points out, there is considerable room for interpretation here, especially amid the chaotic and rapid changes of warfare and regime change. For this reason, the pejorative label of "localist" could be used for political convenience and expedience during factional struggles and political wrangling.[6] It is crucial to note that the perception and misperception of motives diverged greatly between Hainan revolutionaries and their mainland counterparts. While moderate policy implementation on Hainan was carried out by cadres who believed that they were extremely patriotic and loyal to the Party, the same moderation was seen by mainland critics as insidious graft, favoritism, and possibly even separatist sentiment on the part of the Hainanese, in an effort to ensconce their favored leadership in a new Hainan kingdom.

Feng Baiju continued to represent and work for Hainanese interests in this period, and for nearly a year after the Communist conquest he was fully supported by the central leadership. He was not, however, the supreme commander of Hainan, since Deng Hua took that position when he crossed the Qiongzhou Strait with the main army forces. Then, in early 1951, as the land reform campaign on Hainan began in earnest, the perception of an unacceptably slow pace of reform on Hainan led to an influx of outside cadres, also known as the "southbound cadres" (*nanxia ganbu*), whose main charge was to overcome the local obstacles to speedy implementation of land reform policy and power centralization.[7] As land reform accelerated, perceived local resistance continued in various forms.

Questions surrounding personnel were also prominent in disagreements between mainland and Hainan officials in the early PRC. While many of the Hainanese revolutionaries felt that they were most knowledgeable of local conditions, and therefore best qualified to lead in the transition from revolution to rule, mainlanders raised the perennial concerns in Chinese governance (as perhaps in governance anywhere) of nepotism and favoritism. Safeguards like the "law of avoidance" in imperial China, by which an official cannot serve in his own home county or home province, had been diligently implemented even in the final Qing dynasty. The system was by no means perfect in curbing corruption, but it was a long-standing institutional way of aiming to limit local favoritism at the expense of central priorities or loyalties.[8]

The perception of localism and resistance to this acceleration is worth examining. From the perspective of Beijing and Wuhan (the national capital and the headquarters of the Communist southern bureau respectively), the southern regions like Guangdong, and especially Hainan, were resisting the implementation of radical land reform policies out of an alleged desire to create "independent kingdoms." This concern had direct precedents in the southern political and military leaders like Chen Jitang, Bai Zhongxi, Li Zongren, and others who threatened to break away from the earlier regimes of Chiang Kai-shek.

The voices coming out of Hainan in this period express frustration, and ultimately despair, with the failure of Hainanese attempts to moderate and soften the centralization that came with the land reform campaign and military demobilization. Later, Feng Baiju blamed the newly arrived leadership in Guangdong, including Ou Mengjue, Zhao Ziyang, and Tao Zhu for the harsh policies that led to the uprooting of local cadres and the local leadership at the highest levels, including himself. These three high-level officials arrived in Hainan, according to Feng, with an air of superiority and even a sense of their own infallibility. Like the flood of southbound cadres who arrived on the island to implement land reform and radicalize local politics, Feng believed that these three leaders had valued their own personal authority over true national solidarity. This had created a rift that seemed impossible to bridge, and led to a conflict between the local and mainland leadership.[9]

In the early 1950s, however, this type of resistance to newly arrived cadres was difficult to express safely. This resistance manifested itself in different ways, and it was interpreted in different ways by the Hainan and mainland leadership. In some instances, what was perceived as resistance was in fact something else, like obedience to outdated directives or simply abject despair and exhaustion. Indeed, Feng and others later referred to the 1920s and 1930s leadership of Mao and Zhu De in Jinggangshan and Yan'an, asserting that their reliance on local conditions for survival was similar. Feng Baiju reflected on the political consciousness of the Hainan leadership in an article in *Xin Hainan bao* [New Hainan Journal] published on May 8, 1950, referring to those political workers and guerrillas under his command in the twenty-three-year Communist struggle (1926–1950).

> The revolutionary struggle on Hainan has a history of over twenty years, and in that time there have been Communist Party, military, civilian government, and other types of people's organizations. The struggle has been a trial and a tempering for the people. But this is not enough. If the main army did not come to Hainan, liberation would have been impossible. . . . If the main army had not come, we might still be in Wuzhishan. . . . We have many difficult challenges before us, but we can overcome them all. Most important is still our understanding of ideological problems. It is incorrect to try to implement guerrilla work methods in our new environment. Comrades! We have persevered for over twenty years in our struggle on this isolated island, not receiving the direct help of outside revolutionary strength and cooperation. Today is a great opportunity. Not only do we have outside revolutionary strength of help and cooperation, but we

also have an opportunity to study. We must make the most of this time, grasp this opportunity, and study from the main army in order to transform, strengthen, and enrich ourselves.[10]

In this article, as in other speeches and writings, Feng readily acknowledges the need of Hainan Communist workers to study and learn new methods from the main army and the newly arrived cadres. But he also reminds the reader of the revolution's self-reliance and resourceful survival for twenty-three years. Feng would eventually be accused of favoring local cadres over those same newly arrived cadres that he praised in the above quote.[11] He even would be accused of supporting a military insurrection against the mainland political and military operatives who arrived in Hainan in the early 1950s. Those who called him a localist claimed also that he had spread the idea that the Communists of Hainan could have taken over the island without the help of the mainland force.[12] There is no evidence to support these accusations, and they seem to contradict the sentiments Feng expressed in this article published in the early days of Communist rule on Hainan.

Feng's warm rhetoric toward the southbound cadres in the spring of 1950 would be challenged a year later, however, when a much larger contingent of mainland cadres arrived to accelerate land reform. In this context, many local Communist cadres on Hainan began to push back against the increasing loss of autonomy in making local policy as well as military and political staffing.[13] Resistance in this time is difficult to track however, because friendly rhetoric such as Feng's article cited earlier continued through the era. While the focus of this chapter is the early 1950s and the first stage of the localist activities on Hainan, some of the best insights came from events, speeches, and writings from several years later. The "Little Hungarian Incident" in late 1956 reflects the intense frustration of demobilized local military leaders and the soldiers under their command; a recorded speech by Feng in the political calm of 1962 is a frank counterattack, the tenor of which was not possible (or not recorded) in 1952; the official posthumous rehabilitation of Feng in 1983 and Hainan's 1988 provincial status perhaps represents the vindication of the Hainan localists. These all shed light on the early 1950s.

The previous chapters have established the tension between the mainland and Hainan Communist leadership. Within the first three years of Communist rule on Hainan, this conflict was firmly resolved in favor of the mainland command. While Hainan had traditionally been a destination of exiled officials, Feng Baiju was exiled in reverse, sent off the island first to a post in Guangzhou and then in Zhejiang, in 1953 and 1957, respectively. These two changes for Feng were technically promotions within the Party, but their main purpose was to uproot the Hainan leader from his home island, transplanting him into an environment where he could do little of what outsiders perceived to be localist harm, and indeed little of anything because he could not understand the Zhejiang dialect.[14] Perhaps the most indicative of local frustrations with new mainland controls on Hainan came with the series of uprisings in the winter of 1956–1957. This was the culmination of the troubled relationship between local and newly arrived cadres, and a brief examination of this incident will serve to introduce the tensions that pervaded Hainan in the early 1950s.

From Revolution to Rule on Hainan

After the success of the Communist takeover in the spring of 1950, there was a brief celebratory phase in which local leaders were praised and rewarded with high posts in the political and military infrastructures of Communist Hainan. For their part, the Li people, so crucial to the survival of the Communist movement on Hainan in the 1940s, were among the first of fifty-five ethnic minority groups to be officially recognized by the People's Republic of China (PRC), and thus granted special rights and territories under the new national government. As early as June of 1950, the four counties of Baoting, Ledong, Qiongzhong, and Baisha were incorporated in an autonomous district to be governed by the Li and Miao people.[15]

This brief period of relative harmony between local Communist leaders and the new regime continued a long period of localization (*difanghua*), by which regional organizers had been encouraged and supported to embed themselves within local societies. In 1943, this policy had saved the Hainan Communist movement in its alliance with the Li people. But even in the earliest days of Communist rule on Hainan, even while the official celebrations continued, there was tension between the local Communist leaders and those who were newly arrived, in spite of official rhetoric and ceremonial feasts. After a few months, early tensions had escalated into clear political divisions, accusations of corruption and nepotism on the one hand, and what we could loosely call carpetbagging on the other. By 1952, official anti-localism campaigns had begun, and by 1957 they would reach the climax that connected them to the antirightist movement that traumatized and alienated many of the political leaders and intellectuals of the PRC.

In August of 1950, three months after the Communist victory on Hainan, Feng Baiju was invited to Beijing to meet with Mao Zedong for the first time. He ultimately made the trip in November with his secretary, and with Ye Jianying, one of the most prominent military leaders in the Communist revolution. Although Ye had not made Guangdong the base of his revolutionary activities, after the military victory was complete there, he was brought in as the top provincial authority, based in part on his ties to the region. Prior to his trip to Beijing, Feng had met with Ye, Zhou Enlai, and other prominent national leaders, and he had communicated directly with Mao through central commands and responses. On his train ride from the south, Feng turned over in his mind what he would discuss with Mao. The possibility of immediate provincial status for Hainan was a major issue that Feng considered raising in his audience with Mao.[16] The hierarchy of command at the time meant that Hainan had to report to Guangdong provincial leaders, and then to the Southern Party Bureau, and finally to Beijing. Feng would be the obvious candidate for provincial leadership and immediately a player on the national scene if Hainan should be elevated to provincial status.

En route to Beijing, Feng stopped in Wuhan for several days, and there he met with Deng Xiaoping and Deng Zihui, two more high-ranking politicians. While Feng waited to continue his trip north, the two Dengs visited him frequently and the three became well acquainted. Feng later remembered them joking that they were worried he would be lonely in a new city, so they came to his room often to play chess. By the time Feng arrived in Beijing, he must have begun to feel like something of a national celebrity. Immediately upon arrival, a steady stream of notable guests came to his hotel room, along with a package from the Party's Central office containing five million *renminbi*.[17] Three times, Feng sent this back to the office, until finally a personal explanation from Mao accompanied the money, clarifying that this was Feng's "pocket money." Feng then accepted and turned over the funds to his secretary.

Feng met with the Party Vice Chairman Liu Shaoqi and Premier Zhou Enlai, giving them a full report of the Communist movement on Hainan, its history, its current progress, and ideas for its future. Feng also emphasized the ongoing challenges on Hainan, and explained that significant help was needed from the central government. Both Liu and Zhou encouraged Feng to formally submit this report and ask for the funds. He did so, requesting 600 million *renminbi* in economic aid. The request was quickly granted and Feng formally thanked the government on behalf of the three million people of Hainan. In a meeting with Zhu De, commander of the People's Liberation Army (PLA), Feng explained the communication difficulties that had cut off Hainan from the mainland Communist movement. Zhu immediately ordered forty wireless radio devices to be sent back to Hainan with Feng. Perhaps Feng was beginning to feel that he had *carte blanche* in the capital.

Still, ultimately, Feng did not argue forcefully for provincial status for Hainan, and instead he gave an essential report of progress on Hainan island, awaiting Mao's instructions. Mao, for his part, did not take this opportunity to chasten Feng for disobeying central orders when, especially in 1946, the Hainan leadership did not follow explicit central directives to leave Hainan and join forces elsewhere. Neither is there any record that Mao had any critical words for the implementation on Hainan of a relatively moderate land reform policy that made the campaign far slower there than anywhere else in China. Instead, Mao instructed Feng to return to his command on Hainan and to focus on two main areas moving forward: military training and land reform. With the Korean War underway, and expanding Chinese involvement, national defense was a priority in Beijing. Also, Beijing was concerned with real Nationalist and American espionage designs on Hainan that required immediate attention. As for land reform, the relatively moderate policies of Hainan and the island's late inclusion into Communist administered territory meant that there was much work to be done in order to bring economic policy up to speed.[18]

While in Beijing, Feng became ill due to complications related to severe intestinal ailments. Upon Zhou Enlai's insistence, Feng reluctantly postponed his return to Hainan and convalesced in a Beijing hospital. From his "pocket money," to meeting with many of the most prominent figures of the national revolution, and finally to his treatment in a modern Beijing hospital, Feng was a long way from his life as a hard-scrabble guerrilla commander on Hainan. After an operation and ten days in the hospital, the forty-eight-year-old Feng left Beijing in his best health in years. While Feng had only met with Mao briefly, Zhou visited him frequently in the hospital, and before Feng's departure, Zhou reminded him of Mao's final instructions, to focus on both land reform and military training. Feng returned via Guangzhou (Canton) where he received a hero's welcome, and he announced these two priorities of the new regime, doing the same when he returned to Hainan. With him came the promise of 600 million *renminbi* in aid from the central government.

It was during this first year following the Communist victory that Feng Baiju wrote his own account of the Communist movement on Hainan, *Zhongguo gongchandang de guanghui zhaoyao zai Hainan dao shang* (The radiance of the Chinese Communist Party shines on Hainan island).[19] Feng's account marked the thirtieth year of the CCP's existence: "The organization and victory of the Hainan Party is inseparable from the CCP's national victory; it is a very small part of the heroic thirty-year struggle and our Party's great victory."[20]

Feng emphasized the way in which the Hainan movement had relied on the masses, the people of Hainan, as the foundation of its success. This may seem a boilerplate platitude, and perhaps in 1950–1951 it was; but in the coming months, the gap would grow between "relying on the people of Hainan," and "relying on the Southbound cadres (*nanxia ganbu*)," sent by mainland authorities to dictate policy on the island. But for the moment, at least, as Feng made his debut on the national stage and Hainan was embraced by the new regime, it seemed that a honeymoon period would mark the beginning of the new Beijing's relationship with Hainan. Feng's account of the "CCP's radiance" shining on Hainan was, in 1950–1951, no more than a paean to Beijing and the success of the new regime. This same text, however, would take on new meaning in the months and years to come, and it is worth revisiting in an examination of the troubled 1950s on Hainan.

The souring of relations between the Hainan leadership and the mainland Party authorities in Wuhan and Beijing, paralleled in large part throughout Guangdong Province, can be divided into issues related to land reform and civil-military leadership and ideology, those same two crucial issues that Mao and the Party leadership had emphasized to Feng. In both of these areas, relations began very smoothly as reflected in Feng's trip to Beijing and the celebration of the Hainan conquest both in Haikou and Beijing. Land reform began with a period of moderation that quickly shifted into a radical phase that ultimately cleared out the ranks of local leaders in favor of newly arrived cadres from the north. As for the civil-military leadership and ideology, the celebration of the conquest began with praise for the heroics of the Hainan guerrillas, but it then shifted toward a narrative of the main army in wooden junks and fishing boats—a people's flotilla taking on the warships and beach defenses of the Nationalists. This directly reflected the priorities of the people's struggle and national unity as the PRC entered the Korean War.

Land Reform, from Cultivation to Uprooting

Land reform was undoubtedly one of the most important pillars of CCP policy during the civil war and into the early period of Communist rule. It underpinned much of the CCP's support in their territories, from the days of Jinggangshan in the late 1920s, to Yan'an and behind Japanese lines in the late 1930s, and throughout much of northern China in the 1940s. Ever since the split with the Nationalists in 1927 and the shift from an urban to a rural revolution, the CCP either drove or unleashed rural class warfare, calibrating the violence and scale according to their needs. Certain periods saw relatively moderate reforms and rent reductions, while in other periods the CCP implemented violent struggles and radical economic leveling in the countryside. One generalization about land policy leading up to the Communist victory in 1949–1950 was quite self-evident, namely that areas under secure and unrivaled Communist control saw a more systematic and permanent policy of land reform. Those areas that were disputed, either by the Japanese, the Nationalists, or other groups, naturally did not experience as radical or systematic a policy of land reform.

Hainan was one such disputed territory all the way through the Communist takeover in the spring of 1950. This was why, when Mao met with Feng in late 1950, he told Feng to make land reform a top priority in the early work of the new regime. It was not the first time that Feng had received such instructions from the central Party leadership. In 1947, Feng had received a similar directive to "vigorously develop the revolutionary land movement" across Hainan, but this ambitious rhetoric reflected the reality of the increasingly solid hold the Communists had on northern China, not Hainan. While Feng and the Hainan leadership attempted to implement land reform policies in the late 1940s as in earlier periods, the lack of solid administrative control over much of the island made this impossible.[21] The Communists of Hainan had held certain territories with relative impunity, especially following their alliance with the Li and the shift of the movement's locus to the southern mountain bases of Wuzhishan in 1943–1944. In the relative safety of this territory, economic policy could be enforced, but the lack of large landlords in the region, and the need for cooperation from powerful Li leaders, prevented them from implementing any significant policies that radically transformed the social fabric of the Li territories or the rest of Hainan.

Rather, the Hainan Communist fighters made a priority of base-building and disseminating a progressive political ideology that favored sexual equality, broad political participation, universal education, and indeed some degree of economic justice.[22] Some of the Hainanese Communist leaders were familiar with the policies of land redistribution and rent reduction as they were being implemented in more securely held Communist territories in the north. But even by 1950, there was no precedent for the kind of far-reaching successful implementation of these policies on Hainan.

In 1950, the mainland soldiers and cadres arrived to find a fighting force that knew the local terrain and had many local allies. The military conquest and the early transition to Communist rule was facilitated by these local connections, and by the popularity of local leaders, most importantly, Feng Baiju. Among the Li people, Wang Guoxing's unrivaled leadership and his alliance with Feng and the CCP brought in that significant group and bolstered the local credibility of the Party. Feng, Wang, and Ma Baishan all traveled north to Beijing as a way of confirming their loyalties following the success of the Communist conquest.

But it quickly became apparent to the newly arrived cadres and administrators that implementing land reform and class struggle would have to be undertaken almost from scratch. Conditions were very different from northern China, but the initial urban takeover of Guangzhou was a success story in early Communist policy. Fueled by early signs of success in Guangzhou, thousands of young cadres, mostly from northern China of intellectual backgrounds and unfamiliar with southern rural society, spread throughout Guangdong including Hainan. Their initial task was to implement a relatively moderate land reform policy that had been announced in the weeks following the takeover of Hainan.[23]

The initially smooth transition in both political leadership and economic policy can be attributed to several factors. The newly arrived cadres respected the popularity of local leaders and left them in positions of power. Land holdings of overseas Cantonese and Hainanese were not immediately seized, and owing to Hainan's strong connections to commerce throughout the region and the world, but especially in Southeast Asia, this meant that a relatively large portion of Hainan's landowners were abroad. Also, and owing in part to this previous fact, a relatively small percentage of the local population on Hainan was categorized as landlords who deserved punishment and confiscation of their land.

Further contributing to the initial sense of mutual goodwill between natives and newcomers, early land reform development brought with it experts in agricultural development who taught Hainanese farmers how to change their methods and even their crops in order to make better use of their land. The scale of this operation was unprecedented in the economic relationship between Hainan and the mainland, and plans for increasing rubber tree cultivation were realized as soon as March of 1951, when nearly 6,000 hectares of undeveloped land were planted with rubber trees.[24]

Less than a decade later, even while much of the country's agricultural sector hurtled toward disaster in the late 1950s, the improved development of tropical agriculture in Hainan, such as rubber and coconuts, earned the national spotlight in propaganda publications. Improved development methods along with local suitability proved these early policies to have been a success for Hainan.²⁵ A central government loan along with early harmonious leadership between Hainan and the central Party had laid the foundations for success in the early rubber development. A typical rubber tree must grow for between five and six years before it can first be tapped, hence the success story of Hainan's rubber industry came during the late 1950s.

With the successful launching of improved rubber farming in March of 1951, Feng Baiju announced that expectations would be surpassed, and that the first phase of land reform would be complete before the end of that year. This vitality and enthusiasm spurred much of the early work, as thousands of Hainan revolutionary cadres were employed by the effort. The ebullience of this period, however, stands in stark contrast to the revolutionary land reform that took place during wartime throughout northern China. The military success was celebrated across Hainan, and it became increasingly difficult to discern who among the population were in fact deserving of having their land confiscated, either for political crimes or excessive wealth. From the perspective of mainland cadres, local Hainanese cadres went about land reform, especially the task of confiscation and punishment, with insufficient urgency and zeal. This was the basis of what later would be labeled "peaceful land reform," a crime of the highest order in a time of violent revolutionary class struggle.²⁶

In an era of modernization and class struggle, the charge of "peaceful land reform" was a crime that was both premodern ("feudal" in the imprecise jargon of the time), and counterrevolutionary. The lineage and village ties that connected communities of Hainanese were targeted by mainland cadres newly arrived on Hainan, for they were the "feudal" remnants of an earlier society. More importantly, these ties stood in the way of the kind of radical national policies that would have to carry the day in order for the new regime to collect enough revenue to prosper and to fight the United States on the Korean peninsula. Both nationalism and class struggle were brought to bear as rhetorical and political tools to break down local ties. These ties of local identity and loyalty that were under attack included the family, clan, and village, but by 1952, even island-wide ties of Hainanese identity would become the focus of a larger campaign of anti-localism.

In early 1951, the official land reform campaign began in earnest on Hainan. In official documents from this period, the special conditions on Hainan island were already an issue that preoccupied both Hainanese and central Party planners. In February, Feng Baiju and the Hainan leadership repeated the orders from Beijing to focus on military training and land reform. While military training seemed to be less of a contentious issue, a February 13, 1951, circular issued by the Hainan authorities, declared the launching of the land reform movement on Hainan. Considering the conflicts between local and central leadership that would later develop, the confidence of the local leadership in the February circular is remarkable. The authors declare that although they have recently received a central directive ordering them to speed up the land reform campaign on Hainan, they would be able to complete land reform in two years, completing a third of the campaign's planned land redistribution campaigns by the end of 1951, and the rest of the island by the end of 1952. The authors, presumably Feng Baiju and Deng Hua, immediately note the extensive revolutionary experience of the local Hainanese Communist cadres, emphasizing both their competence and their popularity, which will serve them well in the coming campaign: "After over twenty years of revolutionary struggle, the political consciousness of the masses is rather high. Political organizational work of the Party is very widespread, and land reform has begun in a number of places giving us experience."[27]

In March of 1951, the official tone in Hainan documents was still one of restraint and moderate land reform. Nearly every specific note in one relatively thorough list of provisions about land reform on Hainan emphasizes moderation. A list of potential target groups are listed as not being the immediate or pressing targets for confiscation of their land, including wealthy tenant-peasants (*dianfunong*), Li and Miao villagers in Hainan's mountains, absentee landlords, and counterrevolutionaries who have already been punished. The absentee landlords mentioned were those who were not present or could not be found, and included those who lived in the towns and cities of Hainan or the mainland, and also those who lived abroad, mainly in Southeast Asia. The list of provisions notes that it is not necessary to confiscate the landholdings of these and other groups. Even "traitors" (*Hanjian*), those who had collaborated in some way with the Japanese occupiers (1939–1945), were given special mention in this March 1951 document. While traitors could generally be punished in keeping with usual national policy, this document notes that there will be "special circumstances." These special circumstances are not clearly defined, but it seems likely that those circumstances are "special" in cases where the possible punishment of an individual would significantly disturb the local peace. In this brief stipulation, the document advises any cadre adjudicating such a case should rely on two factors: first, "the opinion of the masses" and second, the cadre's own understanding of the situation.[28]

Overall, the deference to local conditions and the judgment of cadres on the ground is striking in this March 1951 document. Feng Baiju was then serving as vice-chairman of Hainan's civil-military committee. The chairman, Deng Hua, was not Hainanese, but had commanded the main Communist army's assault on Hainan a year earlier, and the two worked together closely in this year following the conquest. While some of their policies reflected moderation compared to what was to follow, there were areas of strictness in their policies. These included confronting the real threats of espionage and sabotage from Nationalist remnants, and also the continuation of flagrantly exploitative behavior by landlords. In a document they issued several days after the above March 1951 proclamation, they stipulated that the hasty selling or giving away of land and property by landlords was forbidden. This was done to avoid the adjudication of Party cadres who were on their way to officially parcel out land. The assumption was that a landlord could divide up his land among friendly locals and naturally benefit from these favors, rather than facing the harsher arbitration and redistribution of his land by Communist officials. Also noted in the document was the duty of every Hainanese to report any kind of sabotage or espionage. "It is not permitted to connive and cover for saboteurs. Those harboring violators will be brought to justice."[29]

In this early period on Hainan, it was pragmatism and not ideological purity that made a priority of dealing with sabotage and the illegal preemptive sale of large plots of land and significant amounts of property. On the Guangdong mainland, harsher land reform policies were already being implemented, but it seems these were delayed on Hainan.[30] This variation may be explained by the experimental nature of these early policies. Indeed a circular (*tongzhi*) announcement made regarding Hainan's land reform policies refers to problems with the "land reform experiment" (*tugai shidian*) on Hainan.[31] But while Deng Hua and Feng Baiju continued to issue quite moderate reports and announcements that emphasized stability and consideration of the "opinion of the masses" over radical policy, on the neighboring mainland, and within the same province, a shift was underway. In the case of Hainan, it seems that the "opinion of the masses" could indeed be contrasted with aspects of radical land reform policy, which engages the question of whether the Chinese Communist Party, in its early years, was effectively unleashing the pent-up fury of the masses or stirring up class struggle that might not have been as potent a dormant force as is still sometimes assumed by historians. Ultimately, the example of Hainan showed that from one region to the next, local realities and local "masses" had different ideas about the appropriate degree of radical reform to be implemented.

By April of 1951, a critical mass of northern cadres had arrived in Guangdong and on Hainan so that their presence gradually came to dominate the local cadres, and soon the tone of the land reform movement began to shift. In that month, Fang Fang, a hugely popular local Guangdong revolutionary, made a public self-criticism in which he confessed to having put too much emphasis on orderly transition and peaceful land reform.[32] By mid-April, a circular on land reform and class designations showed early signs of conflict. Work teams had become aware of some individuals hiding land (*mantian*) in order to avoid assignment to a higher class, and naturally to avoid having the land confiscated and redistributed. This problem was a common one, and the work teams and cadres implementing land reform on Hainan were ordered to pay more attention to this type of deceit.[33]

This circular ends by acknowledging a phenomenon that would cause some concern in the coming months and years: local "tyrants" (*eba*) were committing suicide in great enough numbers that it was noticed as a trend, and that the work teams and cadres should compile statistics and rosters of these suicides. Over the coming months, suicides of those targeted by land reform policies, usually referred to as local "tyrants," became a frequent topic in the circulars and directives regarding the calibration of land reform. Studies of suicide in China, as in any other society, usually do not employ "single-cause models," which fail to convey the complex fabric of social and individual factors that might lead to suicide.[34] Still, the cause of the suicides mentioned in the directives and circulars of the Hainan land reform movement seem to share some aspect of the trauma of that movement as their common cause. In fact, while the writers of these documents insist on using the term "suicide" (*zisha*), most of the deaths referred to result from being driven to such an act through coercion, threats, and only then, resulting desperation.

And yet, a citizen of the nation committing suicide as opposed to subjecting himself or herself to the laws of that government is certainly problematic. When it occurs on the scale that it gains the attention of the government, it is more likely that the epidemic is due to a clumsily or brutally enforced policy, rather than simply being due to the wickedness of certain class elements. Suicide was generally considered by authorities to be an admission of guilt, if it came in the case of a persecuted official or landlord. In either case of political suicide, either as protest or admission of guilt, it represents the most absolute impasse between the ruler and the powerless ruled. Whether an inward revolution or a shameful confession, political suicide is the final claim and perhaps the only vestige of individual power.

In Yang Kuisong's 2008 study of the campaign to suppress counter-revolutionaries (*zhenya fan'geming*), the author examines the ways in which a revolutionary regime must continue its violent ways beyond the transition from revolution to rule. Yang explains the use of "executions by quota" in this campaign of the early 1950s, in which a "contest among officials of different places to execute large numbers of people was propelled by these officials' eagerness to prove themselves to higher levels by filling and overfilling quotas."³⁵ Some officials stood against this policy in the early years of the campaign, at the local, provincial, and even at the national levels. Yang quotes a report on the campaign by Ye Jianying from May of 1951, almost at exactly the same time as the beginning of the reports noted above by local land reform work teams on the increasing incidence of suicides and violent deaths. Ye wrote that many of the executions carried out in Guangdong and Guangxi were not even based on the slightest bit of information about the accused. Victims were killed without knowledge of their age or family background, let alone any clear charges of any crime. According to Ye, only a single character—*huai* (wicked)—was enough of a criminal dossier to lead to one's execution.³⁶ Ye's outspoken criticism of the implementation of this campaign at the local level, which employed the very quotas that Mao himself had determined, would soon lead to Ye's own removal from authority in his native southern China.

Besides Ye's report quoted by Yang, Ye also remarked that the best results in the land reform campaign in Guangdong were found in those areas that had been old guerrilla bases, which is relevant to our story. This observation was taken by the central authorities as evidence of Ye's "localist" tendencies—favoring the work of local cadres in the guerrilla bases to the work of newly arrived southbound cadres—and in the later anti-localism campaign, Ye would be "promoted" to a post in Beijing and away from the possibility of affecting policy in his native Guangdong.³⁷

While considering the many campaigns and factors that overlapped in this period, it is difficult and indeed inadvisable to connect suicides and violent deaths to a single cause. It is noteworthy that in the Hainan case, many of the references to a troubling number of suicides, especially among wealthier peasants and landlords, and the actions that should be taken in response, are noted in directives and circulars relating to the land reform movement. It is clear from these directives and from the later urgency in the anti-localist crackdown in Guangdong and Hainan, that the land reform movement was certainly a traumatic period in Hainan's relationship with the mainland.

By February of 1952, increasing incidence of suicide drew the attention of the South China Bureau of the Party leadership, as well as the attention of Party central in Beijing. Party authorities in Guangdong (including Hainan), Hunan, Henan, and other provinces were reporting an increase in suicide, which included not only the "local tyrants," but also middle and lower peasants. Directives and circulars that were issued in this time outlined different ways of dealing with suicide or attempted suicide pertaining to different class elements as well as those peasants who had been tainted by some counterrevolutionary activity as opposed to those who had not.[38] Each suicide case was to be dealt with according to class, family background, and/or revolutionary history.

By the spring of 1952, it was clear that the local cadres had become one of the most important obstacles to the implementation of centrally dictated land reform. The main line of accusation was that these cadres were "rightists," and that their methods were too moderate for the planned land reform policy. In Li territory, land reform was also a special problem. As in the rest of Hainan, cadres familiar with the language, culture, and farming practices of the north were frustrated by the ways in which the Hainanese reality did not fit their training.[39] By July of 1952, the central Party authority in Beijing issued a directive to rely on the southbound cadres and the main army in order to complete land reform. Guangdong was the slowest province to enact and complete land reform, and Hainan was the slowest part of Guangdong to do so, a dubious superlative in the early PRC. Even the Guangdong ally of Hainan, Ye Jianying, pointed out to the central leadership that within the province of Guangdong, Hainan needed the most spurring along in its completion of the campaign. The new slogan was, "Rely on the Southbound Cadres, rely on the main army, complete land reform."[40] It was in the implementation of this stage of land reform that the first anti-localism campaign began in Guangdong. The main purpose was to eliminate any local obstructions to the work of the newly arrived cadres.

Wang Guoxing, the leader of the Li people who brought them into alliance with Hainan Communists, was celebrated as a paragon of the ethnic minority groups and their service to the revolution. Mao Zedong and Zhou Enlai lectured on Wang's exemplary leadership, and granted him a post as a representative in the national government. The southern territories of Hainan that had long been the home of the Li and Miao people were granted status of autonomous districts, and Wang was appointed their leader. Land reform in the Li-Miao district, however, also did not go smoothly. The southbound cadres who arrived in Hainan to complete land reform, especially in large numbers in 1952, also moved into the Li-Miao district for their work. The ethnic distinction was obvious, and the "Han chauvinism" of the newly arrived cadres was clear in their relationship with the Li.[41] The CCP leadership made room for dissent and differing opinions in the early years of the PRC. This meant that Zhou Enlai and others could court the big capitalists and landlords, and convince them that their wealth would not be completely nationalized, and that indeed there was a place for them in the new regime. For many moderates, this was not needed and the ebullient atmosphere of the early years of the regime was enough to attract their loyalty even if they did not share the same radical ideology that had occasionally been revealed in CCP policies of the 1930s and 1940s. The "national bourgeoisie" and the moderates would eventually be incorporated into a new society with varying degrees of force and persuasion.

But sometimes more threatening than outright opponents to an ideological regime is the critic within the political establishment who claims that current policies are straying from the founding ideology. These individuals claim a truer truth—often an earlier truth—and they are the first target in the purges and inquisitions of history. The decision to criticize an authoritarian regime on its own ideological terms can come only from a special kind of audacity, or the belief that one's ideas will be respected, heeded, and not punished.

In the case of Feng Baiju, he became a loyal dissenter when he referred to his own reading of Marx as being inconsistent with the policies he saw implemented on his Hainan island. As the southbound cadres and the main army began to dictate policy, running roughshod over local Hainanese interests, the Hainanese cadres were told to respect this group. The policy directive was to "rely on the southbound cadres, rely on the main army." Feng witnessed this shift away from local policy and local leadership, and in a 1952 speech he bluntly stated his opposition. "I can find no mention in the teachings of Marxism-Leninism of relying on any minority segment of the population. The Southbound Cadres and the main army are a minority segment of the Hainanese population. In Marx's *Das Kapital* there is no prescription for relying on such a minority segment of the population. In my policies, I rely on the will of the masses, and not on the will of a minority segment of the population. This has been the foundation of the Hainanese revolution."[42]

Ten years later, Feng criticized this statement himself, saying that he was mistaken and should not have said it. He does not elaborate, however, and while his self-criticism acknowledges that he was wrong, he does not substantiate how such a statement is mistaken. The confession seems pro forma, and should be treated with some skepticism. Ultimately, the accusations of localism that destroyed his career and ended his service on Hainan would be overturned, and in 1983 Feng was completely exonerated, ten years after his death.[43]

For centuries, Hainan has been perceived with appetite and grand designs from the mainland, "suspended like a baroque green gem from the south coast of China."⁴⁴ Such was still the case in 1921 with Peng Chengwan's survey, and still on the eve of the Communist takeover with T.V. Soong's plans for the island and Chen Zhi's Hainan gazetteer. With each successive mainland regime or individual's plans to develop the island came an acknowledgment of the obstacles to development and modernization. These obstacles were often Hainan's backward infrastructure, and the localist and sometimes nativist mentality that resisted outsiders' schemes and efforts, embodied by both the island's Li and Han populations.

By 1950, the local Communist movement had made common cause with these perennial obstructions to progress in helping to fight the Japanese and Nationalist occupiers of the island. This leap of faith on the part of a portion of the island's Han and Li population anticipated a new kind of relationship with the mainland in which they would hold more control over their political fate. Ultimately, there was no room for this in the early PRC, and the priority of nation-building and political streamlining served to sideline any attempts to assert provincial or regional autonomy. The military victory had been shared, but the peace that followed could not be.

EPILOGUE

Following the Anti-Localism Campaigns of the 1950s, Hainan's political and economic development seemed to be headed for another frustrating disappointment, with the new mainland regime failing to develop the significant strategic and agricultural potential of the island. With the nationwide economic disasters of high Maoism, in the late 1950s and through the first years of the following decade, Hainan's lack of development was no exception in China, where one of the greatest man-made famines following the disastrous Great Leap Forward policies took years of recovery. In the early 1960s, while relative political and economic moderation prevailed throughout most of the country and led to recovery, on Hainan, the Anti-Localism Campaigns were impossible to reverse for Feng Baiju. Feng had been exiled first to Guangzhou (Canton), and later to Zhejiang.

In 1962 Feng spoke openly at a Party meeting about the duplicity and character assassination by Zhao Ziyang, Tao Zhu, and Ou Mengjue, but this speech indicated limits of his freedom. He was not allowed to serve on his home island, but remained in Zhejiang, where he successfully managed a schistosomiasis outbreak. As a result of this and other local governing successes, Feng became a popular figure in the province even though he could not speak the local dialect. By 1973, Feng's chronic illnesses overcame him, and he passed away in Beijing. He had been summoned to the capital for treatment when he became gravely ill. According to several accounts, this transfer was on Zhou Enlai's orders, and his family was also brought to Beijing to be by his side. His eldest daughter told me that she brought his favorite snack of dried shrimp to cheer him. In the Cultural Revolution, Hainan's Communist history was patronizingly essentialized in the model dramatic ballet, *Red Detachment of Women* (Hongse niangzi jun), with intentional manipulations of the actual female unit's history, including a fictitious male character who was born on the mainland. In conversations with nearly anyone outside of Hainan, a discussion of Hainan's revolutionary history invariably seems to lead toward whether I am an expert on this high-flying fable, which has eclipsed all other narratives including an accurate retelling of the women fighters themselves. In an upcoming study, I hope to address the history and mythology of the unit and the prejudice of mainland depictions that are evident in the hugely popular ballet, which has seen a recent revival touring elite stages around the world.

Following Mao's death and the economic opening of China in the early 1980s, there was a revived campaign for Hainan's elevation to provincial status. This effort was marred by a corruption scandal in which officials allocated funds marked for developing Hainan's import economy and transportation infrastructure as a Special Economic Zone. In the "Hainan Car Incident" of 1984–1985, many Hainan officials were approved to use government funds to purchase more vehicles than the island had imported in the past thirty-five years, including vans, which some of the officials then promptly tried to sell for their own profit rather than use in their work units. Other officials, however, hoped to simply use the authorization to bring in the vehicles as an opportunity to enrich their local work units or towns, and did not consider the relatively large shipments of vehicles to be incongruent with general plans for economic development and opening.[1] Ultimately, this conflict between local ambition and national control was resolved with the dismissal of the officials in charge of the operation, and it was only a bump in the road to Hainan's eventual ascension to provincial status in 1988.

The 1990s saw a real estate bubble in Hainan grow and burst by the end of the decade. Hotels and high-rises sprouted across the island, especially in the southern resort of Sanya. Some of them stood empty or incomplete when the tourists and pensioners did not follow the ambitious developments. In the early twenty-first century, as the unflagging growth of the Chinese economy caught up with the dreams of the developers of Hainan, the real estate market stabilized and again began growing with an increase in retirement communities, golf courses, and luxury hotels.

Today, Hainan's importance for Beijing and the region has changed from the early and mid-twentieth-century agricultural plans for the island to become a new breadbasket of China. Most importantly, efforts by both the provincial and national government have begun to shape the island into a major tourist destination for both Chinese and international visitors. Another factor that puts Hainan in recent headlines is its proximity to maritime disputes in the South China Sea, mainly with Vietnam and the Philippines, but also involving Malaysia, Brunei, and other countries.

With these new priorities for Hainan—as an international vacation destination and as a maritime border region—the plans for the island to become a new Taiwan or Singapore, or a breadbasket, have faded. New plans, unlike the ambitious development plans of the past, are built more realistically on Hainan's past. As a maritime border area, unavoidable geography puts Hainan in a position to monitor and police the South China Sea and its potential wealth of energy resources.[2] Historical claims to many islands throughout the South China Sea and a massive maritime region actually make Hainan (otherwise the country's smallest province) the largest province in the People's Republic of China, if we accept Beijing's maritime borders, which put nearly the entire sea under Hainan's jurisdiction. Speculation about natural resources under the water make Hainan a global flashpoint, and even Hainanese fishermen can become national celebrities if they bump into a patrolling Japanese coast guard vessel, as was the case in the fall of 2010.[3]

The detention of this fishing captain by the Japanese led to broader implications for Japan and China in the form of a temporary suspension of rare earth mineral shipments (essential to many high-technology devices) from Japan to China. Beyond regional maritime boundary disputes, the importance of regional waters as major shipping lanes has even led the Chinese foreign ministry to warn the United States about "playing with fire" when the United States declared its national interests in the sea.[4] The Chinese patrols of the region are based out of naval headquarters in Hainan, and if the rhetoric of all parties involved can be trusted, the importance of these conflicting maritime claims cannot be overestimated.

As a tourist destination, Hainan is like some Southeast Asian countries and Pacific or Caribbean Islands, in that its undeveloped economy and infrastructure is hardly an obstacle to decadent vacationers; on the contrary, for some well-heeled visitors, this relative poverty can serve to add rich enjoyment to the experience of the island's quaint, exotic, and seemingly timeless charm. Some regions of the island have been highly developed for wealthy visitors, from golf resorts that sprawl green across the island's hills, to the resort city of Sanya, and the major political conference center of Bo'ao.[5] Other regions are on display as authentic ethnic communities, where the local people dance for tourists and perform rituals in traditional costume. This "ethnic tourism" is a significant draw for Hainan, as are the beaches, golf resorts, and luxury hotels.[6] The glitz of international beauty contests and sporting events has also served to attract the kind of attention that local and national developers of the island hope will translate into major tourist revenue. In the spring of 2011 and again in the winter of 2015–2016, Hainan's provincial government launched a further attempt to draw wealthy travelers with a tax rebate program that allowed foreign and domestic tourists to the island to regain approximately 30 percent of the price of luxury goods that they purchased during their stay.[7]

The past forty years in China have revealed that major shifts in direction can take place in a very short time. Hainan's economy seems poised to continue to benefit from tourist revenue and favorable government policy. Certainly, the island's popularity with domestic tourism continues to rise as the number of middle class Chinese who can afford a vacation there continues to grow. Sustainable tiers of authority and autonomy are based on the stable point in the power negotiation among the different levels. Hainan's position as watchtower of the South China Sea and major tourist destination seem to have provided that stasis.

NOTES

Introduction

1. Edward H. Schafer, *Shore of Pearls: Hainan Island in Early Times* (1969).

2. The recent work of Frank Dikötter, *The Tragedy of Liberation: A History of the Chinese Revolution, 1945–1957* (New York: Bloomsbury, 2013), spans the final years of the revolutionary struggle and moves into the early years of PRC rule, demonstrating how the ebullient atmosphere of revolutionary victory quickly gave way to an atmosphere of purges and terror. Academic historians have analyzed this period in a clear-eyed way for over a decade now, moving past the myth of a honeymoon that followed the victory of the revolution, but Dikötter significantly presents a complex and nonideological narrative here for the general reader.

3. Gregor Benton, *Mountain Fires: The Red Army's Three-Year War in South China, 1934–1938* (1992), *New Fourth Army: Communist Resistance Along the Yangtze and the Huai, 1938–1941* (1999); Hans J. Van de Ven, *War and Nationalism in China, 1925–1945* (2003); Edward A. McCord, *The Power of the Gun: The Emergence of Modern Chinese Warlordism* (1993); Stephen C. Averill, *Revolution in the Highlands: China's Jinggangshan Base Area* (2006).

4. Chalmers Johnson, *Peasant Nationalism and Communist Power: The Emergence of Revolutionary China* (1962).

5. Jung Chang and Jon Halliday, *Mao: The Unknown Story* (2005).

6. Stephen C. Averill, *Revolution in the Highlands: China's Jinggangshan Base Area* (2006).

Chapter 1. Cultivating and Exploiting a "Primitive" Island

1. Anne Csete, "Ethnicity, Conflict, and the State in the Early to Mid-Qing: The Hainan Highlands, 1644–1800," in Pamela Kyle Crossley, Helen F. Siu, and Donald S. Sutton, eds., *Empire at the Margins: Culture, Ethnicity, and Frontier in Early Modern China* (2006), 229–230.

2. Joseph W. Esherick, "How the Qing Became China," in Joseph W. Esherick, Hasan Kayali, and Eric Van Young, eds., *Empire to Nation: Historical Perspectives on the Making of the Modern World* (Lanham, MD: Rowman & Littlefield, 2006), 229–252.

3. Peng Chengwan 彭程萬, *Diaocha Qiongya shiye baogao shu* 調查瓊崖实业报告书 [A report on the investigation of the industry and commerce of Hainan] (1920), "Peng Chengwan Preface." (Hereafter cited as DQSBS. There are several Prefaces and Forewords in the frontmatter of this report, each by a different author and each with its own page numbering. I will refer to each by the name of its author. Other references to this report will be listed by the subject or chapter and page number, as page numbers begin anew in each chapter.)

4. Peng, DQSBS (1920), "Cen Chunxuan Preface."

5. "Chronique," T'oung Pao, vol. 9, no. 4 (1898), 338.

6. N.D.H. "Growing Interest in Hainan Mainly Strategic," *Far Eastern Survey* (1938), 203–204.

7. Peng, DQSBS (1920), "Zhao Fan Preface."

8. Ibid., "Li Genyuan Preface."

9. Howard L. Boorman, Biographical Dictionary of Republican China (New York: Columbia University Press, 1971), vol. 2 (305–307, 455–457), vol. 3 (305–308).

10. B.C. Henry, *Ling-Nam or Interior Views of Southern China Including Explorations in the Hitherto Untraversed Island of Hainan* (London: S.W. Partridge and Co., 1886), 336–337.

11. Kathleen L. Lodwick, *Educating the Women of Hainan: The Career of Margaret Moninger in China, 1915–1942* (1995), 2.

12. Margaret M. Moninger, *Isle of Palms* (1919), 104.

13. Zhonggong Hainan shengwei dangshi yanjiushi 中共海南省委党史研究室 [Historical research office of the Chinese Communist Party provincial committee of Hainan], eds., Zhongguo gongchandang Hainan lishi 中国共产党海南历史 [Chinese Communist Party history of Hainan] (2007), 5.

14. R.P. Mouly, *Hai-nan: L'Ile aux Cent Visages* [Hainan: The island of a hundred faces] (1944), 11.

15. Henry (1886), 8.

16. Ibid., 332–333.

17. R.T. Phillips, "The Japanese Occupation of Hainan"(1980); M. Tayor Fravel, "China's Strategy in the South China Sea," *Contemporary Southeast Asia*, vol. 33, no. 3 (December 2011), 307; James Bussert, "Hainan is the Tip of the Chinese Navy's Spear," *Signal* (June 2009).

18. In a 1931 mission newsletter, one American observer noted "[Yulin], the best harbor in all Hainan, is there, but so far removed from all inland trading centers as to be of no commercial value." See *American Presbyterian Mission: Island of Hainan, Commemorating Fifty Years of Mission Work in Hainan, 1881–1931* (Haikou: American Presbyterian Mission Newsletter, Autumn 1931), 2.

19. Peng, DQSBS (1920), "Transportation," 1–8.

20. Hainansheng difang zhi bangongshi 海南省地方志办公室 [Hainan Provincial Office of Local Gazetteers], eds., *Hainan shengzhi: Tudizhi* 海南省志: 土地志 [Hainan provincial gazetteer: Land gazetteer] (2007), 123–124.

21. Map: Guangdong tong sheng shui dao tu: Call Number: G7823.G8A5 1817.G8; Repository: Library of Congress Geography and Map Division Washing-

ton, DC., USA dcu; digital Id: g7823g ct003406; http://hdl.loc.gov/loc.gmd/g7823g.ct003406; Library of Congress catalog no. Gm71002467.

22. Maritime claims in the South China Sea are a hotly disputed topic at the time of writing (winter 2017), and various actors in the region make widely varying claims. The PRC maritime claim, which is also Hainan's provincial claim, currently includes about 80 percent of the sea, and is based on the "nine-dash line" established by the Nationalist government in 1947. For a more complete examination of this topic, see the epilogue of this work, and Stein Tønnesson, "The History of the Dispute," in *War or Peace in the South China Sea?*, ed. Timo Kivimäki (Copenhagen: Nordic Institute of Asian Studies Press, 2002); Jianming Shen, "China's Sovereignty over the South China Sea Islands: A Historical Perspective," *Chinese Journal of International Law* 1:1 (2002): 94–157; M. Taylor Fravel, "Hainan's New Maritime Regulations: A Preliminary Analysis," *The Diplomat*, December 1, 2012, accessed February 14, 2013, http://thediplomat.com/china-power/hainans-new-maritime-regulations-a-preliminary-analysis/

23. M. Savina, *Monographie de Hainan: Conference faite de 10 décembre 1928 a la Société Géographique de Hanoi*, M. Savina (Missionaire apostolique) (1929), 3.

24. Leonard Clark, "Among the Big Knot Lois of Hainan," (1938), 391. Margaret Moninger also uses the figure of 14,000 square miles in *Isle of Palms* (1919).

25. Hainansheng difang zhi bangongshi, eds., *Hainan shengzhi: Tudi zhi* [Land Gazetteer] (2007), 123–124. This is also my source for the figures of Hainan's current area.

26. Peng, DQSBS (1920), "Peng Preface," "Transportation."

27. Ibid., "Li situation."

28. Hainansheng difang zhi bangongshi, eds., *Hainan shengzhi: Tudizhi* [Land Gazetteer] (2007), 157–158.

29. Phillips (1980).

30. Robert Benewick and Stephanie Hemelryk Donald, *State of China Atlas: Mapping the World's Fastest Growing Economy* (2009), 43. Citing a 2006 study here, Hainan was the only province in the PRC that still owed over a third of its gross domestic product to agricultural production.

31. Moninger (1919), 39, 44–45.

32. *American Presbyterian Mission: Island of Hainan, Commemorating Fifty Years of Mission Work in Hainan, 1881–1931* (1931), 3.

33. This bipolar perception is also analyzed in Gary Y. Okihiro's study of Hawaii, *Island World: A History of Hawaii and the United States* (2008).

34. Burton Watson, tr., *Su Tung-p'o: Selections from a Sung Dynasty Poet* (1965), 130.

35. Wu Lien-teh, "Hainan: The Paradise of China," (1937), 233–234.

36. Peng, DQSBS (1920). In the forewords to this survey, Beijing and Guangdong officials praise the courage of the surveyors who braved the scorching sun and the zhangqi (miasma) of Hainan to conduct their work.

37. Bonnie Tsui, "The Surf's Always Up in the Chinese Hawaii," (2009). Wu Lien-teh, "Hainan: The Paradise of China" (1937).

38. Wu Lien-teh (1937), 241.

39. I refer to the Muslim population of Hainan as Hui because that is the expeditious official classification of this ethnic group on the island, dating from the ethnic minority work of the central government in the 1950s and 1960s. It is noteworthy, however, that most in this group of the Hainan population do not put themselves in the same ethnic category as the Hui Muslims of mainland China, and their origins are probably in southeast Asia. They are, more correctly, the Utsat, and they number about six thousand on Hainan. On the strained relations between Hainanese Han and the island's Muslim minority, see Keng-Fong Pang, "Unforgiven and Remembered: The Impact of Ethnic Conflicts in Everyday Muslim-Han Social Relations on Hainan Island," in William Safran, ed., *Nationalism and Ethnoregional Identities in China* (London: Frank Cass, 1998), 142–162.

40. Peng, DQSBS (1920), "Li Situation," 3.

41. Stevan Harrell, "Introduction: Civilizing Projects and the Reaction to Them," in Stevan Harrell, ed., *Cultural Encounters on China's Ethnic Frontiers* (1995), 23–24.

42. Hu Yaling 胡亚玲, *Hainan Li cun Miao zhai* 海南黎村苗寨 [English title: The Li and Miao Villages in Hainan] (Haikou: Hainan chubanshe, 2012).

43. Csete (2006), 239.

44. Ibid., 247.

45. Wang Xueping 王学萍, *Zhongguo Lizu* 中国黎族 [The Li of China] (2004), 81. One example of such an uprising came as a result of duplicitous behavior by salt merchants in 1829.

46. Moninger also notes this practice of deserting soldiers joining Li communities in Isle of Palms (1919), 28.

47. Peng, DQSBS (1920), "Zhao Fan preface."

48. Ibid., "Li Situation."

49. Henry (1886), 377.

50. Clark (1938).

51. Moninger (1919), 16.

52. Wang (2004), 83–84.

53. Peng, DQSBS (1920), "Li Situation."

54. Ibid., 2, 4.

55. Kunio Odaka, *Economic Organization of the Li Tribes of Hainan Island* (1950) (Originally published in Japanese, 1942); Hans Stübel, *Die Li-stämme der insel Hainan; ein beitrag zur volkskunde südchinas* [The Li of Hainan Island: A Contribution to the Folk Studies of Southern China] (1937).

56. Odaka (1942), 3.

57. Phillips (1980), 93–109.

58. Peng, DQSBS (1920), "Transportation," 20.

59. Chen Daya et al. (2007).

60. Peng, DQSBS (1920), "Transportation," 20–21. In 1919, Margaret Moninger also remarked on the short road and novelty of a couple of automobiles connecting Fucheng and Haikou. (Moninger, *Isle of Palms*, 30). By 1938, however, the

development of passable Hainan roads had extended deep into the island's interior, allowing Leonard Clark and his National Geographic team to ride 60 miles by automobile to Nada, in northwestern Hainan.

61. Savina (1929).
62. *American Presbyterian Mission: Island of Hainan, Commemorating Fifty Years of Mission Work in Hainan, 1881–1931* (1931), 3.
63. Peng, DQSBS (1920), "Transportation," 18–19.
64. L. Carrington Goodrich and L. Chaoying Fang, eds., *Dictionary of Ming Biography, 1368–1644* (New York: Columbia University Press, 1976), 474.
65. The Chinese stone inscription reads Yishou chengtian (一手撑天 "single-handedly hold up the heavens"). An image of the rock is featured on the Qiongzhong County government website: http://www.qiongzhong.gov.cn/view%20spot_info.aspx?id=7500
66. Peng, DQSBS (1920), "Transportation," 18–19.

Chapter 2. Political Prospects in the Early Republic

1. Jean Chesneaux, "The Federalist Movement in China, 1920–1923" in Jack Gray, ed., *Modern China's Search for a Political Form* (London: Oxford University Press, 1969), translation of "Le Mouvement Fédéraliste en China, 1920–1923," in *Revue Historique* (Octobre–Décembre 1966), 347–384.
2. John Fitzgerald, "The Province in History," in John Fitzgerald, ed., *Rethinking China's Provinces* (2002), 20.
3. Stephen R. Platt, *Autumn in the Heavenly Kingdom: China, the West, and the Epic Story of the Taiping Civil War* (New York: Knopf, 2012); Tobie Meyer-Fong, *What Remains: Coming to Terms with Civil War in the 19th Century* (Stanford: Stanford University Press, 2013).
4. John Fitzgerald, "Increased Disunity: The Politics and Finance of Guangdong Separatism, 1926–1936," in *Modern Asian Studies*, vol. 24, no. 4 (October 1990), 745–775; also Boorman (1971), vol. 1, 160–163.
5. Chen Keqin 陈克勤, *Hainan jiansheng* 海南建省 [Hainan becomes a province] (2008), 11–12.
6. Hainansheng difang shizhi bangongshi 海南省地方史志办公室 [Hainan Provincial Office of Local Gazetteers], eds., *Hainan shengzhi: Minzhengzhi, waishizhi* 海南省志: 民政志, 外事志 [Hainan provincial gazetteer: Civil Administration gazetteer, Foreign affairs gazetteer] (Haikou: Nanhai chuban gongsi, 1996), 194–200.
7. Kathleen L. Lodwick, *The Widow's Quest: The Byers Extraterritorial Case in Hainan, China, 1924–1925* (2003).
8. Harry A. Franck, *Roving through Southern China* (New York: The Century Co., 1925), 338.
9. Charles E. Ronan, S.J. and Bonnie B.C. Oh, eds., *East Meets West: The Jesuits in China, 1582–1773* (Chicago: Loyola University Press, 1988), 30.
10. Qiongya wuzhuang douzheng shi bangongshi 琼崖武装斗争史办公室 [Office of the history of Hainan's military struggle], eds. *Qiongya zongdui shi* 琼崖纵

队史 [History of the Hainan Column] (1986), 2. Hainan baikequanshu bianzuan weiyuanhui 海南百科全书编纂委员会 [Committee of compilers of the Hainan encyclopedia], eds., *Hainan baikequanshu* 海南百科全书 [Hainan encyclopedia] (1999), 45.

11. Hainan, People's Republic of China Provincial Government official website: http://en.hainan.gov.cn/englishgov/AboutHaiNan/200904/t20090408_1228.html

12. Sterling Seagrave, *The Soong Dynasty* (New York: Harper & Row, 1985).

13. Xing Yilin, Han Qiyuan, Huang Liangjun 邢益森, 韩启元, 黄良俊, *Qiongqiao cangsang* 琼侨沧桑 [The ups and downs of overseas Hainanese] (1991), 44–45.

14. Hainansheng difang shizhi bangongshi 海南省地方史志办公室 [Hainan Provincial Office of Local Gazetteers], eds., *Hainan shengzhi: Baoyezhi, Di shiyi juan* 海南省志: 报业志, 第十一卷 [Hainan provincial gazetteer: Newspaper gazetteer, vol. 11] (Haikou: Nanhai chuban gongsi, 1997), 10–11.

15. Ezra Vogel, *Canton Under Communism: Programs and Politics in a Provincial Capital, 1949–1968* (1971 [originally published by Harvard University Press, 1969]), Prologue, 21.

16. Rhoads (1975), 222–223, 80–81.

17. See the works of Adam McKeown, including "Conceptualizing Chinese Diasporas, 1842–1949," *Journal of Asian Studies* (May 1999), 306–337; *Chinese Migrant Networks and Cultural Change: Peru, Chicago, Hawaii, 1900–1936* (Chicago: University of Chicago Press, 2001).

18. Victor Purcell, *The Chinese in Malaya* (1948), 204.

19. Moninger (1919), 24–25.

20. See also Philip A. Kuhn, *Chinese Among Others: Emigration in Modern Times* (2008).

21. Vogel (1971 [1969]), 20.

22. Biographical material here on Lin Wenying comes from the following materials: Fan Yunxi 范运晰, *Qiongji minguo renwuzhuan* 琼籍民国人物传 [Biographies of Hainanese in the republic], Haikou: Nanhai chuban gongsi, 1999 (293–300); Zhonggong wenchang xianwei dangshi yanjiushi, eds., 中共文昌县委党史研究室编 [Chinese Communist Party Committee of Wenchang county historical research office], *Wenchang yinghun* 文昌英魂 [The spirit of Wenchang heroes] (1993), 1–7.

23. Kuhn (2008), 80.

24. Kuhn (2008) reproduced a 1914 document titled, "The Jews of the Orient," in which Rama VI denounced the Chinese living in Siam, noting the "racial loyalty which prevents their absorption into other nations" (Kuhn, 298).

25. Fan Yunxi (1999), 294.

26. Zhonggong wenchang xianwei dangshi yanjiushi, eds., 中共文昌县委党史研究室编 [Chinese Communist Party Committee of Wenchang county historical research office], *Wenchang yinghun* 文昌英魂 [The spirit of Wenchang heroes] (1993). In this volume, Lin Wenying has pride of place as the first biographical entry.

27. Fu Heji 符和积, "Shixi Xinhai nian Qiongya zhengju de shanbian" 试析辛亥年琼崖政局的嬗变 [Analysis of the evolution of the political situation on

Hainan in 1911], in *Hainan daxue xuebao shehui kexue ban* 海南大学学报社会科学版 [Social Science Journal of Hainan University] (September 1998), 1–6.

28. Ibid., 2.

29. Zhonggong Wenchang xianwei dangshi yanjiushi 中共文昌县委党史研究室 [Party history research office for the Wenchang County Committee of the Chinese Communist Party], eds., *Wenchang Yinggui: Wenchang dangshi ziliao* 文昌英魂: 文昌党史资料 [Spirits of Wenchang's martyrs: Wenchang Party history materials] (1993), 5–7.

30. Xing Yilin et al. (1991), 43–44.

31. Hainansheng difang shizhi bangongshi, eds., *Hainan shengzhi: Baoyezhi, Di shiyi juan* [Hainan provincial gazetteer: Newspaper gazetteer, vol. 11] (1997), 257.

32. Henry (1886), 334; also see Moninger (1919).

33. Zhonggong Hainan shengwei dangshi yanjiushi 中共海南省委党史研究室 [Historical research office of the Chinese Communist Party provincial committee of Hainan], eds., *Zhongguo gongchandang Hainan lishi* 中国共产党海南历史 [Chinese Communist Party history of Hainan] (2007), 14–15.

34. Fan Yunxi (1999), 299–300. Lin was also celebrated in the Hainanese community in Thailand, and he continues to be a hero there as well as in his home province. In 1984, during a revival of local history and in a time of exoneration of local heroes, Lin's hometown was renamed Gelan village, for Lin's courtesy or style name (Gelan 格兰).

35. Chen Fatan 陈发檀, "Qiongzhou gaisheng liyou shu" 琼州改省理由书 [Reasons for making Hainan a province] (1912), reprinted in Fan Yunxi 范运晰, *Qiongji minguo renwu zhuan* 琼籍民国人物传 [Biographies of Hainanese in Republican China] (1999), 197–200. Also see Liang Kun 梁昆, 1912 海南改省风云 "Hainan gaisheng fengyun" [1912, The controversy over making Hainan a province], in *Hainan zhoukan* (November 18, 2008).

36. John Fitzgerald, "Increased Disunity: The Policy and Finance of Guangdong Separatism, 1926–1936," *Modern Asian Studies* (October 1990), 250–254.

37. Ibid., "The Misconceived Revolution: State and Society in China's Nationalist Revolution, 1923–26," *Journal of Asian Studies* (May 1990), 333.

38. Gordon Y.M. Chan, "The Communists in Rural Guangdong, 1928–1936," *Journal of the Royal Asiatic Society* (April 2003), 86.

39. Hainansheng difang shizhi bangongshi 海南省地方史志办公室 [Hainan Provincial Office of Local Gazetteers], eds., *Hainan shengzhi: Baoyezhi, Di shiyi juan* 海南省志: 报业志, 第十一卷 [Hainan provincial gazetteer: Newspaper gazetteer, vol. 11] (1997), 259–261.

40. *Zhongguo gongchandang Hainan lishi* (2007), 23.

41. "Japanese Activities in South China: Naval Intelligence Officer's Reports, June 1922," reprinted in Kenneth Bourne and D. Cameron Watt, eds., *British Documents on Foreign Affairs: Reports and Papers from the Foreign Office Confidential Print, Part II* (From the First to the Second World War), Series E, Asia, 1914–1939, ed. Ann Trotter, vol. 27, China, March 1922–May 1923 (1994), 249.

42. N.D.H., "Growing Interest in Hainan Mainly Strategic," *Far Eastern Survey* (August 24, 1938), 203–204; Etienne Dennery, "A French View of the Situation in the Far East," *International Affairs (Royal Institute of International Affairs 1931–1939)* (July–August 1938), 528–540; Norman D. Hanwell, "France Takes Inventory in China," *Far Eastern Survey* (September 28, 1938), 217–225.

43. Li Yisheng 李毅生, *Fenzhan ershisan nian de Hainan dao* 奋战二十三年的海南岛 [Twenty-three years of fighting on Hainan island] (Hankou: Renmin chubanshe, 1951), 3.

44. Xu Chengzhang 徐成章, "'Qiongya Xunbao' chuanban zhi Jingguo" "琼崖旬报" 创办之经过 [Since the founding of the Hainan Xunbao] (April 1922), reprinted in Hainansheng difang shizhi bangongshi 海南省地方史志办公室 [Hainan Provincial Office of Local Gazetteers], eds., *Hainan shengzhi: Baoyezhi, Di shiyi juan* 海南省志: 报业志, 第十一卷 [Hainan provincial gazetteer: Newspaper gazetteer, vol. 11] (1997), 316.

45. Kuhn (2008), 269–270.

46. Zhonggong Hainan shengwei dangshi yanjiushi [Chinese Communist Party History Research Office for the Provincial Committee of Hainan], eds., *Zhonggong Qiongya difang zuzhi de guanghui licheng* 中共琼崖地方组织的光辉历程 [The glorious history of the local organization of the Chinese Communist Party on Hainan], for internal Provincial Government circulation (Document YK060) (June 2001), 6–7 (pages not numbered).

47. Ibid., 6 (pages not numbered).

48. Xu Chengzhang (1922), 316–320.

49. Ulises Granados, "As China Meets the Southern Sea Frontier: Ocean Identity in the Making, 1920–1937," *Pacific Affairs* (Fall 2005), 454–457.

50. "Consul-General Jamieson to Sir B. Alston, Document number 42, Secret, Canton, July 11, 1922," reprinted in Kenneth Bourne and D. Cameron Watt, eds., *British Documents on Foreign Affairs: Reports and Papers from the Foreign Office Confidential Print, Part II* (From the First to the Second World War), Series E, Asia, 1914–1939, ed. Ann Trotter, vol. 27, China, March 1922–May 1923 (1994), 238–240.

51. M. Savina, *Monographie de Hainan: Conference faite de 10 décembre 1928 a la Société Géographique de Hanoi* [Monograph on Hainan: 10 December 1928 Conference of the Geographical Society of Hanoi] (Missionaire apostolique) (1929), 7.

52. Xing Yikong, Peng Changlin, Qian Yue 邢诒孔, 彭长霖, 钱跃, *Feng Baiju jiangjun zhuan* 冯白驹将军传 [Biography of General Feng Baiju] (1998), 3–4.

53. A slightly broader interpretation of the name does not include the character of Hong Xiuquan's family name, but ascribes the "three dot" or "three drop" name to the ways in which members of the society wrote secret signs with the three dot water sign in front of them as part of a code. (See Mary Somers Heidhues, "Chinese Organizations in West Borneo and Bangka: Kongsis and *Hui*," in David Ownby and Mary Somers Heidhues, eds., *"Secret Societies" Reconsidered: Perspectives on the Social History of Modern South China and Southeast Asia* [1993], 86, footnote 7.)

54. David Ownby, *Brotherhoods and Secret Societies in Early and Mid-Qing China: The Formation of a Tradition* (1996), 5.

55. David Ownby (1996), 13–14, 182–183.

56. As cited in Feng Chongyi and David S.G. Goodman, "Hainan: Communal Politics and the Struggle for Identity," in David S.G. Goodman, *China's Provinces in Reform: Class, Community, and Political Culture* (London: Routledge, 1997), 57.

Chapter 3. From Globetrotters to Guerrillas

1. Feng Yunxi's letter is reproduced in Wu Zhi and He Lang, *Feng Baiju zhuan* 冯白驹传 [Biography of Feng Baiju] (1996), 19.

2. Stephen C. Averill, "The Origins of the Futian Incident," in Tony Saich and Hans van de Ven, eds., *New Perspectives on the Chinese Communist Revolution* (Armonk, NY: M.E. Sharpe, 1995), 79–115.

3. Zhonggong Hainan shengwei dangshi yanjiu shi (2007), 180.

4. Many retrospective essays on the Communist revolution on Hainan bear this phrase, such as Lin Hongsheng 林鸿盛, "Hongqi budao yu Qiongya hongse geming laoqu" 红旗不倒与琼崖红色革命老区 [The red flag never fell on the old revolutionary base areas of Hainan], in *Hainan gemingshi yanjiu* 海南革命史研究 [Research on the revolutionary history of Hainan], vol. 9 (December 2002), 91–99.

5. Yuan Bangjian and Chen Yongjie 元邦建, 陈永阶, "Xu Chengzhang" 徐成章 [Xu Chengzhang], in Qiongdao xinghuo bianjibu 琼岛星火编辑部 Qiongdao xinghuo editorial board, eds., *Qiongdao Xinghuo* (hereafter *QX*), vol. 4, 1981, 48–84.

6. Qiongya wuzhuang douzheng shi bangongshi (1986), 6.

7. Hainansheng difang zhi bangongshi 海南省地方志办公室 [Hainan Provincial Office of Local Gazetteers], eds., *Hainan shengzhi: Gongchandang* 海南省志: 共产党 [Hainan provincial gazetteer: Communist Party gazetteer] (2005), 311.

8. Feng Baiju, "Guanyu wo canjia geming guocheng de lishi qingkuang" (1968), 412–413.

9. Hainansheng difang zhi bangongshi 海南省地方志办公室 [Hainan Provincial Office of Local Gazetteers], eds., *Hainan shengzhi: Gongchandang* 海南省志: 共产党 [Hainan provincial gazetteer: Communist Party gazetteer] (2005), 57.

10. Zhonggong Hainan shengwei dangshi yanjiu shi (2007), 95–96.

11. Qiongya wuzhuang douzheng shi bangongshi 琼崖武装斗争史办公室 [Office of the history of Hainan's military struggle], eds. *Qiongya zongdui shi* 琼崖纵队史 [History of the Hainan Column] (1986), 13–14.

12. Zhonggong Guangdongsheng Qiongya tewei 中共广东省琼崖特委 [Special Committee for Hainan of the Chinese Communist Party of Guangdong Province], *Qiongya tewei yiyufen zongbaogao, di liu ci* 琼崖特委一月份总报告, 第六次 [The sixth January summary report from the Hainan special committee], January 25, 1928, reprinted in the Zhongyang dang'anguan (Central archives), 755, Guangdong Provincial Archives.

13. Ibid.

14. Qiongya wuzhuang douzheng shi bangongshi (1986), 33; Diana Lary, *Region and Nation: The Kwangsi Clique in Chinese Politics, 1925–1937* (1974), 197.

15. "Zai geming kunnan shiqi de Feng Baiju" 在革命困难时期的冯白驹 [Feng Baiju in the difficult period of the revolution], a summary of activities on Hainan sent to the Southern Party Bureau, reprinted in *FBYS*, October 23, 1937, 466–467.

16. Haikoushi bingwei 海口市兵委 [Haikou municipal military committee], *Haikou xingshi ji gongzuo qingkuang* 海口形势及工作情况 [Haikou circumstances and work situation], June 6, 1928, reprinted in the Zhongyang dang'anguan (Central Archives), reprint no. 1069, Guangdong Provincial Archives, folio 18.

17. *Haikou xingshi ji gongzuo qingkuang* (June 6, 1928).

18. Ibid.

19. "Huang Xuezeng gei shengwei de baogao" 黄学增给省委的报告 [Huang Xuezeng's report to the Provincial Committee], July 16, 1928, cited in *Zhongguo gongchandang Hainan lishi* (2007), 134–135.

20. Qiongya wuzhuang douzheng shi bangongshi (1986), 37–38.

21. Zhonggong Hainan shengwei dangshi yanjiu shi (2007), 150–151.

22. Luo Wenyan zhi Zhongyang xin 罗文淹致中央信 [Luo Wenyan's letter to Party Central], September 6, 1929, Shanghai.

23. Zhonggong Hainan shengwei dangshi yanjiu shi (2007), 103.

24. Luo Wenyan zhi Zhongyang xin 罗文淹致中央信 [Luo Wenyan's letter to Party Central], September 6, 1929, Shanghai.

25. Feng Baiju, "Guanyu wo canjia geming guocheng de lishi qingkuang" (1968), 359. Feng remembered there being twenty-six in his mountain gang in Muruishan in 1932–1933.

26. Hainansheng difang zhi bangongshi 海南省地方志办公室 [Hainan Provincial Office of Local Gazetteers], eds., *Hainan shengzhi: Gongchandang* 海南省志: 共产党 [Hainan provincial gazetteer: Communist Party gazetteer] (2005), 58–59.

27. "Qiongya tewei baogao" 琼崖特委报告 [Hainan special committee report] (October 27, 1929), cited in Qiongya wuzhuang douzheng shi bangongshi (1986), 44–45.

28. Ibid., 41.

29. Ibid., 53.

30. Zhou Shike, Feng Qihe, Ou Yingqin, Wei Jingzhao 周仕科, 冯启和, 欧英钦, 韦经照, "Zhongguo gongnong hongjun Qiongya duli er shi nüzi jun tewu lian" 中国工农红军琼崖独立二师女子军特务连 [The women's special services (spy) company of the Hainan independent second division of the Chinese Red Army of Workers and Peasants], in Qiongdao xinghuo (Hainan spark) editorial board, eds., *Qiongya funü geming douzheng zhuanji* 琼崖妇女革命斗争专辑 [Hainan women's revolutionary struggle album], vol. 5, 1981, Internal Circulation, pp. 1–8.

31. Feng Baiju 冯白驹, "Gei Zhongyang de baogao: tewei yu shangji shiqu lianxi de qingxing" 给中央的报告: 特委与上级失去联系的情形 [Report to Party Central: The situation of the loss of communications between the Special Committee and its superiors] (December 12, 1934), reprinted in Zhonggong Hainanqu dangwei dangshi bangongshi 中共海南区党委党史办公室 [The Party history office of the Chinese Communist Party of Hainan district committee], eds., *Feng Baiju yanjiu shiliao* 冯白驹研究史料 [Research materials on Feng Baiju] (1988), 3–4.

32. Hainansheng difang zhi bangongshi 海南省地方志办公室 [Hainan Provincial Office of Local Gazetteers], eds., *Hainan shengzhi: Gongchandang* 海南省志: 共产党 [Hainan provincial gazetteer: Communist Party gazetteer] (2005) 383, 385.

Chapter 4. An Outrage of Little Consequence

1. "Southward Advance of Japanese Expansionist Movement: Hainan and the Spratly Islands," Telegram from U.S. ambassador to Japan (Grew) to the U.S. Secretary of State (Hull), February 10, 1939, in *Foreign Relations of the United States (FRUS), United States Diplomatic Papers, 1939, The Far East (1939)*, p. 103.

2. "Japanese Landing on Hainan Island," February 12, 1939, in Chiang Kai-shek, *The Collected Wartime Messages of Generalissimo Chiang Kai-shek 1937–1945* (New York: John Day Company, 1946), 184–186.

3. Ibid., 186.

4. Most significantly, see Rana Mitter's *Forgotten Ally: China's World War II, 1937–1945* (New York: Houghton Mifflin Harcourt, 2013); and Jay Taylor's *The Generalissimo: Chiang Kai-shek and the Struggle for Modern China* (Cambridge, MA: Belknap, 2009).

5. Diana Lary, *Region and Nation: The Kwangsi Clique in Chinese Politics, 1925–1937* (1974), 197–199; Gregor Benton, *Mountain Fires: The Red Army's Three-Year War in South China, 1934–1938* (1992), 104–106.

6. The most obvious and extreme example of this came with the New Fourth Army Incident, also known as the Southern Anhui Incident (*Wannan shibian* 皖南事变), in January of 1941. Gregor Benton treats this incident and its context masterfully in his work, *New Fourth Army: Communist Resistance Along the Yangtze and the Huai, 1938–1941* (1999). Benton also deals with the longer context in an earlier work, *Mountain Fires: The Red Army's Three-Year War in South China, 1934–1938* (1992).

7. See Kathleen L. Lodwick's excellent treatment of this case in *The Widow's Quest: The Byers Extraterritorial Case in Hainan, China, 1924–1925* (2003).

8. David S. Tappan, "Communist Echoes: Dreaded Reds Still Taking Their Toll," *Hainan Newsletter*, American Presbyterian Mission (Fall 1937).

9. Qiongya wuzhuang douzheng shi bangongshi, eds. (1986), 96–99; also Wu Zhi and He Lang 吴之, 贺朗, *Feng Baiju zhuan* 冯白驹传 [Biography of Feng Baiju] (1996), 275–287.

10. Luella Rice Tappan's *Grandfather's China Story* is a modestly titled, self-published, volume of recollections covering the many years spent on Hainan by Mrs. Tappan and her husband, Reverend David S. Tappan. The volume was printed for the couple's grandchildren in 1967 and is held in the University of Oregon's special collection of the David S. and Luella R. Tappan Papers, Collection 103, Box 5, Folder 9.

11. David S. Tappan, "War Shadows," *Hainan Newsletter*, American Presbyterian Mission (Christmas 1938), 21.

12. Cited in R.T. Phillips, "The Japanese Occupation of Hainan," *Modern Asian Studies* (1980), 95.

13. Dai Xiuli 戴秀丽, "'Wo shi Zhongguoren,'" "我是中国人" ["I am Chinese"], in Hainan gemingshi yanjiu hui, eds. [Hainan revolutionary history research association, eds.] 琼崖风云 *Qiongya fengyun* [Hainan wind and clouds]. Haikou: Hainan chubanshe, 2006, 347–353.

14. "Japan Seeks Needed Pot of Gold on Hainan Isle," *Sunday Mercury* (November 5, 1940).

15. Zhuang Tian, quoting Zhou Enlai in his work *Qiongdao fengyan* 琼岛烽烟 [Hainan island beacon fire] (Guangdong renmin chubanshe, 1979), as cited in *FBYS*, 519.

16. Feng Baiju, "Zhihan Haiwai qiaobao baogao Qiong zhan bing qing nuanzhu" 致函海外侨胞报告琼战并请援助 [Letter to overseas Hainanese abroad with report and request for assistance], November 2, 1939; Feng Baiju, "Zhi Qiongya Huaqiao lianhe zonghui jiuji weiyuanhui zhuren Wang Taosong han liang feng" 至琼崖华侨联合总会救济委员会主任王兆松函两封 [Two letters to Wang Zhaosong, director of the Relief Committee of the Overseas Hainanese Federation], 1940; "Women ying jieshou Qiongqiao zonghui ji Feng Zongduizhang zhi huyu wei nan bao jiangshi quanmu hanyi" 我们应接受琼侨总会及冯总队长之呼吁为难胞将士劝募寒衣 [We should accept the Overseas Hainanese Committee's and Captain Feng's appeal for soldiers, funds, and winter clothes], October 30, 1940, all reprinted in *FBYS*, 6–13.

17. Feng Baiju, "Hongqi budao," 红旗不倒 [The Red flag didn't fall], written for *Hongqi piaopiao* 红旗飘飘 [The fluttering red flag], vol. 3, 1957, reprinted in Zhu Yihui 朱逸辉, ed. *Qiongya qizhi* 琼崖旗帜 [The Colors of Hainan] (Haikou: Hainan chubanshe, 2004), 513.

18. Lin Ping to Zhou Enlai, "Lin Ping guanyu Qiongya qingkuang zhi Zhou Enlai bing Zhongyang junwei dian" 林平关于琼崖情况致周恩来并中央军委电 [Lin Ping's telegam to Zhou Enlai and the Central Military Commission on the situation on Hainan], May 7, 1945, reprinted in Zhonggong Hainanqu dangwei dangshi bangongshi, 中共海南区党委党史办公室, eds. [Chinese Communist Party History Office of Hainan District, eds.], in *Feng Baiju yanjiu shiliao* 冯白驹研究史料 [Historical Research Materials on Feng Baiju] (Guangzhou: Guangdong renmin chubanshe, 1988), 478–481.

19. Fan Yunxi 范运晰, *Qiongji minguo renwu zhuan* 琼籍民国人物传 [Biographies of Hainanese in Republican China] (1999), 319–321.

20. Li Bo 李勃, *Hainan dao: Lidai jianzhu yange kao* 海南岛: 历代建置沿革考 [Hainan island: A study of the establishment and evolution of previous regimes] (2005), 456–463.

21. Sato Shojin 佐藤 正人 publishes his findings in the reports of his *Hainan Modern Historical Research Association* (海南岛近现代史研究).

22. Zhang Qianyi 张茜翼, "Riben xuezhe Sato Shojin 22 ci lai Hainan souji Riben jun qinlüe Qiong shiliao" 日本学者佐藤正人 22 次来海南搜集日军侵琼史料 [Japanese scholar, Sato Shojin, comes to Hainan for the twenty-second time to

gather historical materials on the Japanese military invasion of Hainan], *Zhongguo Xinwen Wang* 中国新闻网 [China News], October 30, 2012, accessed July 25, 2014, http://www.chinanews.com/sh/2012/10-30/4288752.shtml

23. Su Zhiliang, Hou Jiafang, Hu Haiying 苏智良, 侯桂芳, 胡海英, *Riben dui Hainan de qinlue jiqi baoxing* 日本对海南的侵略及其暴行 [The Japanese invasion and atrocities on Hainan] (2005).

24. Phillips (1980), 96–98.

25. Lin Ping to Zhou Enlai, "Lin Ping guanyu Qiongya qingkuang zhi Zhou Enlai bing Zhongyang junwei dian" 林平关于琼崖情况致周恩来并中央军委电 [Lin Ping's telegam to Zhou Enlai and the Central Military Commission on the situation on Hainan], May 7, 1945, reprinted in Zhonggong Hainanqu dangwei dangshi bangongshi, eds. 中共海南区党委党史办公室, eds. [Chinese Communist Party History Office of Hainan quarter, eds.], in *Feng Baiju yanjiu shiliao (FBYS)*, 478–479.

26. Ibid.

27. Interviews, Lin'cheng, March 1, 2008; Xianlai, March 26, 2008.

28. Su Zhiliang et al. (2005), 49.

29. Ibid. The account of the public gang-rape of women and the burning alive of Changtai villagers as written by Su Zhiliang et al., was confirmed in an interview by the author with the witness of these events in Changtai village, March 2008.

30. Major General John K. Singlaub, *Hazardous Duty: An American Soldier in the Twentieth Century* (1991), 94.

31. Ibid., 94, 91.

32. Su Zhiliang et al. (2005), 41.

33. Sato Shojin 佐藤 正人 has done the work of uncovering this and many other burial and massacre sites. The "Korea-town" mentioned here was excavated and reported on by Professor Sato in October 1999 reports of his *Hainan Modern Historical Research Association* (海南島近現代史研究).

34. Singlaub (1991), 99.

35. As a standard of Chinese Communist historiography on the subject, see Zhonggong Hainan shengwei dangshi yanjiu shi, eds. 中共海南省委党史研究室 [The research office of Hainan province's Chinese Communist Party history], *Zhongguo gongchandang Hainan lishi* 中国共产党海南历史 [The history the Chinese Communist Party on Hainan] (2007).

36. Feng Baiju 冯白驹, "Guanyu wo canjia geming guocheng de lishi qingkuang" 关于我参加革命过程的历史情况 [Regarding the historical situation of my participation in the revolutionary process], June 25, 1968, reprinted in *Feng Baiju yanjiu shiliao*, 447.

37. Qiongya wuzhuang douzheng shi bangongshi, eds. (1986) frontmatter.

38. "Women zai junshi shang shi zenyang fensui diren de qingjiao," 我们在军事上是怎样粉碎敌人的清剿 [How we militarily crushed the enemy's attempt to wipe us out], undated report from the Hainan Communist leadership to the mainland Communist leadership, probably late 1946 or early 1947.

39. Guenther Stein, "Japan's Army on China's Fronts," *Far Eastern Survey*, vol. 12, no. 1 (July 14, 1943), 141–143.

Chapter 5. New Allies

1. Feng Baiju, "Wuzhishan jian wu duo hongxia" 五指山尖五朵红霞 [Wuzhishan points to five red mists], December 1957, reprinted in *FBYSL*, 364–371.
2. Peng Chengwan 彭程萬, *Diaocha Qiongya shiye baogao shu* 调查琼崖实业报告书 [A report on the investigation of the industry and commerce of Hainan] (1920).
3. Wu Lien-teh (1937); Clark (1938), 391–418.
4. Li Bo 李勃, *Hainan dao: Lidai jianzhu yange kao* 海南岛: 历代建置沿革考 [Hainan island: A study of the establishment and evolution of previous dynasties] (2005), 287.
5. Anne Alice Csete, *A Frontier Minority in the Chinese World: The Li People of Hainan Island from the Han through the High Qing* (April 1995).
6. Anne Csete, "Ethnicity, Conflict, and the State in the Early to Mid-Qing: The Hainan Highlands, 1644–1800," in Pamela Kyle Crossely, Helen F. Siu, and Donald S. Sutton, eds., *Empire at the Margins: Culture, Ethnicity, and Frontier in Early Modern China* (2006), 231.
7. Csete (1995), 171.
8. Ibid., 84–85. Citing Ming histories, Csete notes that the source of the problem was attributed to unprecedented avarice and cruelty of local officials during large Ming uprisings.
9. Peng Chengwan, *Diaocha Qiongya* (1920), Li section, p. 4.
10. Ibid., 3.
11. Zhang Qingchang, *Liqi jiwen* [A record of the Li people], preface dated 1756, in Yu Quan, ed., *Linghai wenlu* [A record of unusual reports from Linghai], as noted in Csete (1995), 176.
12. Su Ke 肃克, ed., *Zhonghua wenhua Tongzhi: Minzu wenhua* 中华文化通志: 民族文化 [Annals of Chinese culture: People's culture] (1998), 418–419. The policy of the Ming was called *tu she, tu guan* (local house, local official) and that of most of the Qing era was simply called *zongguan zhidu*. This meant a steward system, roughly translated, though literally it simply meant, "to be in charge of."
13. Robert Swinhoe, "The Aborigines of Hainan" (Article 2), read before the Society on 25th March 1872, 26.
14. Ibid., 28–29.
15. Stevan Harrell, ed., *Cultural Encounters on China's Ethnic Frontiers* (1995), 7.
16. Hainan sheng difangzhi ban'gongshi 海南省地方志办公室 [The office of Hainan provincial gazetteers], eds., *Hainan shengzhi: Minzu zhi* 海南省志: 民族志 [Hainan provincial gazetteer: Nationalities gazetteer] (2006), 32–38. A brief account of their population figures through a few sample years is as follows. In 1412 there were 296,093 Han Chinese on Hainan, and 41,386 (12 percent of the total population). By 1935 the Li were almost 9 percent (almost 200,000 total) of the total Hainan population of more than 2 million. By 1953, the Li numbered about 358,000, and by 1990 they were more than one million. The dramatic increase from 1953 to

1990 (almost a trebling) is accounted for by health improvements, a more flexible child-bearing policy for ethnic minorities, and due to the custom of an intermarried couple counting itself and its descendants as fully and officially Li.

17. One American linguist working in Taiwan has presented the possibility of a connection between the origins of the aborigines of Taiwan and Hainan. Since Taiwan's aborigines have definitively traced their ancestral tracks to the Pacific and what is today Indonesia, this would shift the received knowledge on the Li origins. It seems likely, however, that linguistic interaction and exchange throughout the region caused any similarities between the aborigines of the two islands, since all other indicators point the Li ancestral tracks to mainland Southeast Asia. (Csete [1995], 13). The Li language was one of the most interesting aspects of the culture of these indigenous people of Hainan island to early twentieth-century scholars. These ethnologists and anthropologists focused a disproportionate amount of their studies on Li language, establishing a Romanized system of writing the language that was most likely quickly relegated to library shelves and left for only a handful of later scholars of Hainan to ponder. It is not clear that any military or political missions to Hainan ever brought with them a scholar of the Li language, and the compilation of Li linguistic information seems rather to have been an effort to establish their Southeast Asian origins, rather than to preserve the language and culture. See Walter Strzoda, *Die Li auf Hainan und ihre Beziehungen zum asiatischen Kontinent* [The Li on Hainan and their relations with the Asian continent] (1911), 196. Nearly every page of Strzoda's text is dedicated to Li linguistics, and it includes an extensive explanation of the sounds and meanings of many words in the Li language. The preeminent Hainan scholar of the Li, Wang Xueping, also dedicates a chapter of his most recent study of the Li to their language, but it is not the primary focus of his study (Wang Xueping [2004], 43–74). The Li language still does not have an official script.

18. Wang Xueping (2004), 72. This group has its roots in the Sino-Tibetan family, but it has since been accorded its own category by linguists. Kra-Dai languages are restricted for the most part to the Southeast Asian and southern Chinese mainland, with Hainan as the one notable island exception. Grouping the Li language and most of Hainan's Chinese dialects in this language groups orients the island toward the Asian continent rather than toward the surrounding island chains. This linguistic connection, and other characteristics of the Li people suggest that their ancestral roots are in Southeast Asia, and not in what is today Malaysia or the Philippines. See Ouyang Jueya, *The Cun Language* (1998); Graham Thurgood, *From Ancient Cham to Modern Dialects: Two Thousand Years of Language Contact and Change* (1999). This is a rich area of exploration, with perceived high stakes for the cultural and linguistic claims on all sides of the sometimes-contentious scholarly discussion.

19. *Hainan shengzhi: Minzu* (2006), frontmatter.

20. Leonard Clark, while researching his article for *National Geographic Magazine* cited above, shot some footage that was later made into the short documentary film, *Beyond the Mountains of the Red Mist in Hainan* (1938). The author is grateful to the staff of the American Museum of Natural History for digitizing this film and

making it available for Interlibrary Loan (American Museum of Natural History, 1985). This film is purportedly the first moving images of the Li people. Hans Stübel recorded the intricate distinctions in the dress of both Li men and women across the island in his exhaustive 1937 ethnographic study. His photographs are reprinted in this chapter. (Hans Stübel, *Die Li-Stämme der Insel Hainan: Ein Beitrag zur Volkskunde Südchinas* [The Li tribes of Hainan island: A contribution to the ethnography of South China]) (1937).

21. Harrell (1995), 10–13.

22. Cl. Madrolle, *Hai-nan: Le Pays et Ses Habitants* [Hainan: The land and its inhabitants] (1909), 22.

23. B.C. Henry, *Ling-Nam or Interior Views of Southern China Including Explorations in the Hitherto Untraversed Island of Hainan* (London: S.W. Partridge and Co., 1886), 350–351.

24. Harry A. Franck, *Roving through Southern China* (New York: The Century Co., 1925), 327.

25. Harrell (1995), 18.

26. Csete (2006).

27. Zhong Yuanxiu 中元秀, *Lizu renmin lingxiu Wang Guoxing* 黎族人民领袖王国兴 [The leader of the Li people, Wang Guoxing], *Qiongdao xinghuo* 琼岛星火 [Hainan spark], vol. 6 (Guangdong Province, publication for internal circulation, 1980). There are two editions of this biography by the same author. One is for "internal circulation" (*neibu faxing*), and contains more sensitive accounts of critiques by and of Wang Guoxing. This is the edition I use throughout. The differences between this edition and the one published in 1983 by "Nationalities Press" (*Minzu chubanshe*) are negligible for the portions used in this chapter, but they are more substantial in the post-1950 sections. The 1983 edition is Zhong Yuanxiu 中元秀, *Lizu renmin lingxiu Wang Guoxing* 黎族人民领袖王国兴 [The leader of the Li people, Wang Guoxing] (1983).

28. *Hainan shengzhi: Minzu* (2006), 756–757.

29. Zhong Yuanxiu (1983), 13–21.

30. Odaka (1942), 24–27.

31. Ibid., 26.

32. Wu Lien-teh (1937), 240.

33. Lloyd E. Eastman. *Seeds of Destruction: Nationalist China in War and Revolution, 1937–1949* (1984).

34. Zhong Yuanxiu (1983), 15.

35. Ibid.

36. Preserving Li culture has become a priority recently, and efforts especially in the realm of education have been made to document and encourage the distinctiveness of the Li of Hainan. See Zhang Hongxia and Zhan Changzhi, "A Library's Efforts en Route to Salvaging a Vanishing Culture," a paper presented at The World Library and Information Congress: 73rd Annual International Federation of Library Associations (IFLA) General Conference and Council (19–23 August 2007, Durban, South Africa).

NOTES TO CHAPTER 5

37. In this period, the anthropological interest that was shown in the Li people was mostly from the foreign community, and not from mainland China. Hans Stübel (Germany), Kunio Odaka (Japan), M. Savina (France), and earlier, Robert Swinhoe (Great Britain) all toured the island as well as other foreigners cited here, and wrote extensively on the Li people. Meanwhile the cultural and political interest of mainlanders seems to have been at a low point in Hainan's history. Mainly economic concerns can be found in the mainland perspective in this period, as is reflected in the Peng Chengwan survey, Chen Zhi's *Hainan dao xin zhi* [New Gazetteer of Hainan], and the Wu Lien-teh English-language article.

38. Wu Lien-teh (1937), 225–226.

39. Csete (1995), 215; Chen Keqin 陈克勤, *Hainan jiansheng* 海南建省 [Hainan is made a province] (2008), 20–33.

40. Peng Chengwan, *Diaocha Qiongya* (1920), Li situation.

41. Clark (1938), 404–405.

42. Peng Chengwan, *Diaocha Qiongya* (1920), Introduction.

43. Wang Guoxing 王国兴, "Gongchandang shi Lizu Miaozu renmin de jiuxing" 共产党是黎族苗族人民的救星 [The Communist Party is the savior of the Li and Miao people], in Qiongdao xinghuo bianji bu 琼岛星火编辑部 [Hainan Spark editorial department], eds., *Qiongdao xinghuo: Baisha qiyi zhuan* 琼岛星火: 白沙起义专辑 [Hainan Spark: Baisha Uprising special edition]. Vol. 12 (Guangdong Province, publication for internal circulation, 1983), 15.

44. Yuan jizheng 原吉征, "Chen Hanguang jingweilü zai Qiongya de cansha" 陈汉光警卫旅在琼崖的残杀 [Slaughter by Chen Hanguang's Hainan guards brigade], in Hainansheng zhengxie wenshiziliao weiyuanhui 海南省政协文史资料委员会 [Hainan Province *wenshiziliao*], eds., *Qiongdao fengyu* 琼岛风雨 [Hainan wind and rain], vol. 1 (1989), 60.

45. Li Duqing 李独清, *Lizu renmin guanghui de zhandou licheng* 黎族人民光辉的战斗历程 [The glorious struggle of the Li people], in Qiongdao xinghuo bianji bu 琼岛星火编辑部 [Hainan Spark editorial department], eds., *Qiongdao xinghuo* 琼岛星火 [Hainan spark] vol. 2 (1980), 121.

46. Zhong Yuanxiu (1983), 19.

47. Clark (1938), 408.

48. Zhong Yuanxiu (1983), 13–15.

49. Su Ke (1998), 418–419. Passing hereditary titles among ethnic groups at the margins of the Chinese empire precluded the need to send unwelcome officials from Beijing. These marginal groups were not required to follow the "rule of avoidance" for Chinese officials, which traditionally dictated that an official could not serve in his home district—a measure that was intended to prevent corruption and nepotism.

50. Zhong Yuanxiu (1983), 17–18.

51. Ibid.

52. *Hainan shengzhi: Minzu zhi* (2006), 782. Wang Xueping (2004), 92.

53. Zhong Yuanxiu (1983), 18.

54. *Hainan shengzhi: Minzu zhi* (2006), 774–775.

55. Wang Xueping (2004), 90–91.

56. Li Duqing (1980), 120–121. A later, more scholarly account of the Li uprising of 1897 also notes that it involved more than four thousand Li fighters, but makes no mention of an alliance with the Han. See Cheng Zhaoxing and Xing Yikong 程昭星, 邢诒孔. *Lizu renmin douzheng shi* 黎族人民斗争史 [A history of the struggles of the Li people] (1999), 505.

57. Swinhoe (1872), 71.

58. Cheng Zhaoxing and Xing Yikong (1999), 507.

59. In 1943, Wang Yujin remembered that the Lingshui Communist movement had included a mixture of Han and Li fighters (Zhong Yuanxiu [1980], 45).

60. Csete (1995), 174, citing a report from 1756, during the high Qing by the official, Zhang Qingchang. Zhang Qingchang, *Liqi jiwen* [A record of the Liqi people], preface dated 1756, in Yu Quan, ed., *Linghai Wenlu* [A record of unusual reports from Linghai (Lingnan)], Guangxu gengyin. The practice of circulating an "arrow of war" or "sending around an arrow" was not limited to the Li, and also a tradition among the warring peoples of early Iceland. See chapter 1, section 3 in Jane Smiley, ed., *The Sagas of Icelanders* (New York: Penguin, 2001).

61. Feng Baiju, "五指山尖五朵红霞" "Wuzhishan jianwuduo hongxia" [Wuzhishan red dusk glow], in Zhonggong Hainanqu dangwei dangshi ban'gongshi 中共海南区党委党史办公室 [The history office for the Chinese Communist Party Committee of Hainan district], eds., *Feng Baiju yanjiu shiliao* 冯白驹研究史料 [Feng Baiju research materials] (Guangzhou: Guangdong renmin chubanshe [article originally written in 1957], 1988), 364–371.

62. Odaka (1942), 14.

63. Ibid., 17.

64. Zhong Yuanxiu (1980), 21.

65. Ibid., 22–24.

66. Ibid., 35–37.

67. Ibid., 41.

68. Ibid., 42.

69. Ibid., 43.

70. You Qi 尤淇, *Qiongya Limin shanqu fangwen sanji* [Notes and Interviews on the Li people of Hainan's mountain region] 琼崖黎民山区访问散记 (1950), 1–4. In fact, Wang would certainly have known that the sudden appearance of a bright red mist is not unheard of in the mountains of Hainan, though it is striking to observe for the newcomer to the island. This might account for You Qi's eagerness to weave the dramatic natural phenomenon into his account of the events. In his 1937 *National Geographic* article cited above, Leonard Clark was also impressed by the sudden appearance of the "ox-blood red" mist (Clark [1938], 399–400), and it inspired the name of his short documentary film, also mentioned above, *Beyond the Mountains of the Red Mist in Hainan* (1938) (American Museum of Natural History, 1985).

71. Zhong Yuanxiu (1980).

72. The following accounts use the smaller figures of twenty thousand Li fighters and three hundred Nationalist casualties: Qiongya wuzhuang douzheng shi

ban'gongshi, eds. (1986), 171. Zhong Yuanxiu's biography of Wang Guoxing (1980) uses the larger figures for both Li participation and Nationalist casualties.

73. *Hainan shengzhi: Minzu zhi* (2006), 787.

74. Csete (1995), 109.

75. Zhonggong zhongyang shuji chu 中共中央书记处 [Chinese Communist Central secretary], "对琼崖工作指示" "Dui Qiongya gongzuo zhishi" [Directive on Hainan work], July 1940, as quoted in Qiongya wuzhuang douzheng shi ban'gongshi, eds. (1986), 171.

76. Zhan Lizhi 詹力之, "Suqing fandong shili, gonggu minzhu zhengquan: Huiyi yu Wang Guoxing tongzhi gongshi de rizi 肃清反动势力 巩固民主政权: 回忆与王国兴同志公事的日子 [Eliminating the influence of reactionaries, consolidating the power of democracy: A recollection of days working together with Comrade Wang Guoxing], in Zhonggong Guangdongsheng Hainan Lizu Miaozu zizhizhou wei dang shi ban'gongshi 中共广东省海南黎族苗族自治州委党史办公室 [Office of the Chinese Communist Party history committee of the Hainan Li-Miao autonomous region, Guangdong Province], eds., *Baisha qiyi: sishi zhounian jinian wenji* 白沙起义: 四十周年纪念文集 [Baisha Uprising: 40th anniversary commemoration writings]. Vol. 1 (1983).

Chapter 6. Holding Aloft Hainan's Red Flag

1. "Statement by President Truman on U.S. Policy towards China, Dec. 15, 1945," *Department of State Bulletin*, December 16, 1945.

2. Letter from Zhou Enlai to Australian Legation First Secretary, Patrick Shaw, May 14, 1946, Australian National Archives documents (321/46/3).

3. Singlaub (1991), 83.

4. Yu Maochun, *OSS in China: Prelude to Cold War* (New Haven: Yale University, 1997), 232.

5. Yu, Maochun (1997), 232. Ho's relationship with the OSS was a complex and perhaps paradoxical one that involved cooperation and confrontation, but in this instance of evacuating French personnel from Vietnam, a mutual enmity between the United States and the Vietnamese Communists was evident.

6. Singlaub (1991), 83.

7. Though the beginning of the full-scale Japanese invasion of China (starting in July1937 and the occupation of Hainan beginning in February of 1939) did not immediately prompt the withdrawal of the American Presbyterians, the bombing of Pearl Harbor in December of 1941 led to the missionaries' departure first to Hong Kong and then back to America. From 1939 through the end of 1941, the Japanese occupiers appear to have maintained rather close ties to the American Presbyterians on Hainan. The new eastern masters of the island simply became the power that the Americans attempted to work with to spread their faith through schools and hospitals (Lodwick, *Educating the Women of Hainan*, 1995).

8. Lionel Max Chassin (Timothy Osato and Louis Gelas, trans.), *The Communist Conquest of China: A History of the Civil War, 1945–1949* (1965).

9. Singlaub (1991), 99.

10. Ibid., 99–100.
11. Odd Arne Westad, *Decisive Encounters: The Chinese Civil War* (2003), 31.
12. Singlaub (1991), 99.
13. Ibid., 100.
14. Ibid., 98–99.
15. Phillips (1980).
16. Ibid., 109.
17. Zhonggong Hainan shengwei dangshi yanjiu shi, eds. 中共海南省委党史研究室 [The research office of Hainan province's Chinese Communist Party history], *Zhongguo gongchandang Hainan lishi* 中国共产党海南历史 [The history of Hainan's Chinese Communist Party] (2007), 411.
18. Phillips (1980), 98.
19. "Liang-Guang zongdui shi" bianxie lingdao xiaozu "两广纵队史" 编写领导小组 [Leading group editors of the "History of the Guangdong and Guangxi Column"], eds., *Liang-Guang zongdui shi* 两广纵队史 [History of the Guangdong and Guangxi Column] (1988), 1–8.
20. R.T. Phillips, "The Japanese Occupation of Hainan," *Modern Asian Studies* (1980), 107–109.
21. Fan Yunxi 范运晰, *Qiongji minguo renwu zhuan* 琼籍民国人物传 [Biographies of Hainanese in Republican China] (1999), 319–321.
22. Interview, Lin'cheng, March 1, 2008; Xianlai, March 26, 2008.
23. Westad (2003), 46.
24. Phillips (1980). Phillips notes that this was the Japanese view that the Communists were more active in their resistance fighting, and this view is not surprisingly shared by the contemporary and historical Chinese Communist views.
25. Lin Ping 林平 "Guanyu Qiongya gongzuo fangzhen gei Zhongyang de baogao" 关于琼崖工作方针给中央的报告 [Report to Party Central on the direction of work done on Hainan], October 26, 1945. As cited in Zhonggong Hainan shengwei dangshi yanjiushi, eds., 中国共产党海南历史 *Zhongguo gongchandang Hainan lishi* [Hainan's history of the Chinese Communist Party] (2007), 411.
26. Lloyd E. Eastman, *Seeds of Destruction: Nationalist China in War and Revolution, 1937–1949* (1984), 156–157.
27. Zhonggong Hainan shengwei dangshi yanjiushi, eds. (2007), 418–421.
28. Shi Dan 史丹, "Haikou tanpan" 海口谈判 [Haikou negotiations], in *Qiongdao xinghuo* 琼岛星火 [Hainan spark] (1987), 454.
29. Zhonggong Hainan shengwei dangshi yanjiushi, eds. (2007), 411.
30. Feng Baiju, "Zai Qiongya jian jun shi zhou nian jinian dahui shang de yanshuo" 在琼崖建军十周年纪念大会上的演说 [Speech at the commemorative meeting for the tenth anniversary of the founding of the Hainan army], December 5, 1948, reprinted in *Feng Baiju yanjiu shiliao*, 150.
31. "Zhonggong zhongyang guanyu XX Qiongya budui jixu fenzhan gei Feng, Huang, Li dian" 中共中央关于鼓励琼崖部队奋战给冯黄李电 [Telegram from Party Central to Feng (Baiju), Huang (Kang), and Li (Ming) regarding encouragement of the Hainan army's struggle], September 30, 1946, in *Feng Baiju yanjiu shiliao*, 485.

32. Chen Dagui, Chen Qin, and Wang Jun were among the leaders of the Hainan Communist military who lost their lives in this attempt to reestablish this vital line of communication between the mainland Chinese Communists and the Hainan movement. See Qiongya wuzhuang douzhengshi bangongshi, eds. (1986), 212.

33. Xing Yikong, Peng Changlin, Qian Yue 邢诒孔, 彭长霖, 钱跃, *Feng Baiju jiangjun zhuan* 冯白驹将军传 [The Biography of General Feng Baiju] (1998), 327. This account is taken from a personal recollection of Wang Yuzhang, who was tasked with organizing the communications of the Hainan Column.

34. Gregor Benton, *New Fourth Army: Communist Resistance Along the Yangtze and the Huai, 1938–1941* (1999), 59.

35. Huang Yunming, as told to Zhou Longjiao 黄运明口述, 周龙蛟整理 "Wo tong Qiongya diantai de qingyuan" 我同琼崖电台的情缘 [My love for Radio Hainan], in Hainan gemingshi yanjiu hui, eds. [Hainan revolutionary history research association, eds.] 琼崖风云 *Qiongya fengyun* [Hainan wind and clouds] (2006), 228–229.

36. Singlaub (1991), 95.

37. Xing Yilin, Han Qiyuan, Huang Liangjun, *Qiongqiao cangsong* 琼侨沧桑 [The ups and downs of Overseas Hainanese (English title)] (1991), 47.

38. Xing Yilin et al. (1991), 76–78.

39. As was noted in chapter 2, the British were also most likely in part clandestinely responsible for the arrest and execution of a prominent Hainan operative, newly arrived from Hong Kong in the early years of the Communist Party on Hainan. See Chan Lau Kit-ching, *From Nothing to Nothing: The Chinese Communist Movement and Hong Kong, 1921–1936* (New York: St. Martin's Press, 1999), 188–189. This operative was Sichuan native, Li Shuoxun, who arrived in Hainan in 1931 and was executed within weeks. He left his son (the now well-known Li Peng) and wife in the care of Zhou Enlai. Also see Hainan gemingshi yanjiu hui, eds. [Hainan revolutionary history research association, eds.] 琼崖风云 *Qiongya fengyun* [Hainan wind and clouds] (2006), 9–10.

40. "Zhonggong zhongyang guanyu guli Qiongya budui jixu fenzhan gei Feng, Huang, Li dian" 中共中央关于鼓励琼崖部队奋战给冯黄李电 [Telegram from Party Central to Feng (Baiju), Huang (Kang), and Li (Ming) regarding encouragement of the Hainan army's struggle], September 30, 1946, in *Feng Baiju yanjiu shiliao*, 485.

41. Ma Biqian 马必前, "Qiongya dianbo" 琼崖电波 [Hainan broadcast], in Hainan gemingshi yanjiu hui, eds. [Hainan revolutionary history research association, eds.] 琼崖风云 *Qiongya fengyun* [Hainan wind and clouds] (2006), 211.

42. Wu Zhi, He Lang 吴之, 贺郎, *Feng Baiju zhuan* 冯白驹传 [Biography of Feng Baiju] (1996), 588.

43. Ibid., 591.

44. Feng Baiju, "Gongbu san nian ziwei zhanzheng zhi zhanji" 公布三年自卫战争只战绩 (Report on the successes in three years of the struggle of self-defense," December 10, 1948, in *Feng Baiju yanjiu shiliao*, 156.

45. Feng Baiju, "Zai Qiongya jian jun shi zhou nian jinian dahui shang de yanshuo" 在琼崖建军十周年纪念大会上的演说 [Speech at the commemorative

meeting for the tenth anniversary of the founding of the Hainan army], in *Feng Baiju yanjiu shiliao*, 150–155. Han Hanying was the military leader of the Nationalist forces on Hainan in 1948.

46. Benton (1992), xxxvii.
47. Ibid.
48. Vogel (1971 [1969]).

Chapter 7. Sharing Victory

1. "Zhongguo renmin geming junshi weiyuanhui dianhe Hainandao quanbu jiefang" 中国人民革命军事委员会电贺海南岛全部解放 [Telegram of congratulations from the Chinese People's Revolutionary Military Committee on the complete liberation of Hainan island], May 5, 1950, reprinted in Zhu Yihui 朱逸辉, ed., *Qiongya qizhi* [The Colors of Hainan] (2004), 8.

2. Li Xiaobing, *A History of the Modern Chinese Army* (2007), 133. This assessment is not incorrect, and it is not within Li's stated goals to include the nuance of every regional struggle in the Communist revolution. However, this brief treatment does perpetuate the notion that the Hainan campaign was fought and won by an overwhelming landing force that simply swept the enemy before them.

3. Liu Zhenhua, *Hainan jiefang* 海南解放 [Liberating Hainan] (1998), 81.

4. Han Xianchu, "Hainandao saotao zhan" 海南岛扫讨战 [The Hainan island mop-up campaign], from *Xinghuo liaoyuan* 星火燎原 [A single spark can start a prairie fire], translated and reprinted in the appendix of Reed Richard Probst, *The Communist Conquest of Hainan* (1982), 228.

5. Ibid., 235.

6. "Zhongguo Gongchandang de guanghui zhaoyao zai Hainan shang" 中国共产党的光辉照耀在海南上 [The glory of the Chinese Communist Party shines on Hainan], 1951. Reprinted in Zhu Yihui 朱逸辉, ed., *Qiongya qizhi* [The Colors of Hainan] (2004), 492–498.

7. "Hainan's saviors," Hainan anti-Japanese wartime song, reprinted in He Lang and Wu zhi 贺朗, 吴之, eds., *Chengqi Qiongya banbi tian* 撑起琼崖半壁天 [Lifting up half of the Hainan sky] (1992), 440.

8. This phrase was General John Burgoyne's (1722–1792) description of American troops. He referred to the Americans as a "rabble in arms, flushed with success and insolence," and Kenneth Roberts used the phrase as the title of his Revolutionary War novel, *Rabble in Arms* (Doubleday: New York, 1936). It is interesting to note that with the distance of time, Americans embrace the culture of a "rabble in arms," and this may be the direction in the PRC. In 1950, I believe, it was more important for the PRC leadership to point to its transformation from such a rabble into a massive and effective conventional fighting force.

9. Michael Szonyi, *Cold War Island: Quemoy on the Front Line* (2008). Quemoy is a Hokkien romanization that is still sometimes used for Jinmen. Crossing the Qiongzhou Strait with the Fourth Field Army was a Soviet documentar-

ian whose footage has become the source for seminal images of the campaign. Some of this footage has been compiled in historical documentary film accounts of the campaign at: http://v.ifeng.com/his/201005/b8a742dd-e53b-44ec-bfe5-7eeb6ffc65b2.shtml

10. Suzanne Pepper emphasizes corruption and incompetence in her unsurpassed 1978 study of the Chinese Civil War. The Nationalists' administrative corruption and incompetence lost the war as much as any Communist attributes won it (Suzanne Pepper, *Civil War in China: The Political Struggle, 1945–1949* [Berkeley: University of California Press, 1978], 423). On Hainan this nepotism was embodied by Chen Jitang and Han Hanying. The military leadership of Xue Yue in the final days of Nationalist rule on Hainan offered a glimpse of another road of efficiency and responsibility in Nationalist rule, but Xue's tenure was quickly ended by the Communist campaign.

11. Seymour Topping, *On the Front Lines of the Cold War: An American Correspondent's Journal from the Chinese Civil War to the Cuban Missile Crisis and Vietnam* (Baton Rouge: Louisiana State University Press, 2010), 115–116.

12. Deng Hua, "Jiefang Hainan" 解放海南 [Liberating Hainan], in He Lang and Wu zhi 贺朗, 吴之, eds., *Chengqi Qiongya banbi tian* 撑起琼崖半壁天 [Lifting up half of the Hainan sky] (1992), 415–423. Liu Zhenhua, *Hainan jiefang* 海南解放 [Liberating Hainan] (1998).

13. Interview with three guerrilla veterans from Xianlai village of Qiongshan county provided eye-witness accounts of their first meetings with the mainland PLA forces, October 8, 2008.

14. This interview with a PLA captain, then living in Haikou, provided eye-witness account and opinion of the first interactions between PLA regulars and the Hainan guerrillas, October 15, 2008. (Numbers of casualties are wildly divergent in contemporary sources, based on propaganda, especially in a specific engagement like the initial crossing of the Qiongzhou Strait. Today most estimates of total Communist casualties in the Hainan campaign are around four thousand. Most of these were probably incurred in the earliest phase of the fighting, namely in the initial crossing, when Nationalist warships and planes were able to sink entire unarmed junks full of PLA soldiers.)

15. Interview with PLA captain, October 15, 2008. In late 1949 and early 1950, both the *New York Times* and *Los Angeles Times* provided daily updates on the progress of the Communist conquest of Hainan, with information coming via press offices on Hong Kong and with little delay. The world watched intently as half of the Nationalists territory (considered by some to be "free China") was on the verge of falling to the Reds.

16. Han Xianchu, "Hainandao saotao zhan," 225–241.

17. Ma Baishan and Ma Biqian 马白山, 马必前, *Yuxue tianya* 浴血天涯 [Bloody Horizon] (2007 [vol. 2]), 387–389.

18. Chen Keqin, *Hainan jiansheng* 海南建省 [Making Hainan a province] (2008), 20–33.

19. Zhou Quangen 周泉根, *Sui, Tang, Wudai Hainan renwu zhi* 隋唐五代海南人物志 [Prominent figures of the Sui, Tang, and Five Dynasties] (Haikou: Sanhuan chubanshe, 2007), 164–204.

20. Jeremy Brown and Paul G. Pickowicz, eds., *Dilemmas of Victory: The Early Years of the People's Republic of China* (2007).

21. Zhonggong Hainan shengwei dangshi yanjiu shi [Hainan Provincial Committee for Historical Research, Chinese Communist Party], eds., *Zhongguo renmin jiefangjun: Hainan jiangling zhuan* 中国人民解放军: 海南将领传 [Chinese People's Liberation Army: Biographies of Hainan's Military Officers] (Guangzhou: Guangdong renmin chubanshe, 1991), 201–203.

22. Lu Jun and Xing Yikong 陆军, 邢诒孔, "Dui Qiongya genjudi 23 nian hongqi budao de chubu tantao" 对琼崖革命根据地 23 年红旗不倒的初步探讨 [A preliminary inquiry into the Hainan base areas "holding aloft the red flag for twenty-three years"], in Zhonggong Hainan shengwei dangshi yanjiu shi, eds., *Qiongya geming yanjiu lunwenxuan* (1994), 19.

23. "Dongyuan xuesheng canjia Qiongya gongxue xuexi tongzhi" 动员学生参加琼崖公学学习通知 [Notice on mobilizing students to attend Hainan Public School]. Issued by Chairman Feng Baiju, Hainan Interim Democratic Government, October 24, 1948.

24. "Guanyu Qiongzong fuban junzheng xuexiao de zhishi" 关于琼纵复办军政学校的指示 [Directive on the Hainan Independent Column reestablishing the military and political schools]. Issued by Chairman Feng Baiju, Hainan Interim Democratic Government, January 12, 1949.

25. Pepper (1980), 95–131.

26. *Hainan sheng zhi: Jinrong zhi*, 533–534.

27. Ibid., 28, 72, 532–533. Most recently there had been two notable attempts. In December of 1948 a small run of about 80 *yuan* was printed in denominations of 1 and 2 *jiao*, and 5 *fen* notes (1 *yuan* = 10 *jiao* = 100 *fen*). This was clearly only an experiment, and the notes were recalled in May of the following year. At the time of the recall, though, the Hainan Column authorities printed another run of paper money. This was presumably a more ambitious venture, though there are no records of how much money was printed in this second issuance. The notes issued in this second run were also recalled, but not until the Communist takeover a year later, in May of 1950, when the Communist government essentially bought the old money using the new currency, the mainland *renminbi* ("the people's money").

28. *Hainan sheng zhi: Jinrong zhi*, 533–534.

29. Telegrams between Feng Baiju and Deng Hua, *Feng Baiju yanjiu shiliao*, 183–191.

30. He Lang and Wu Zhi 贺朗, 吴之, *Feng Baiju zhuan* 冯百驹传 [Biography of Feng Baiju] (1996), 726–727. Lin accomplished the task of collecting the Nationalist reserves nearly perfectly. Feng only scolded him on one point. When Lin and his men were collecting the gold reserves, Lin suggested Feng's wife take a bauble for herself—"a souvenir of the revolution." For the austere Feng, this type

of behavior would not stand, and according to this account in Feng's biography, Lin quickly acknowledged his mistake under Feng's criticism.

31. Hainan sheng zhi: Jinrong zhi, 72, 75, 533–534. The name of the bank would be changed in November 1950, and the Hainan Branch would become simply a division of the Guangdong Branch of the People's Bank of China.

32. Ma Baishan and Ma Biqian 马白山, 马必前, Yuxue tianya 浴血天涯 [Bloody Horizon] (2007 [vol. 2]), 387–389.

33. Ibid.

34. Ma Baishan 马白山, "Beishang canjia zhengxie huiyi" 北上参加政协会议 [Going north to attend the Political Consultative Conference], in Ma Baishan and Ma Biqian 马白山, 马必前, Yuxue tianya 浴血天涯 [Bloody Horizon] (2007) [vol. 2], 122–125.

35. Hainansheng difang shizhi bangongshi [Hainan provincial local history and gazetteer office], eds. Hainan shengzhi: Renkou zhi, fangyan zhi, zongjiao zhi 海南省志: 人口志, 方言志, 宗教志 [Hainan provincial gazetteer: Population gazetteer, dialect gazetteer, religion gazetteer] (1994), 67–69.

36. Yang Dechun 杨德春, Hainandao gudai jianshi 海南岛古代简史 [A brief history of Hainan island in ancient times] (Jilin: Dongbei shifan daxue chubanshe, 1988), 143–148.

37. Zhong Yuanxiu 中元秀, Lizu renmin lingxiu Wang Guoxing 黎族人民领袖王国兴 [The leader of the Li people, Wang Guoxing] (1983), 33–38.

38. Ma Baishan 马白山, "Beishang canjia zhengxie huiyi" 北上参加政协会议 [Going north to attend the Political Consultative Conference], in Ma Baishan and Ma Biqian 马白山, 马必前, Yuxue tianya 浴血天涯 [Bloody Horizon] (2007) [vol. 2], 123–124.

39. A. Doak Barnett, *China on the Eve of the Communist Takeover* (1963), 296–303.

40. Deng Hua speech, FBYS.

41. Qiongya wuzhuang douzheng shi bangongshi [Hainan military struggle history office], eds., Qiongya zongdui shi 琼崖纵队史 [History of the Hainan Column] (1986), 209–217.

42. Chen Keqin, Hainan jiansheng 海南建省 [Making Hainan a province] (2008), 54.

43. Han Xianchu, "Hainandao saotao zhan" 海南岛扫讨战 [The Hainan island mop-up campaign], from Xinghuo liaoyuan 星火燎原 [A single spark can start a prairie fire], translated and reprinted in the appendix of Reed Richard Probst, *The Communist Conquest of Hainan* (1982), 227.

44. Dangdai Zhongguo de Hainan 当代中国的海南 [Hainan in modern China] (1993), 77.

45. *China Handbook, 1951* (1952), 151.

46. "Chen Jitang yao zuo Hainan wang," [Chen Jitang wants to be king of Hainan] in Xinwen tiandi (December 4, 1949), 9.

47. Xinwen tiandi (December 31, 1949).

48. Yan Xishan, Taiwan ji Hainan dao baowei an [A plan for the protection of Taiwan and Hainan Islands], 17–24.

49. Hainan shengzhi: Junshi zhi, 690.

50. Yuan Jizheng "Chen Hanguang jingweilü zai Qiongya de cansha" [Chen Hanguang's guard brigade's massacre in Hainan], He Kaiqia "Chen Hanguang dui Hainan shaoshuminzu de xuexing tongzhi" [Chen Hanguang's bloody rule over the ethnic minorities of Hainan].

51. Barnett (1963), 296–303.

Chapter 8. Bringing Hainan to the Nation's Heel

1. Tiewes (1979), 368.

2. Zhengxie Lingaoxian wenshi ziliao yanjiu weiyuanhui 政协临高县文史资料研究委员会 [Chinese People's Political Consultative Conference (CPPCC) Lingao County Historical Research Committee], eds., *Lingao Wenshi* 临高文史 [Lingao literature and history], vol. 12, Hainansheng feiyingli chuban (1998).

3. For a major 1962 retrospective speech by Hainan's most prominent Communist leader in the 1930s, 1940s, and 1950s, see Feng Baiju's February 5, 1962, speech, "Zai Zhonggong Guangdong shengwei zhaokai de tanxin hui shang de fayan" 在中共广东省委召开的谈心会上的发言 [Speech at the meeting of the Chinese Communist Party Guangdong Provincial Committee], reprinted in Guangdong Qiongya gemingshi yanjiuhui 广东琼崖革命史研究会 [Guangdong, Hainan revolutionary history research association], eds., *Feng Baiju huiyilu* 冯白驹回忆录 [Feng Baiju recollection volume] (2000). For official communications between the Hainan and mainland leadership during land reform of the early 1950s, see 海南省史志工作办公室，海南省档案局(馆) [Hainan provincial historical office, Hainan provincial archives (museum)], eds., *Hainan tudi gaige yundong ziliao xuanbian, 1951–1953* 海南土地改革运动资料选编, 1951–1953 [Selected materials on the land reform movement in Hainan, 1951–1953] (2002).

4. The work, translated into English by Stacy Mosher and Guo Jian, is Yang Jisheng's *Tombstone: The Great Chinese Famine, 1958–1962* (New York: Farrar, Straus and Giroux, 2012).

5. Feng Baiju, "Zai Zhonggong Guangdong shengwei zhaokai de tanxin hui shang de fayan" 在中共广东省委召开的谈心会上的发言 [Speech at the meeting of the Chinese Communist Party Guangdong Provincial Committee], February 5, 1962, reprinted in Guangdong Qiongya gemingshi yanjiuhui 广东琼崖革命史研究会 [Guangdong, Hainan revolutionary history research association], eds., *Feng Baiju huiyilu* 冯白驹回忆录 [Feng Baiju recollection volume] (2000), 253–254.

6. Xiaorong Han, "Localism in Chinese Communist Politics Before and After 1949: The Case of Feng Baiju," *The Chinese Historical Review* 11, 1 (Spring 2004): 23–56.

7. Ye Ding 叶顶, *Nanxia Nanxia! Xin Zhongguo de jijiehao* [Advance South, Advance South!: New China's call to arms] 南下南下! 新中国的集结号 (2010).

8. William T. Rowe, *China's Last Empire: The Great Qing* (Cambridge, MA: Belknap/Harvard, 2009), 38–39.

9. Feng Baiju 冯白驹, "Feng Baiju tanpan Ou Mengjue qingkuang" 冯白驹谈攀区梦觉情况 [Feng Baiju discusses the situation with Ou Mengjue], undated, hand-written document, probably a speech in a closed Party meeting, dating to 1961 or 1962.

10. Feng Baiju 冯白驹, "Zhaojin jihui xiang jiefang dajun xuexi" 抓紧机会向解放大军学习 [Seize the opportunity to study from the PLA main army], originally printed in *Xin Hainan bao* 新海南报 [New Hainan Journal], May 8, 1950, and reprinted in Zhonggong Hainanqu dangwei dangshi ban'gongshi 中共海南区党委党史办公室 [The history office for the Chinese Communist Party Committee of Hainan district], eds., *Feng Baiju yanjiu shiliao* 冯白驹研究史料 [Historical Research Materials on Feng Baiju] (1988), 192–195.

11. Ou Mengjue. "What Have Been the Mistakes of Ku Ta-ch'un and Feng Pai-chu?" in *Survey of China Mainland Press* 1899, pp. 16–23. (Originally published in the first issue of 上游 *Shangyou* [1958]).

12. Ibid.

13. Frederick C. Tiewes, *Politics and Purges in China: Rectification and the Decline of Party Norms, 1950–1965* (1979), 357–358, 366–367.

14. Wu Zhi, He Lang 吴之, 贺郎, *Feng Baiju zhuan* 冯白驹传 [Biography of Feng Baiju] (1996), 844–845.

15. Wang Xueping 王学萍, *Zhongguo Lizu* 中国黎族 [The Li Ethnic Group in China] (2004), 465.

16. Chen Keqin 陈克勤, *Hainan jiansheng* 海南建省 [Hainan is made a province] (2008), 50–51.

17. This took place following the shift in name of the currency to renminbi, or "people's money," but prior to the adjustment in denominations in 1955 from the inflated Nationalist currency. So Feng's 5,000,000 would actually be the equivalent of 500 *yuan*, following the adjustment.

18. Hu Tichun, Xu Chunhong, Wang Huanqiu 胡提春, 许春宏, 王焕秋, *Feng Baiju jiangjun zhuan* 冯白驹将军传 [Biography of General Feng Baiju], *Qiongdao Xinghuo* (Hainan Spark) Series, vol. 3 (1981), 108–111.

19. Feng Baiju 冯白驹, *Zhongguo gongchandang de guanghui zhaoyao zai Hainandao shang* 中国共产党的光辉照耀在海南岛上 [The radiance of the Chinese Communist Party shines on Hainan island] (1951).

20. Ibid., 1.

21. Hainansheng difangzhi bangongshi 海南省地方志办公室 [Hainan provincial gazetteer office], eds., *Hainan shengzhi: Tudi zhi* 海南省志: 土地志 [Hainan provincial gazetteer: Land gazetteer] (2007), 357–359.

22. Hainansheng difangzhi bangongshi 海南省地方志办公室 [Hainan provincial gazetteer office], eds., *Hainan shengzhi: Haiyang zhi, Geming genjudi zhi* 海南省志: 海洋志, 革命根据地志 [Hainan provincial gazetteer: Maritime gazetteer, revolutionary base area gazetteer] (2006), 186, 193, 195.

23. Vogel (1971 [1969]), 95.

24. Hainansheng difangzhi bangongshi 海南省地方志办公室 [Hainan provincial gazetteer office], eds., *Hainan shengzhi: Tudi zhi* 海南省志：土地志 [Hainan provincial gazetteer: Land gazetteer] (2007), 360.

25. Cai Dizhi 蔡迪支, *Guangdong 1949–1959* 广东 1949–1959 [Guangdong, 1949–1959] (1959), 104–105.

26. Tiewes (1979), 367.

27. "Zhonggong Hainan qu wei guanyu tugai gongzuo jihua," 中共海南区委关于土改工作计划 [Chinese Communist Party Hainan District Committee plan regarding land reform work], February 13, 1951, reprinted in 海南省史志工作办公室，海南省档案局(馆) [Hainan provincial historical office, Hainan provincial archives (museum)], eds., *Hainan tudi gaige yundong ziliao xuanbian, 1951–1953* 海南土地改革运动资料选编，1951–1953 [Selected materials on the land reform movement in Hainan, 1951–1953], Haikou, 2002, p. 6.

28. "Hainan junzheng weiyuanhui guanyu tugai zhong ruogan teshu wenti de guiding" 海南军政委员会关于土改中若干特殊问题的规定 [Provisions regarding a number of special problems in land reform by the Hainan military administrative committee] March 17, 1951, reprinted in 海南省史志工作办公室，海南省档案局(馆) [Hainan provincial historical office, Hainan provincial archives (museum)], eds., *Hainan tudi gaige yundong ziliao xuanbian, 1951–1953* 海南土地改革运动资料选编，1951–1953 [Selected materials on the land reform movement in Hainan, 1951–1953] (Haikou, 2002), 19–22.

29. Hainan junzheng weiyuanhui shishi tudi gaige de bugao 海南军政委员会实施土地改革的布告 [Hainan military administrative committee announcement on the implementation of land reform] March 22, 1951, reprinted in 海南省史志工作办公室，海南省档案局(馆) [Hainan provincial historical office, Hainan provincial archives (museum)], eds., *Hainan tudi gaige yundong ziliao xuanbian, 1951–1953* 海南土地改革运动资料选编，1951–1953 [Selected materials on the land reform movement in Hainan, 1951–1953] (Haikou, 2002), 24–25.

30. Vogel (1971 [1969]), 99–110. The precision with which Guangdong land reform is striking in Vogel's account. January and February are labor-intensive in the Guangdong calendar since these are the planting months. According to Vogel, January and February of 1951 saw moderate policies that did not alienate farmers while their planting labor was needed, and then the spring brought a flood of radicalized northern cadres to take over the process.

31. "Hainan tugaiwei guanyu tugai shidian ji ge wenti de tongzhi" 海南土改委关于土改试点几个问题的通知 [Circular by the Hainan land reform committee regarding some problems with the land reform experiment], April 13, 1951, reprinted in 海南省史志工作办公室，海南省档案局(馆) [Hainan provincial historical office, Hainan provincial archives (museum)], eds., *Hainan tudi gaige yundong ziliao xuanbian, 1951–1953* 海南土地改革运动资料选编，1951–1953 [Selected materials on the land reform movement in Hainan, 1951–1953] (Haikou, 2002), 28–29.

32. Vogel (1971 [1969]), 112.

33. "Hainan tugai gongzuo di yi tuan guanyu huafen jieji gongzuo wenti de tongzhi" 海南土改工作第一团关于划分阶级工作问题的通知 [Circular by the

Hainan first land work group regarding some problems with class divisions], April 14, 1951, reprinted in 海南省史志工作办公室, 海南省档案局(馆) [Hainan provincial historical office, Hainan provincial archives (museum)], eds., *Hainan tudi gaige yundong ziliao xuanbian, 1951–1953* 海南土地改革运动资料选编, 1951–1953 [Selected materials on the land reform movement in Hainan, 1951–1953] (Haikou, 2002), 30–31.

34. Michael R. Phillips, Huaqing Liu, and Yanping Zhang, "Suicide and Social Change in China," *Culture, Medicine, and Psychiatry* (1999), 25–50.

35. Yang Kuisong, "Reconsidering the Campaign to Suppress Counterrevolutionaries," *The China Quarterly* (2008), 109, 115.

36. Ibid., 116. Yang quoted Ye Jianying's report on the *zhenfan* work in southern China from May 17, 1951.

37. Vogel (1971 [1969]), 115, 119.

38. "Zhonggong Hainan quwei zhuanfa 'Zhongnanju guanyu chuli nongmin zisha shijian de si zhong banfa' de tongzhi" 中共海南区委转发 "中南局关于处理农民自杀事件的四种办法" 的通知 [Circular by the Hainan Chinese Communist Party district committee "Central Southern Bureau regarding four methods of handling peasant suicides"], February 12, 1952, reprinted in 海南省史志工作办公室, 海南省档案局(馆) [Hainan provincial historical office, Hainan provincial archives (museum)], eds., *Hainan tudi gaige yundong ziliao xuanbian, 1951–1953* 海南土地改革运动资料选编, 1951–1953 [Selected materials on the land reform movement in Hainan, 1951–1953] (Haikou, 2002), 436–437.

39. "Zhonggong Hainan qu wei guanyu kefu ganbu youqing sixiang shenru fanba tuizu douzheng de tongbao" 中共海南区委关于克服干部右倾思想深入反霸退租斗争的通报 [Circular by the Chinese Communist Party district committee of Hainan regarding overcoming the rightist tendencies among cadres and deepening the anti-tyrant rent remission struggle], April 19, 1952, reprinted in 海南省史志工作办公室, 海南省档案局(馆) [Hainan provincial historical office, Hainan provincial archives (museum)], eds., *Hainan tudi gaige yundong ziliao xuanbian, 1951–1953* 海南土地改革运动资料选编, 1951–1953 [Selected materials on the land reform movement in Hainan, 1951–1953] (Haikou, 2002), 510–514.

40. Hu Tichun, Xu Chunhong, Wang Huanqiu 胡提春, 许春宏, 王焕秋, *Feng Baiju jiangjun zhuan* 冯白驹将军传 [Biography of General Feng Baiju], *Qiongdao Xinghuo* (Hainan Spark) Series, vol. 3 (1981), 112.

41. Zhong Yuanxiu 中元秀, *Lizu renmin lingxiu Wangguoxing* 黎族人民领袖王国兴 [Wang Guoxing, leader of the Li people], Qiongdao xinghuo (Hainan Spark series), vol. 6 (Haikou, 1981), 142–144.

42. Feng Baiju, "Zai Zhonggong Guangdong shengwei zhaokai de tanxin hui shang de fayan" 在中共广东省委召开的谈心会上的发言 [Speech at the meeting of the Chinese Communist Party Guangdong Provincial Committee], February 5, 1962, reprinted in Guangdong Qiongya gemingshi yanjiuhui 广东琼崖革命史研究会 [Guangdong, Hainan revolutionary history research association], eds., *Feng Baiju huiyilu* 冯白驹回忆录 [Feng Baiju recollection volume] (2000).

43. Zhongyang jilü jiancha weiyuanhui 中央纪律检查委员会 [Central committee on disciplinary inspection], *Guanyu Feng Baiju, Gu Dacun tongzhi de wenti*

shenli yijian de baogao 冯白驹, 古大存同志的问题审理意见的报告 [Report of opinions on the hearing over the problems of Comrades Feng Baiju and Gu Dacun] (1983), in *Feng Baiju yanjiu shiliao*, 527–528.

44. Edward H. Schafer, *Shore of Pearls: Hainan Island in Early Times* (Berkeley: University of California Press, 1970), 5.

Epilogue

1. Ezra Vogel, *One Step Ahead In China: Guangdong Under Reform* (Cambridge, MA: Harvard University Press, 1989), 291–294.
2. Li Jinming, "Nansha Indisputable Territory," *China Daily* (June 15, 2011).
3. James Manicom, "Understanding the Nature of China's Challenge to Maritime East Asia," *Harvard Asia Quarterly* (December 24, 2010).
4. Edward Wong, "Beijing Warns US About South China Sea Disputes," *New York Times* (June 22, 2011).
5. The annual Bo'ao Forum for Asia draws an impressive roster of dignitaries, including current and former heads of state, whose expressed aim is to increase the economic integration of the region. This economic integration has prevailed in recent years, even over any escalation of regional tensions. (http://www.boaoforum.org/html/home-en.asp)
6. Philip Feifan Xie, *Authenticating Ethnic Tourism* (Bristol: Channel View Publications, 2011).
7. "Hainan to Expand Tax Rebate Program to Domestic Tourists," *People's Daily Online* (March 22, 2011).

BIBLIOGRAPHY

Anderson, Benedict. *Imagined Communities: Reflections on the Origin and Spread of Nationalism*. New York: Verso, 1991.
Appadurai, Arjun. *Modernity at Large: Cultural Dimensions of Globalization*. Minneapolis: University of Minnesota Press, 1996.
Averill, Stephen C. *Revolution in the Highlands: China's Jinggangshan Base Area*. Lanham, MD: Rowman & Littlefield, 2006.
Barnett, A. Doak. *China on the Eve of the Communist Takeover*. New York: Frederick A. Praeger, 1961.
Benewick, Robert, and Stephanie Hemelryk Donald. *State of China Atlas: Mapping the World's Fastest Growing Economy*. Berkeley: University of California Press, 2009.
Benton, Gregor. *Mountain Fires: The Red Army's Three-Year War in War in South China, 1934–1938*. Berkeley: University of California Press, 1992.
———. *New Fourth Army: Communist Resistance Along the Yangtze and the Huai, 1938–1941*. Berkeley: University of California Press, 1999.
Blythe, Wilfred. *The Impact of Chinese Secret Societies in Malaya: A Historical Study*. London: Oxford University Press, 1969.
Bourne, Kenneth, and D. Cameron Watt, eds. *British Documents on Foreign Affairs: Reports and Papers from the Foreign Office Confidential Print*. University Publications of America, An imprint of CIS, 1994.
Brødsgaard, Kjeld Erik. *Hainan: State, Society, and Business in a Chinese Province*. Routledge: London, 2009.
Brown, Jeremy, and Paul Pickowicz, eds. *Dilemmas of Victory: The Early Years of the People's Republic of China*. Cambridge, MA: Harvard University Press, 2007.
Cai Dizhi 蔡迪支. *Guangdong 1949–1959* 广东 1949–1959 [Guangdong, 1949–1959]. Guangzhou: Guangdong hua bao she, 1959.
Chan, F. Gilbert, and Thomas H. Etzold, eds. *China in the 1920s: Nationalism and Revolution*. New York: New Viewpoints/Franklin Watts, 1976.
Chan, Gordon Y.M. "The Communists in Rural Guangdong, 1928–1936." *Journal of the Royal Asiatic Society* 3 (13.1) (2003): 77–97.
Chan Lau Kit-ching. *From Nothing to Nothing: The Chinese Communist Movement and Hong Kong, 1921–1936*. New York: St. Martin's Press, 1999.

Chang, Jung, and Jon Halliday. *Mao: The Unknown Story*. London: Jonathan Cape, 2005.

Chassin, Lionel Max (Timothy Osato and Louis Gelas, trs.). *The Communist Conquest of China: A History of the Civil War, 1945–1949*. Cambridge, MA: Harvard University Press, 1965.

Chen Daya 陈达娅. *Zaihui ba Nanyang: Hainan Nanyang huaqiao jigong huiguo kangzhan huiyi* 再会吧南洋: 海南南洋华侨机工回国抗战回忆 [See you again, South Pacific: Recollections of the Southern Pacific overseas Hainanese Chinese mechanics and chauffeurs returning to China to resist the Japanese]. Beijing: Zhongguo Huaqiao chubanshe, 2007.

Chen Dengqiao 陈登乔. "Er zhan shiqi Guomindang 'weijiao' Qiongya geming genjudi zongshu" 二战时期国民党 '围剿' 琼崖革命根据地综述" [Summary of Guomindang "encirclement and suppression" of the local Qiongya revolution in the period of the second war]. In *Hainan wenshiziliao* 海南文史资料 1 (1989).

"Chen Jitang yao zuo Hainan wang," 陈济棠要做海南王 [Chen Jitang wants to be king of Hainan]. In *Xinwen tiandi* 新闻天地 December 4, 1949, 9.

Chen Keqin 陈克勤. *Hainan jiansheng* 海南建省 [Hainan becomes a province]. Beijing: Renmin chubanshe, 2008.

Chen Pixian 陈丕显, ed. *Nanfang sannian youji zhanzheng* 南方三年游击战争 [The Three-year guerrilla war in South China]. Beijing: Jiefangjun chubanshe, 1995.

Chen Wenmin 陈文敏. "Feng Baiju junzi ye" 冯白驹君子耶! [Isn't Feng Baiju a man of noble character!]. In *Shanxi shen ji* 陕西审计 1 (1998): 37.

Cheng Zhaoxing and Xing Yikong 程昭星, 邢诒孔. *Lizu renmin douzheng shi* 黎族人民斗争史 [A history of the struggles of the Li people]. Beijing: Minzu chubanshe, 1999.

Chen Zhi 陈植. *Hainan dao xin zhi* 海南岛新志 [A New Gazetteer of Hainan Island]. Shanghai: Shangwuyin shuguan, 1949.

"China to Develop Strategic Island of Hainan." *Far Eastern Survey* 6 (3) (February 3, 1937), 34–35.

China Handbook, 1951. Taipeh (Taibei): China Publishing Company, 1951.

Ching, Leo T.S. *Becoming Japanese: Colonial Taiwan and the Politics of Identity Formation*. Berkeley: University of California Press, 2001.

Clark, Leonard. "Among the Big Knot Lois of Hainan." *National Geographic Magazine* 74 (3) (September 1938).

Cochran, Sherman, and Paul G. Pickowicz, eds. *China on the Margins*. Ithaca, NY: Cornell University Press, 2010.

Crossley, Pamela Kyle, Helen F. Siu, and Donald S. Sutton, eds. *Empire at the Margins: Culture, Ethnicity, and Frontier in Early Modern China*. Berkeley: University of California Press, 2006.

Csete, Anne. "Ethnicity, Conflict, and the State in the Early to Mid-Qing: The Hainan Highlands, 1644–1800." In *Empire at the Margins: Culture, Ethnicity, and Frontier in Early Modern China*. Berkeley: University of California Press, 2006.

———. *A Frontier Minority in the Chinese World: The Li People of Hainan Island from the Han through the High Qing*. State University of New York, Buffalo: Doctoral Dissertation, April 1995.

———. "The Li Mother Spirit and the Struggle for Hainan's Land and Legend." *Late Imperial China* 22 (2) (December 2001), 91–123.

Dai Fu 戴夫. *Haishang lianbing ji* 海上练兵记 [A record of troop training at sea]. Beijing: Gongren chubanshe, 1950.

"Dangdai Zhongguo" congshu bianji weiyuanhui "当代中国"丛书编辑委员会 [The editorial committee for the "Modern China" series], ed. *Dangdai Zhongguo de Hainan* 当代中国的海南 [Modern China's Hainan]. Beijing: Dangdai Zhongguo chubanshe, 1993.

Deleuze, Gilles. *Desert Islands and Other Texts, 1953–1974*. Cambridge, MA: Semiotext(e) (Distributed by MIT Press), 2004.

Dennery, Etienne. "A French View of the Situation in the Far East." *International Affairs (Royal Institute of International Affairs 1931–1939)* 17 (4) (July–August 1938).

Duara, Prasenjit. *Rescuing History from the Nation: Questioning Narratives of Modern China*. Chicago: University of Chicago Press, 1997.

Eastman, Lloyd E. *Seeds of Destruction: Nationalist China in War and Revolution, 1937–1949*. Stanford: Stanford University Press, 1984.

Fan Yunxi 范运晞. *Qiongji minguo renwu zhuan* 琼籍民国人物传 [Biographies of Hainanese in Republican China]. Haikou: Nanhai chubanshe, 1999.

Fang Tian, Chang Qing, Jian Hua 方天, 常青, 建华. *Siye zuihou yi zhan* 四野最后一战 [The Last Campaign of the Fourth Field Army]. Beijing: Guofang daxue chubanshe, 1995.

Feng Anquan 冯安全. "Hainan geming douzheng qinliji" 海南革命斗争亲历记 [A Record of Personla Experiences in the Revolutionary Struggle on Hainan]. In *Guangdong wenshi ziliao* 广东文史资料. April 1981, 30.

Feng Baiju 冯白驹. *Zhongguo gongchandang de guanghui zhaoyao zai Hainan dao* 中国共产党的光辉照耀在海南岛 [The radiance of the Chinese Communist Party illuminates Hainan Island]. Guangzhou: Huanan renmin chubanshe, 1951.

———, Zeng Sheng 冯白驹, 曾生, eds. *Guangdong renmin kangri youji zhanzheng huiyi* 广东人民抗日游击战争回忆 [Recollections of the Guangdong People's Guerrilla War of Resistance Against the Japanese]. Guangzhou: Huanan renmin chubanshe, 1951.

"Feng Baiju dui Lizu renmin de gongxian," 冯白驹对黎族人民的贡献 *Qiongzhou daxue xuebao* 琼州大学学报 (3) (2000):18.

Feng Chongyi. "Seeking Lost Codes in the Wilderness." *China Quarterly* 160 (December 1999): 1036–1056.

———, and David S.G. Goodman. *China's Hainan Province: Economic Development and Investment Environment*. Nedlands: University of Western Australia Press, 1995.

Feng Dachun 冯大椿. *Hainan dao gong kuangye jiqi jihua* 海南岛工矿业及其计划 [Industry and Mining on Hainan Island and Future Plans]. n.p.: Xin Zhongguo chubanshe, 1947.

Feng Qiuhong. 冯秋泓. "Hainan bai nian jian sheng shi" 海南百年建省史 [The hundred-year history of building Hainan province]. In *Haikou wenshiziliao* 海口文史资料 (Hainan) 4 (1987).

Feng Renhong 冯任鸿. "Haikoushi yange shi" 海口市沿革史 [The history of the evolution of Haikou]. In *Haikou wenshiziliao* 海口文史资料 (Hainan) 2 (1985).

Fitzgerald, John. "Increased Disunity: The Politics and Finance of Guangdong Separatism, 1926–1936." *Modern Asian Studies* 24 (4) (October 1990), 745–775.

———. "The Misconceived Revolution: State and Society in China's Nationalist Revolution, 1923–26." *Journal of Asian Studies* 49 (2) (May 1990).

———, ed. *Rethinking China's Provinces*. London: Routledge, 2002.

Foreign Relations of the United States, United States Department of State.

Fu Heji 符和积. "Shixi Xinhai nian Qiongya zhengju de shanbian" 试析辛亥年琼崖政局的嬗变 [Analysis of the evolution of the political situation on Hainan in 1911]. *Hainan daxue xuebao shehui kexue ban* 海南大学学报社会科学版 [Social Science Journal of Hainan University] 16 (3) (September 1998).

Fu Yan 符炎. "Duhai zuozhan huiyi" 渡海作战回忆 [A recollection of crossing the sea to fight (to take over Hainan Island)]. In *Haikang wenshi* 海康文史 (Guangzhou) 4 (1985).

Gan Xianqiong 甘先琼, ed. *Qionghai xianzhi* 琼海县志 [Qionghai provincial records]. Guangzhou: Guangdong liaoji chubanshe, 1995.

Goh, S.Y. "Hainan Development Plans Laid: Governor T.V. Soong's program for South China includes country's second largest island. Various Nanking Ministries and Chinese navy to participate." *China Economist* 1 (April 26, 1948): 110–111.

Goldman, Dara E. *Out of Bounds: Islands and the Demarcation of Identity in the Hispanic Caribbean*. Lewisburg, PA: Bucknell University Press, 2008.

Gongnong de shubian weihui 工农的书编委会 [Workers and peasants editorial committee], ed. *Jiefang Hainan dao* 解放海南岛 [Liberating Hainan Island]. Beijing: Renmin meishu chubanshe, 1950.

Granados, Ulises. "As China Meets the Southern Sea Frontier: Ocean Identity in the Making, 1920–1937." *Pacific Affairs* 78 (3) (Fall 2005).

Gray, Jack, ed. *Modern China's Search for a Political Form*. London: Oxford University Press, 1969.

Guan Xin 关欣. "Zai Hainan geming genjudishang" 在海南革命根据地上 [Making Revolution in Hainan on the Basis of Local Conditions]. *Renmin ribao* [People's Daily] August 8, 1960 (7).

Guangdong Qiongya gemingshi yanjiuhui 广东琼崖革命史研究会 [Guangdong, Hainan revolutionary history research association], eds. *Feng Baiju huiyilu* 冯白驹回忆录 [Feng Baiju recollection volume]. (Hong Kong: Xianggang dongxi wenhua shiye gonsi, 2000).

Guo Wenyong 郭仁勇. *Wenchang jiangjun zhuan* 文昌将军传 [Biographies of Wenchang generals]. Tianma tushu youxian gongsi: Hong Kong, 2002.

"Guomindang jundui Qiongya geming genjudi weijiao dashiji" 国民党军对琼崖革命根据地围剿大事纪 [Chronicle of the Guomindang army's encirclement and suppression of the Hainan local revolution]. In *Hainan wenshiziliao* 海南文史资料 1 (1989).

Hainan baikequanshu bianzuan weiyuanhui 海南百科全书编纂委员会 [Committee of compilers of the Hainan encyclopedia], eds. *Hainan baikequanshu* 海南百科全书 [Hainan encyclopedia]. Beijing: Zhongguo da baikequanshu chubanshe, 1999.

"Hainan dao zhi zhan" 海南岛之战 [The battle for Hainan]. In *Jianzai wuqi* 舰载武器[Shipborne Weapons] 11 (2003): 79–81.

Hainan gemingshi yanjiu hui, eds. [Hainan revolutionary history research association, eds.] 琼崖风云 *Qiongya fengyun* [Hainan wind and clouds]. Haikou: Hainan chubanshe, 2006.

Hainan junqu dangshiban 海南军区党史办 [Hainan military command office of Party history], ed. *Qiongdao nuchao* 琼岛怒潮 [Hainan's raging tide]. Beijing: Jiefangjun chubanshe, 1987.

Hainansheng difang shizhi bangongshi 海南省地方史志办公室 [The office of local historical records of Hainan province], eds. *Hainan shengzhi: Baoye zhi*. 海南省志: 报业志 [Hainan provincial annals: Newspaper annals]. Haikou: Nanhai chuban gongsi, 1993.

———, eds. *Hainan shengzhi: Gongchandang* 海南省志: 共产党 [Hainan provincial gazetteer: Communist Party gazetteer]. Haikou: Nanhai chuban gongsi, 2005.

———, eds. *Hainan shengzhi: Haiyang zhi, Geming genjudi zhi* 海南省志: 海洋志,革命根据地志 [Hainan provincial gazetteer: Maritime gazetteer, revolutionary base area gazetteer]. Haikou: Nanhai chuban gongsi, 2006.

———, eds. *Hainan shengzhi: Jiancha zhi* 海南省志: 检察志 [Hainan provincial annals: Procuratorate annals]. Haikou: Nanhai chuban gongsi, 1997.

———, eds. *Hainan shengzhi: Jiancha zhi* 海南省志: 金融志 [Hainan provincial annals: Financial annals]. Haikou: Nanhai chuban gongsi, 1993.

———, eds. *Hainan shengzhi: Junshi zhi* 海南省志: 军事志 [Hainan provincial annals: Military annals]. Haikou: Nanhai chuban gongsi, 1993.

———, eds. *Hainan shengzhi: Kouanzhi, haiguanzhi, shangjianzhi, di jiu juan* 海南省志: 口岸志, 海关志, 商检志, 第九卷 [Hainan provincial gazetteer: Ports, customs, inspection, vol. 9]. Haikou: Nanhai chuban gongsi, 1996.

———, eds. *Hainan shengzhi: Minzhengzhi, waishizhi* 海南省志: 民政志, 外事志 [Hainan provincial gazetteer: Civil Administration gazetteer, Foreign affairs gazetteer]. Haikou: Nanhai chuban gongsi, 1996.

———, eds. *Hainan shengzhi: Minzu zhi* 海南省志:民族志 [Hainan provincial gazetteer: Nationalities gazetteer]. Haikou: Nanhai chubanshe, 2006.

———, eds. *Hainan shengzhi: Nongye zhi* 海南省志: 农业志 [Hainan provincial annals: Agricultural annals]. Haikou: Nanhai chuban gongsi, 1997.

———, eds. *Hainan shengzhi: Renkou zhi, Fangyan zhi, Zongjiao zhi* 海南省志: 人口志, 方言志, 宗教志 [Hainan provincial gazetteer: Population gazetteer, dialect gazetteer, religion gazetteer]. Haikou: Nanhai chuban gongsi, 1994.

———, eds. *Hainan shengzhi: Shangjian, haiguan, kou'an* 海南省志: 商检, 海关, 口岸 [Hainan provincial annals: Ports annals]. Haikou: Nanhai chuban gongsi, 1993.

———, eds. *Hainan shengzhi: Shenpanzhi* 海南省志: 审判志 [Hainan provincial gazetteer: Judicial gazetteer]. Haikou: Nanhai chuban gongsi, 2006.

———, eds. *Hainan shengzhi: Tudizhi* 海南省志: 土地志 [Hainan provincial gazetteer: Land gazetteer]. Haikou: Nanhai chuban gongsi, 2007.

Hainansheng shizhi gongzuo bangongshi, Hainansheng dang'anju (guan) 海南省史志工作办公室, 海南省档案局(馆) [Hainan provincial historical office, Hainan provincial archives (museum)], eds. *Hainan tudi gaige yundong ziliao xuanbian, 1951–1953* 海南土地改革运动资料选编, 1951–1953 [Selected materials on the land reform movement in Hainan, 1951–1953] (Haikou, 2002).

Hainansheng tongji ju 海南省统计局 [Hainan province statistics bureau], ed. *Hainan 50 nian, 1949–1999* 海南50年, 1949–1999 [50 years in Hainan, 1949–1999]. Beijing: Zhongguo tongji chubanshe, 1999.

Han Xianchu 韩先楚. "Kua hai zhi zhan" 跨海之战 [The campaign across the sea (to take Hainan)]. In *Xinghuo liao yuan* 星火燎原 [Sparks Set Fire to the Plain], ed. Zhongguo renmin jiefangjun sanshi nian zhengwen bianji weiyuanhui 中国人民解放军三十年征文编辑委员会 [The Editorial Committee of Writings on the Thirtieth Year of the PLA], 486–502 (vol. 10). Beijing: Renmin wenxue chubanshe, 1958.

Han Xiaorong. "Localism in Chinese Communist Politics Before and After 1949: The Case of Feng Baiju." *Chinese Historical Review* 11 (1) (Spring 2004): 23–56.

Hanwell, Norman D. "France Takes Inventory in China." *Far Eastern Survey* 7 (19) (September 28, 1938).

Harrell, Stevan, ed. *Cultural Encounters on China's Ethnic Frontiers*. Seattle: University of Washington Press, 1995.

He Kaiqia 何凯洽. "Chen Hanguang dui Hainan shaoshuminzu de xuexing tongzhi" 陈汉光对海南少数民族的血腥统治 [Chen Hanguang's bloody rule over the ethnic minorities of Hainan]. In *Hainan wenshiziliao* 海南文史资料 1 (1989).

Hou Wenqiang 侯文强. "Gudao yingxiong Feng Baiju" 孤岛英雄冯白驹 [Feng Baiju: Hero on an Isolated Island]. In *Dangshi bocai* (3) 2004: 14–17.

Hu Tichun, Xu Chunhong, Wang Huanqiu 胡提春, 许春宏, 王焕秋. *Feng Baiju jiangjun zhuan* 冯白驹将军传 [Biography of General Feng Baiju], *Qiongdao Xinghuo* (Hainan Spark). Series, vol. 3, Internal Circulation. Haikou: Guangdong Province, Hainan New China Press, 1981.

Huang Fei 黄飞. "Jie fang Hainan" 解放海南 [The liberation of Hainan]." In *Zhishi jiu shi liliang* 知识就是力量 [Knowledge is strength] 7 (2001).

Huang Jinxian 黄进先. "Jiefang qian Haikou de jiaotong yunshu ye" 解放前海口的交通运输业 [Haikou's transportation and communications industries prior to liberation]. In *Haikou wenshiziliao* 海口文史资料 3 (1986).

Huang, Philip C.C. "Civil Adjudication in China, Past and Present." *Modern China* 32 (2) (April 2006): 135–180.

Huang Yijing 黄奕荆. "Jiefang qianxi Guomindang junzheng yaoyuan zai Haikou de pinfan huodong" 解放前夕国民党军政要员在海口的频繁活动 [The frequent activities of important military and political Guomindang officials in Haikou on the eve of liberation]. In *Haikou wenshiziliao* 海口文史资料 3 (1986).

Huebner, Jon W. "The Abortive Liberation of Taiwan." *China Quarterly* 110 (June 1987): 256–275.

Ienaga, Saburo. *The Pacific War, 1931–1945: A Critical Perspective on Japan's Role in World War II*. New York: Pantheon Books (1968), 1978.

Jiefangjun jiangling zhuan 解放军将领传 [Biographies of High-Ranking PLA Officers]. Beijing: Jiefangjun chubanshe, 1984.

Johnson, Chalmers. *Peasant Nationalism and Communist Power: The Emergence of Revolutionary China*. Stanford: Stanford University Press, 1962.

Jueya, Ouyang. *The Cun Language*. Shanghai: Far East Publishers, 1998.

Klein, Donald W., and Anne B. Clark. *Biographic Dictionary of Chinese Communism, 1921–1965*. Cambridge, MA: Harvard University Press, 1971.

Kuhn, Philip A. *Chinese Among Others: Emigration in Modern Times*. Lanham, MD: Rowman & Littlefield, 2008.

Lary, Diana. *The Kwangsi Clique in Chinese Politics, 1925–1937*. Cambridge: Cambridge University Press, 1974.

Lee, Joseph, ed. *Ireland: Towards a Sense of Place*. Cork: Cork University Press, 1985.

Lei Feng, Cao Ke, Xie Yuexiong 雷锋, 曹轲, 谢岳雄, eds. *Nan Yue zhi jian: Yue-Hai kangzhan shilu* 南粤之剑: 粤海抗战实录 [The Sword of Southern Guangdong: A Record of Guangdong and Hainan in the War of Resistance]. Beijing: Jiefangjun wenyi chubanshe, 1995.

Lewis, Martin, and Karen Wigen. *The Myth of Continents: A Critique of Metageography*. Berkeley: University of California Press, 1997.

Li Bo 李勃. *Hainan dao: Lidai jianzhu yange kao* 海南岛: 历代建置沿革考 [Hainan island: A study of the establishment and evolution of previous dynasties]. Haikou: Hainan chubanshe, 2005.

Li Boqiu, Yin Canzhen 李伯秋, 尹灿贞. "Hainan dao zhanyi zhong de Xie Fang tongzhi: Hainan dao jiefang 45 nian zhuiyi" 海南岛战役中的解方同志: 海南岛解放45年追忆 [Comrade Xie Fang in the campaign to take Hainan: Looking back on the liberation of Hainan after 45 years]. In *Dangshi bocai* 党史博菜 5 (1995): 22–25.

Li Daichen 李待琛. *Hainan dao zhi xianzhuang* 海南岛之现状 [Hainan's current situation]. Shanghai: Shijie shuju, 1947.

Li Duqing 李独清. *Lizu renmin guanghui de zhandou licheng* 黎族人民光辉的战斗历程 [The glorious struggle of the Li people]. In Qiongdao xinghuo bianji bu 琼岛星火编辑部 [Hainan Spark editorial department], eds., *Qiongdao xinghuo* 琼岛星火 [Hainan spark] 2. Guangdong Province, publication for internal circulation, 1980.

Li Nan. *Chinese Civil-Military Relations: The Transformation of the People's Liberation Army*. New York: Routledge, 2006.

Li Ren 李任. "Hainan dao xiezhen" 海南岛写真 [A True Depiction of Hainan Island]. In *Beijhua yuekan* 北华月刊 2:2 (95–98) 1941 (12).

Li Xiaobing. *A History of the Modern Chinese Army*. Lexington: University Press of Kentucky, 2007.

Li Ying 李盈. *Qiongya gudao shang de menzhen* 琼崖孤岛上的门争 [Struggle on Isolated Hainan Island]. Hong Kong: Xin minzhu chubanshe, 1947.

Li Yingmin 李英敏. *Nan dao feng yun* 南岛风云 [Storm over the southern island]. Beijing: Tongsu wenyi chubanshe, 1957.

———. *Ye feng jiao yu* 椰风蕉雨 [Coconut winds and banana rains]. Nanning: Guangxi renmin chubanshe, 1978.

Li Yisheng 李毅生. *Fenzhan ershisan nian de Hainan dao* 奋战二十三年的海南岛 [Twenty-three years of fierce fighting on Hainan Island]. Hankou: Zhongnan renmin chubanshe, 1951.

Liang Bingshu 梁秉枢. "Kangzhan shengli qianhou Hainan dao ji dian jianwen" 抗战胜利前后海南岛几点见闻 [Some Observations on Hainan Island Before and After Victory in the War of Resistance]. In *Guangdong wenshi ziliao* 4:173.

———. "Qiongya gongnong hongjun zhandou shi pianduan" 琼崖工农红军战斗史片断 [Fragments of the history of the struggle of the workers' and peasants' Red army of Hainan]. In *Wanning wenshi* 万宁文史 1 (1984).

"Liang-Guang zongdui shi" bianxie lingdao xiaozu "两广纵队史" 编写领导小组 [Leading group editors of the "History of the Guangdong and Guangxi Column"], eds. *Liang-Guang zongdui shi* 两广纵队史 [History of the Guangdong and Guangxi Column]. Guangzhou: Guangdong renmin chubanshe, 1988.

Liang Guowu 梁国武. "Chen Jitang, Xue Yue zai Hainan dao de zuihou tongzhi jianwen" 陈济棠, 薛岳在海南岛的最后统治见闻 [The last reports on the rule of Chen Jitang and Xue Yue on Hainan Island]. In *Guangdong wenshiziliao* 广东文史资料 17 (1964).

Liang Kun 梁昆, 1912 海南改省风云 "Hainan gaisheng fengyun" [1912, The controversy over making Hainan a province]. In *Hainan zhoukan* 海南周刊 (November 18, 2008).

Liang Zhenqiu 梁振球, ed. *Hainan jiefang wushi zhounian jinian wenji* 海南解放五十周年纪念文集 [Collected works in commemoration of the fiftieth anniversary of the liberation of Hainan]. Haikou: Nanhai chubanshe, 2001.

Lin Huicun 林荟村. "Wo zai Hainan canjia qiyi de jingguo" 我在海南参加起义的经过 [My experience in participating in the revolt on Hainan]. In *Hainan wenshiziliao* 海南文史资料 3 (1990).

———. "Zai Hainan 'jiao gong' 'fu Li' 'suijing' de zhenxiang" 在海南 "剿共" "抚黎" "绥靖" 的真相 [The truth behind "suppressing the Communists," "nurturing the Li," and "pacification" on Hainan]. In *Hainan wenshiziliao* 海南文史资料 1 (1989).

Lin Keze 林克泽. "Wo de huiyi—er zhan shiqi Qiong xi nan douzheng pianduan" 我的回忆—二战时期琼西南斗争片断 [My recollections—Fragments of the struggle in western and southern Hainan in the period of the second war]. In *Dongfang wenshi* 东方文史 3 (1987).

Lin Longyou 林龙由. "Baisha geming genjudide jianli" 白沙革命根据地的建立 [Building a revolution in Baisha according to local conditions]. In *Baisha wenshi* 白沙文史 3 (1988).

Lin Yuhua 林玉华. "Hainan dao shang diyi mian wuxinghongqi" 海南岛上第一面五星红旗 [The First Five-Star (PRC) Flag on Hainan]. *Renmin ribao* November 14, 1979 (6).

Liu, F.F. *A Military History of Modern China, 1924–1949*. Princeton, NJ: Princeton University Press, 1956.
Liu Zhenhua 刘振华. *Jiefang Hainan* 解放海南 [Liberating Hainan]. Shenyang: Liaoning renmin chubanshe, 1998.
Lodwick, Kathleen L. *Educating the Women of Hainan: The Career of Margaret Moninger in China, 1915–1942*. Lexington: University Press of Kentucky, 1995.
———. *The Widow's Quest: The Byers Extraterritorial Case in Hainan, China, 1924–1925*. Bethlehem, PA: Lehigh University Press, 2003.
Lu Jun and Xing Yikong 陆军, 邢诒孔. "Dui Qiongya genjudi 23 nian hongqi budao de chubu tantao" 对琼崖革命根据地23年红旗不倒的初步探讨 [A preliminary inquiry into the Hainan base areas "holding aloft the red flag for twenty-three years"]. Zhonggong Hainan shengwei dangshi yanjiu shi, eds. *Qiongya geming yanjiu lunwenxuan*. Beijing: Zhonggong dangshi chubanshe, 1994.
Ma Baishan and Ma Biqian 马白山, 马必前. *Yuxue tianya* 浴血天涯 [Bloody Horizon]. Nanhai chuban gongsi: Haikou, 2007.
MacFarquhar, Roderick, and Michael Schoenhals. *Mao's Last Revolution*. Cambridge, MA: Harvard University Press, 2006.
Madrolle, Cl. *Hai-nan: Le Pays et Ses Habitants* [Hainan: The land and its inhabitants]. Paris: Comité de l'Asie Française, 1909.
McCord, Edward A. *The Power of the Gun: The Emergence of Modern Chinese Warlordism*. Berkeley: University of California Press, 1993.
McKeown, Adam. *Chinese Migrant Networks and Cultural Change: Peru, Chicago, Hawaii, 1900–1936*. Chicago: University of Chicago Press, 2001.
———. "Conceptualizing Chinese Diasporas, 1842–1949." *Journal of Asian Studies* 58 (2) (May 1999), 306–337.
Meisner, Maurice J. *Mao Zedong: A Political and Intellectual Portrait*. Cambridge, MA: Polity, 2007.
Moninger, Margaret M. (credited as M.M.M.). *The Isle of Palms: Sketches of Hainan*. Shanghai: Commercial Press, 1919.
Mouly, R.P. *Hai-nan: L'Ile aux Cent Visages* [Hainan: The island of a hundred faces]. Paris: P. Lethielleux, 1944.
N.D.H. "Growing Interest in Hainan Mainly Strategic." *Far Eastern Survey* 7 (17) (August 24, 1938).
Nanfang ribao 南方日报 [South China Daily]. Guangzhou, 1949–1952.
Odaka, Kunio. *Economic Organization of the Li Tribes of Hainan Island*. New Haven: Yale Southeast Asia Studies, 1950. (Originally published in Japanese, 1942)
Okihiro, Gary Y. *Island World: A History of Hawaii and the United States*. Berkeley: University of California Press, 2008.
Ou Mengjue. "What Have Been the Mistakes of Ku Ta-ch'un and Feng Pai-chu?" In *Survey of China Mainland Press* 1899, 16–23. (Originally published in the first issue of 上游 *Shangyou* [1958])
Ownby, David. *Brotherhoods and Secret Societies in Early and Mid-Qing China: The Formation of a Tradition*. Stanford: Stanford University Press, 1996.

———, and Mary Somers Heidhues, eds. *"Secret Societies" Reconsidered: Perspectives on the Social History of Modern South China and Southeast Asia*. Armonk, NY: M.E. Sharpe, 1993.

Pak, Hyobom, ed. *Documents of the Chinese Communist Party: 1927–1930*. Hong Kong: Union Research Institute, 1971.

Pan Youheng 盘有恒. "Changjiangxian Guomindang dang bu renyuan bianzhi" 昌江县国民党党部人员编制 [Changjiang county Guomindang administrative personnel establishment]. In *Dongfang wenshi* 东方文史 3 (1987).

Pan Zhi 潘稚. "Cong jingji shang guofang shang guancha Hainan dao" 从经济上国防上观察海南岛 [An Economic and Strategic Study of Hainan Island]. In *Zhongguo jianshe*, Shanghai, Nanjing: Zhongguo jianshe xiehui (May 1937): 63–70.

Peng Chengwan 彭程萬. *Diaocha Qiongya shiye baogao shu* 调查琼崖实业报告书 [A report on the investigation of the industry and commerce of Hainan]. Haikou: Hainan shuju, 1920.

Pepper, Suzanne. *Civil War in China: The Political Struggle*. Berkeley: University of California Press, 1980.

Phillips, Michael R., Huaqing Liu, and Yanping Zhang. "Suicide and Social Change in China." *Culture, Medicine, and Psychiatry* 23 (1) (1999): 25–50.

Phillips, R.T. "The Japanese Occupation of Hainan." *Modern Asian Studies* 14 (1) (1980): 93–109.

Probst, Reed Richard. *The Communist Conquest of Hainan*. George Washington University, PhD dissertation, 1982.

Purcell, Victor. *The Chinese in Malaya*. London: Oxford University Press, 1948.

———. *The Chinese in Southeast Asia*. Kuala Lumpur: Oxford University Press (1951) 1980.

Qian Yue "Feng Baiju ershiliu nian de mengyuan suiyue" [Twenty-six years of injustices suffered by Feng Baiju]. In *Dangshi bolan* 9 (2004), 24–25.

Qian Yue 钱跃. *Feng Baiju jiangjun zhuan* 冯白驹将军传 [The Biography of General Feng Baiju]. Beijing: Zhonggong dangshi chubanshe, 1998.

Qiongya wuzhuang douzhengshi bangongshi 琼崖武装斗争史办公室 [Office for the History of Military Struggle on Hainan (Qiongya)], ed. *Qiongya zongdui shi* 琼崖纵队史 [The History of the Hainan (Qiongya) Column]. Guangzhou: Guangdong renmin chubanshe, 1986.

Qiongzhongxian zhi bangongshi 琼中县志办公室 [Office of records for Qiongzhong county (Hainan)], ed. "Qiongzhongxian jianzhi yange ji quhua" 琼中县建置沿革及区划 [The establishment and evolution of administrative districts in Qiongzhong county]. In *Qiongzhong wenshi* 琼中文史 1 (1986).

Rhoads, Edward J.M. *China's Republican Revolution: The Case of Kuangtung, 1895–1913*. Cambridge, MA: Harvard University Press, 1975.

"Rikou zai Dingan de sharenchang" 日寇在定安的杀人场 [The Japanese bandits' execution grounds at Dingan]. In *Dingan wenshi* 定安文史 4 (1990).

Ropp, Paul S., Paola Zamperini, and Harriet T. Zurndorfer, eds. *Passionate Women: Female Suicide in Late Imperial China*. Leiden: Brill, 2001.

Röslor, Michael, and Tobias Wendl, eds. *Frontiers and Borderlands: Anthropological Perspectives*. Frankfurt: Peter Land Publishers, 1999.

Ryan, Mark, ed. *Chinese Warfighting: The PLA Experience Since 1949*. New York: M.E. Sharpe, 2003.

Safran, William, ed. *Nationalism and Ethnoregional Identities in China*. London: Frank Cass, 1998.

Savina, M. *Monographie de Hainan: Conference faite de 10 décembre 1928 a la Société Géographique de Hanoi*. Hanoi: Cahiers de la Société de Géographie de Hanoi (17), 1929.

Schafer, Edward. *Shore of Pearls*. Berkeley: University of California Press, 1970.

Scobell, Andrew. *China's Use of Military Force: Beyond the Great Wall and the Long March*. Cambridge: Cambridge University Press, 2003.

Selden, Mark. *Yenan Way in Revolutionary China*. Cambridge, MA: Harvard University Press, 1971.

Shi Dan 史丹. "Haikou tanpan" 海口谈判 [Haikou negotiations]. In *Qiongdao xinghuo* 琼岛星火 [Hainan spark]. Beijing: Jiefangjun chubanshe, 1987.

Singlaub, Major General John K. *Hazardous Duty: An American Soldier in the Twentieth Century*. New York: Summit Books, 1991.

Struve, Lynn A., ed. *Voices from the Ming-Qing Cataclysm: China in Tigers' Jaws*. New Haven, CT: Yale University Press, 1993.

Strzoda, Walter. *Die Li auf Hainan und ihre Beziehungen zum asiatischen Kontinent* [The Li on Hainan and their relations with the Asian continent]. Berlin: Zeitschrift für Ethnologie, 1911.

Stübel, Hans. *Die Li-stämme der insel Hainan; ein beitrag zur volkskunde südchinas* [The Li of Hainan Island: A Contribution to the Folk Studies of Southern China]. Berlin: Klinkhardt & Biermann, 1937.

Su Ke 肃克, ed. *Zhonghua wenhua Tongzhi: Minzu wenhua* 中华文化通志: 民族文化 [Annals of Chinese culture: People's culture]. Shanghai: Renmin chubanshe, 1998.

Su Zhiliang 苏智良. *Riben dui Hainan de qinlüe jiqi baoxing* 日本对海南的侵略及其暴行 [The Extreme atrocities of Japan's invasion of Hainan]. Shanghai: Makesi zhuyi chubanshe, 2005.

Swinhoe, Robert. "The Aborigines of Hainan" (Article 2), "Read before the Society on 25th March 1872."

Szonyi, Michael. *Cold War Island: Quemoy on the Front Line*. Cambridge: Cambridge University Press, 2008.

Tang Kunning 唐昆宁. "Qiongya kangri minzu tongyi zhanxian" 琼崖抗日民族统一战线 [Hainan's anti-Japan people's united front of resistance]. In *Hainan wenshiziliao* 海南文史资料 3 (1990).

Tang Ruen 唐汝恩. "Huiyi Hainan dao zhandou" 回忆海南岛战斗 [A recollection of the struggle to take Hainan Island]. In *Dunhua wenshiziliao* (Jilin) 5 (1988).

Tappan, David S., and Luella R., "David S. and Luella R. Tappan Papers, 1913–1966," Collection 103, Special Collections and University Archives, University of Oregon Libraries.

Teng, Emma. *Taiwan's Imagined Geography: Chinese Colonial Travel Writing and Pictures, 1683–1895.* Cambridge, MA: Harvard University Press, 2004.

Thornton, Richard. *The Communist Conquest of Hainan Island.* PhD dissertation. George Washington University, 1982.

Thurgood, Graham. *From Ancient Cham to Modern Dialects: Two Thousand Years of Language Contact and Change.* Honolulu: University of Hawaii Press, 1999.

Tian Shulan 田曙岚. *Hainan dao lüxingji* 海南岛旅行记 [Diary of Travels on Hainan Island]. Shanghai: Zhonghua shuju, 1936.

Tiewes, Frederick C. *Politics and Purges in China: Rectification and the Decline of Party Norms, 1950–1965.* White Plains, NY: M.E. Sharpe, 1979.

Tsin, Michael. *Nation, Governance, and Modernity in China: Canton, 1900–1927.* Stanford: Stanford University Press, 1999.

Tsui, Bonnie. "The Surf's Always Up in the Chinese Hawaii." *New York Times*, March 15, 2009.

Van de Ven, Hans J. *War and Nationalism in China, 1925–1945.* London: Routledge, 2003.

Vogel, Ezra. *Canton Under Communism: Programs and Politics in a Provincial Capital, 1949–1968.* New York: Harper & Row, 1969.

Wakeman, Frederic Jr., and Carolyn Grant, eds. *Conflict and Control in Late Imperial China.* Berkeley: University of California Press, 1975.

Waley, Arthur. *The Opium War through Chinese Eyes.* Stanford: Stanford University Press, 1958.

Wallerstein, Immanuel. *World-Systems Analysis: An Introduction.* Durham, NC: Duke University Press, 2004.

Wang Bida 王必达. "Lingaoxian 'guoda' daibiao jing xuanji" 临高县"国大"代表竞选记 [Selected representative writings of the Lingao county "National University"]. In *Lingao wenshiziliao* 6 (1990).

Wang Guoxing 王国兴. "Gongchandang shi Lizu Miaozu renmin de jiuxing" 共产党是黎族苗族人民的救星 [The Communist Party is the savior of the Li and Miao people], Qiongdao xinghuo bianji bu 琼岛星火编辑部 [Hainan Spark editorial department], eds., *Qiongdao xinghuo: Baisha qiyi zhuan* 琼岛星火:白沙起义专辑 [Hainan Spark: Baisha Uprising special edition], 12. Guangdong Province, publication for internal circulation, 1983.

Wang Jingxuan 王景暄. "Jiefang Hainan zhiqian pianduan" 解放海南支前片断 [A short account of supporting the front in the liberation of Hainan]. In *Xuwen wenshi* 徐闻文史 (Guangdong) 4 (1989).

Wang Min 王民. "Hainan jiefang qianxi de Qiongya zongdui" 海南解放前夕的琼崖纵队 [The Hainan Column on the Eve of Liberation]. *Hainan ribao* April 3, 1980 (2).

Wang Qixun 王启训. "Baisha qiyi jianjie" 白沙起义简介 [Synopsis of the revolt in Baisha]. In *Baisha wenshi* 白沙文史 1 (1987).

Wang Xingrui 王兴瑞. "Qiongya jianshi" 琼崖简史 [A Concise History of Hainan]. In *Bianzhenggonglun* 边政工论 5:1 (3–7) 1946 (7).

Wang Xueping 王学萍. *Zhongguo Lizu* 中国黎族 [The Li of China]. Beijing: Minzu chubanshe, 2004.

Wang Yuchun 王俞春. *Hainan yimin shizhi* 海南移民史志 [Records of the history of migration of Hainan]. Beijing: Zhongguo wenlian chubanshe, 2003.

Watson, Burton, tr. *Su Tung-p'o: Selections from a Sung Dynasty Poet*. New York: Columbia University Press, 1965.

Westad, Odd Arne. *Decisive Encounters: The Chinese Civil War*. Stanford: Stanford University Press, 2003.

Wilbur, C. Martin. *The Nationalist Revolution in China, 1923–1928*. Cambridge: Cambridge University Press, 1983.

Wolf, Margery. *Women and the Family in Rural Taiwan*. Stanford: Stanford University Press, 1972.

Wu Fei. *Suicide and Justice: A Chinese Perspective*. London: Routledge, 2010.

Wu Lien-teh. "Hainan: The Paradise of China." *China Quarterly* 2, 1937.

Wu Shengping 吴升平. "Dingan xian de 'guoda' daibiao xuanju" 定安县的"国大"代表选举 [Representative selections from Dingan County's "National University"]. In *Dingan wenshiziliao* 定安文史资料 3 (1987).

Wu Zhi, He Lang 吴之, 贺朗. *Feng Baiju zhuan* 冯白驹传 [The Biography of Feng Baiju]. Beijing: Dangdai Zhongguo chubanshe, 1996.

———, eds. *Chengqi Qiongnan banbi tian* 撑起琼南半壁天 [Supporting southern Hainan]. Guangzhou: Huacheng chubanshe, 1992.

Xing Yikong, Peng Changlin, Qian Yue 邢诒孔, 彭长霖, 钱跃. *Feng Baiju jiangjun zhuan* 冯白驹将军传 [Biography of General Feng Baiju]. Beijing: Zhonggong dangshi chubanshe, 1998.

———, Qian Yue 邢诒孔, 钱跃. "Wo shi hong siling, bu shi hei siling: Feng Baiju zai 'wenge' zhong de kangzheng" 我是红司令不是黑司令: 冯白驹在"文革"中的抗争 [I Am a Red commander, Not a Black Commander: Feng Baiju's Struggle of Resistance in the Cultural Revolution]. In *Shanghai dangshi yu dangjian* 6 (1996): 37–39.

Xing Yilin, Han Qiyuan, Huang Liangjun 邢益森, 韩启元, 黄良俊. *Qiongqiao cangsang* 琼侨沧桑 [The ups and downs of overseas Hainanese]. Haikou: Nanhai chubanshe, 1991.

Xu Bing, Qian Yue 徐冰, 钱跃. "Mao Zedong sixiang yu Qiongya geming de shengli" 毛泽东思想与琼崖革命的胜利: 纪念海南解放四十五周年 [Maoism and the victory in Hainan's revolution: Remembering the liberation of Hainan on the fortieth anniversary]. In *Special Economic Zone Outlook* 2 (1995): 32–33.

Xu Chonghao 许崇灏. *Qiongya zhi lüe* 琼崖志略 [A Brief Overview of Hainan]. Shanghai: Zhengzhong zhuju, 1947.

Yan Xishan 阎锡山 (提). *Taiwan ji Hainan dao baowei an* 台湾及海南岛保卫案 [A plan for the protection of Taiwan and Hainan Islands (submitted for consideration by Yan Xishan)]. (Top-secret document, no publisher information, 1949–1950)

Yang Kuisong. "Reconsidering the Campaign to Suppress Counterrevolutionaries." *China Quarterly* 193 (March 2008).

Ye Ding 叶顶.*Nanxia Nanxia! Xin Zhongguo de jijiehao* [Advance South, Advance South!: New China's call to arms] 南下南下！新中国的集结号. (Wuhan: Wuhan chubanshe, 2010).

You Qi 尤淇. *Qiongya Limin shanqu fangwen sanji* [Notes and Interviews on the Li people of Hainan's mountain region] 琼崖黎民山区访问散记. Guangzhou: Huanan chubanshe, 1950.

Yu Guoyang 余国扬. *Nanhai Mingzhu: Hainan Dao* 南海明珠：海南岛 [Jewel of the South China Sea: Hainan Island]. Guangzhou: Guangdong sheng ditu chubanshe, 1985.

Yu Maochun. *OSS in China: Prelude to Cold War*. New Haven: Yale University, 1997.

Yu Yan 余雁. *Wushi nian guoshi jiyao: Junshi juan* 五十年国事纪要：军事眷 [A summary of fifty years of national affairs: Military affairs volume]. Changsha: Hunan renmin chubanshe, 1999.

Yuan jizheng 原吉征. "Chen Hanguang jingweilü zai Qiongya de cansha" 陈汉光警卫旅在琼崖的残杀 [Slaughter by Chen Hanguang's Hainan guards brigade]. In Hainansheng zhengxie wenshiziliao weiyuanhui 海南省政协文史资料委员会 [Hainan Province *wenshiziliao*], eds., *Qiongdao fengyu* 琼岛风雨 [Hainan wind and rain], 1. Haikou: Hainan, 1989.

Zeng Qian 曾骞, ed. *Hainan dao zhi* 海南岛志 [Gazetteer of Hainan]. Shanghai: Shenzhou guoguangshe, 1933.

Zhan Lizhi 詹力之. "Suqing fandong shili, gonggu minzhu zhengquan: Huiyi yu Wang Guoxing tongzhi gongshi de rizi 肃清反动势力 巩固民主政权：回忆与王国兴同志公事的日子 [Eliminating the influence of reactionaries, consolidating the power of democracy: A recollection of days working together with Comrade Wang Guoxing]. In Zhonggong Guangdongsheng Hainan Lizu Miaozu zizhizhou wei dang shi ban'gongshi 中共广东省海南黎族苗族自治州委党史办公室 [Office of the Chinese Communist Party history committee of the Hainan Li-Miao autonomous region, Guangdong Province], eds., *Baisha qiyi: sishi zhounian jinian wenji* 白沙起义：四十周年纪念文集 [Baisha Uprising: 40th anniversary commemoration writings], 1. Guangzhou: Guangdong Provincial publication, for internal circulation, 1983.

Zhang Hongxia, and Zhan Changzhi. "A Library's Efforts en Route to Salvaging a Vanishing Culture." Paper presented at the World Library and Information Congress: 73rd Annual International Federation of Library Associations (IFLA) General Conference and Council (19–23 August 2007, Durban, South Africa).

Zhang Kaitai 张开泰. "Zai Hainan dao de geming hongliu zhong" 在海南岛的革命洪流中 [In the Middle of the Revolutionary Torrent of Hainan]. In *Guangdong wenshi ziliao* 广东文史资料. April 1981, 30.

Zhang Kaiyuan 章开沅, ed. *Xinhai geming cidian* 辛亥革命辞典 [Dictionary of the 1911 revolution]. Wuhan: Wuhan chubanshe, 1991.

Zhang Shijie 张实杰. "Feidu Qiongzhou haixia jiefang Hainan baodao" 飞渡琼州海峡解放海南宝岛 [Flying across the Hainan strait to liberate the precious Hainan Island]. In *Wangshi zhuiyi* 6 (2000): 22–27.

Zhao Zhixian 赵志贤. "Guomindang Changjiangxian dangbu de jianli jiqi chuqi huodong gaikuang 国民党昌江县党部的建立及其初期活动概况 [A survey of the activities of the Guomindang activities in Changjiang county]. In *Changjiang wenshi* 昌江文史 1 (1986).

Zhengxie Lingaoxian wenshi ziliao yanjiu weiyuanhui 政协临高县文史资料研究委员会 [Chinese People's Political Consultative Conference (CPPCC) Lingao County Historical Research Committee], eds., *Lingao Wenshi* 临高文史 [Lingao literature and history], 12. Hainansheng feiyingli chuban (Hainan Provincial nonprofit publication): Lingao, 1998.

Zheng Yaoxin 郑瑶新. "Dongfangxian yange tan" 东方县沿革谈 [A discussion of Dongfang county's evolution]. In *Dongfang wenshi* (Hainan) 3 (1987).

Zhong Yuanxiu 中元秀. *Lizu renmin lingxiu Wang Guoxing* 黎族人民领袖王国兴 [The leader of the Li people, Wang Guoxing]. *Qiongdao xinghuo* 琼岛星火 [Hainan spark], 6. Guangdong Province, publication for internal circulation, 1980.

———. *Lizu renmin lingxiu Wang Guoxing* 黎族人民领袖王国兴 [The leader of the Li people, Wang Guoxing]. Beijing: Minzu chubanshe, 1983.

Zhonggong Hainan shengwei dangshi yanjiu shi 中共海南省委党史研究室 [Hainan Provincial CCP History Committee Office], eds. *Hainan jiangling zhuan* 海南将领传 [Biographies of Hainan's military leaders]. Guangzhou: Guangdong renmin chubanshe, 1991.

———, eds. *Zhonggong Qiongya difang zuzhi de guanghui licheng* 中共琼崖地方组织的光辉历程 [The glorious history of the local organization of the Chinese Communist Party on Hainan], for internal Provincial Government circulation (Document YK060), June 2001, 6–7 (pages not numbered).

———, eds. *Zhongguo gongchandang Hainan lishi* 中国共产党海南历史 [Chinese Communist Party history of Hainan]. Beijing: Zhonggong dangshi chubanshe, 2007.

Zhonggong Hainan shengwei zuzhi bu 中共海南省委组织部 [Hainan province's Chinese Communist Party Committee Organization Unit], ed. *Zhongguo gongchandang Guangdong sheng Hainan xingzhengqu zuzhi shiziliao* 中国共产党广东省海南行政区组织史资料 [Chinese Communist Party of Guangdong province's Hainan administrative region organization of historical materials]. Haikou: Hainan chubanshe, 1994.

Zhonggong Hainanqu dangwei dangshi bangongshi 中共海南区党委党史办公室 [The Party Committee's Office of Party History of the Hainan Region in the Chinese Communist Party], ed. *Feng Baiju yanjiu shiliao* 冯白驹研究史料 [Historical Research Materials on Feng Baiju]. Guangzhou: Guangdong renmin chubanshe, 1988.

Zhonggong Wenchang xianwei dangshi yanjiushi, eds., 中共文昌县委党史研究室编 [Chinese Communist Party Committee of Wenchang county historical research office]. *Wenchang yinghun* 文昌英魂 [The spirit of Wenchang heroes]. Wenchang: Wenchang Communist Party historical materials, 1993.

Zhonggong zhongyang shuji chu 中共中央书记处 [Chinese Communist Central secretary]. "对琼崖工作指示" "Dui Qiongya gongzuo zhishi" [Directive on Hainan work], July 1940, as quoted in Qiongya wuzhuang douzheng shi ban'gongshi 琼崖武装斗争史办公室 [The office of the history of the Hainan military struggle], eds., *Qiongya zongdui shi* 琼崖纵队史 [The history of the Hainan Column]. Guangzhou: Guangdong renmin chubanshe, 1986.

Zhongguo Guomindang: Zhongyang weiyuanhui 中国国民党: 中央委员会 [The Chinese Nationalist Party: Central Committee], ed. "Fei e xuexing tongzhi xia de Hainan dao" 匪俄血腥统治下的海南岛 [Hainan Island under the Bloody Rule of the Bandits (the Chinese Communists) and the Soviets]. In *Diqu feiqing* 地区匪情 [Regional Information on Communist China]. Taibei: Zhongyang wenwu gongyingshe, 1953, 53–78.

Zhongguo renmin jiefangjun lishi ziliao congshu bianshen weiyuanhui 中国人民解放军历史资料丛书编审委员会 [Chinese people's liberation army historical materials series editorial committee], ed. *Zhongguo renmin jiefangjun lishi ziliao congshu: Nanfang sannian youji zhanzheng: Qiongya youjiqu* 中国人民解放军历史资料丛书: 南方三年游击战争: 琼崖游击区 [Chinese people's liberation army historical materials series: Southern three-year guerrilla war: The Hainan guerrilla region]. Beijing: Jiefang chubanshe, 1995.

Zhonghua ribao 中华日报 [China Daily]. Tainan, January–August 1950.

Zhu Yihui 朱逸辉, ed. *Qiongya qizhi* 琼崖旗帜 [The Colors of Hainan]. Haikou: Hainan chubanshe, 2004.

INDEX

Allied prisoners of war on Hainan, 120–125
anti-localism. *See* localism and anti-localism
Australia, prisoners of war, 90, 120–125
automobiles on Hainan, 28–30

Baisha Uprising, 91–92, 95–118, 131, 153
banishment. *See* exile
Barnett, A. Doak, 160–161
Byers, Reverend George D., 37–38, 79

Cai Tingkai, 65, 68, 70
Changtai village, 54–57, 64, 81, 90, 128
Chen Hanguang, 71, 105, 160
Chen Jitang, 7, 34–35, 71–72, 77, 92, 105, 147–152, 160, 168
Chiang Kai-shek (Jiang Jieshi), 3, 7, 35, 39, 69, 71–72, 75–77, 81, 83, 119, 121, 139, 147–148, 151, 166, 168
Chongqing (Chung-king), 77–78, 81, 89, 95
Coconut Stockades (Yezisai), 64–70
collaboration on Hainan. *See* Zhao Shihuan
Confucianism, 23–24, 40, 48, 55, 97, 99, 101
Cultural Revolution, 70, 72–73, 80, 100

Das Kapital. *See* Marx, Karl
Deng Benyin, 47, 62
Deng Xiaoping, 172
Deng Yingchao, 60

economy of Hainan, 18, 126, 135–136, 151, 186–188
exile, 19–20, 23, 149, 170

Fang Fang, 180
Feng Baiju, 1, 4–8, 38, 53–59, 63, 69–73, 80–90, 95, 119–120, 127–140, 144–160, 166–179, 183, 185
Feng Zengmin, 71
Feng Zicai, 30–31
Fitzgerald, John, 34
Five-Finger Mountain. *See* Wuzhishan
Five Ministers Temple, 149, 152, 157
Fourth Field Army, 3, 144, 147–149, 153, 159
French interest in Hainan, 13, 17, 29–30, 37–38, 48–49, 53, 76
Fucheng, 28, 65

Great Leap Forward, 4, 165, 185
Guangzhou (Canton), 34, 37, 39, 46–50, 52, 56–58, 62, 68–69, 73, 83, 89, 103, 107, 129, 135, 138, 152, 171, 176, 185

Hai Rui, 20, 31

Haikou, x, 8, 15–16, 28–30, 36–37, 44, 48, 50–51, 57, 60–61, 63–68, 80–81, 84, 92, 98, 103, 130, 132, 139, 148–149, 152, 154, 160–161, 174
Han chauvinism, 97–98, 105
Han Liancheng, 132
Han Xianchu, 149, 159
Henry, B. C., 24
Hong Kong, x, 13, 16, 28, 41, 45, 48, 50, 68–69, 80, 82, 85–86, 89, 91, 122, 126, 129, 135, 138, 158
Huang Xuezeng, 66–69, 73, 198
Hui, Hainan Muslim population, 21

Indochina. See Vietnam

Japanese on Hainan, 1–7, 12–13, 15–16, 18, 26–27, 32, 35–36, 48–49, 51, 53, 57–59, 65, 71–73, 75–93, 95–96, 107, 107–112, 116, 118–136, 138, 141, 145, 151, 153, 158, 174–175, 178, 187
Jiaji (Kachek), 37, 64–65, 79
Jinmen (Quemoy), 146, 154, 155, 160, 161

Korean War, 3–4, 122, 146, 157, 161, 166, 173–174, 177

Li people of Hainan, 2, 7, 11–12, 15, 20–27, 30–31, 71, 73, 91, 93, 95–118, 140, 153, 171, 176, 182
Li Aichun, 55–58
Li Genyuan, 13–14
Li Jinlong, 28–30
Li Peng, 59–60
Li Shuoxun, 59–61, 73
Li Zhenya, 73
Lin Biao, 159
Lin Wenying, 38, 42–43, 45–52, 60, 62, 69
Lingao, 163–164
Lingshui, 65–66, 107, 109–110, 115
"Little Hungarian Incident" (Xiao Xiongyali shijian), 163–166

Liu Shaoqi, 172
localism and anti-localism, 3–4, 8, 139–141, 163–171, 177, 181–185
Long Jiguang, 14, 25, 45, 51
Long March, 61, 69, 71–73, 85
Luo Wenyan, 68

Ma Baishan, 84, 145, 152–154, 159, 176
Mao Zedong, 6, 128, 154, 159, 171, 182
Marshall, George C., 119
Marx, Karl, 49, 165–166, 183
May Fourth Movement, 35, 48–51, 57, 62
May Thirtieth Movement, 35, 58–59, 61–62
Miao people of Hainan, 108, 110, 182
missionaries, on Hainan, 14, 16, 19, 24, 30, 36, 37, 41, 53, 78–79, 83
Meihe Incident, 131–133
Moninger, Margaret M., 14–16, 18–19, 25, 41
"Mountaintoppism," 139–140
Muruishan, 69–70

Nanchang Uprising, 59, 61, 63, 64
Nanjing (Nanking), 34–35, 58, 66, 71, 76–77, 81, 138–139, 154
New Fourth Army, 133–134, 139
northern retreat order (beiche), 137

Operation Pigeon, 121–126, 136
Opium War, 36, 46, 98
Ou Mengjue, 169, 185
Overseas Hainanese, 18, 36, 66, 82, 86, 135, 137

Peng Chengwan, 12–15, 19–21, 26–33, 96–97, 104
provincial status, Hainan, 4, 47, 104, 156–157, 170, 172–173, 186

Qingming Festival, 8
Qiongshan County, 48, 53, 57, 67, 90, 127

radio communications (wireless radio), 7, 66, 89, 120, 127, 131–138, 173
Red Detachment of Women (Hongse niangzi jun), 70–71, 185
Red May (1930), 70
retreat orders. *See* northern retreat order (beiche); southern retreat order (nanche)

Sanya, 16, 84, 91, 109, 148, 186–187
Sato Shojin, 5, 88, 91
Savina, M., 29, 30, 53
Second United Front (Communist and Nationalist), 81–82, 85–86
Singlaub, John K., 122–126
Snow, Edgar, 80
Soong, Charlie (Song Yaoru), 39
Soong, T.V. (Song Ziwen), 39, 103, 184
"Southbound cadres" (nanxia ganbu), 4, 164, 166, 168–170, 174, 181–183
southern retreat order, 136–137
Southeast Asia, 7, 18, 23, 29, 36, 39, 41, 49–51, 54, 58, 60, 68, 73, 80, 85, 100, 126, 129, 135–137, 176, 187
Stilwell, Joseph, 80
Su Dongpo (Su Shi), 19–20, 149
Sun Yat-sen (Sun Zhongshan), 36, 39–40, 43–47, 51–53, 56, 61–62, 72–73, 151
Swinhoe, Robert, 98–99

Taiwan, 2–3, 9, 12–13, 17, 19, 72, 84, 92, 100, 125, 143, 146–148, 151, 154, 157–161, 166, 187
Tappan, Reverend David S., 78–80, 82–83, 86
Tao Zhu, 169, 185
Thailand (Siam), 41–43, 48, 50
Tibet, 2, 9, 143, 159, 166
Tongmenghui (Chinese Revolutionary Alliance), 43, 48, 69

Topping, Seymour, 147–148
Treaty of Tianjin, 36

Vietnam (Indochina), 3, 7–8, 13, 37, 42, 121–122, 129, 137, 159, 186

Wang Guoxing, 21, 95, 99, 99–101, 106–118, 153, 176, 182
Wang Wenming, 63–64, 67–70, 73
Wang Yujin, 95, 111–117
Wenchang, 28, 39, 42–46, 67–68, 87, 92, 103
"White Terror," 63, 67
White, Theodore, 80
Wuzhishan (Five-Finger Mountain), 18, 31, 117–118, 169, 175

Xinjiang, 2, 9
Xu Chengzhang, 48–52, 57, 60, 62, 69
Xue Yue, 147, 151, 155, 160

Yan Xishan, 160
Yan'an, 1, 7, 61, 68–69, 72, 77–78, 80, 85, 87, 89, 95, 120, 131, 133–134, 136–139, 160, 169, 174
Yaxian, 65
Ye Jianying, 80, 147, 172, 181–182
Yuan Shikai, 14, 35, 44–46, 48, 62
Yunlong Reorganization (Yunlong gaibian), 81–82, 85–86

Zeng Huiyu, 72
Zhang Zhidong, 47, 104, 149
Zhao Fan, 23
Zhao Shihuan, 87, 129
Zhao Ziyang, 169, 185
Zhejiang, 59, 171, 185
Zhou Enlai, 60, 62, 80, 85–86, 120–121, 127, 132, 138, 172–173, 182, 185
Zhou Tangzhen, 110
Zhu De, 169, 172
Zhuang Tian, 73, 85–86, 138

www.ingramcontent.com/pod-product-compliance
Ingram Content Group UK Ltd.
Pitfield, Milton Keynes, MK11 3LW, UK
UKHW021833140426
5217IPUK00021B/1423